Professional Uncertainty, Knowledge and Relationship in the Classroom

The extent to which teachers should make use of theoretical and expert knowledge as opposed to tacit experiential knowledge, and how these might be combined, is a perennial issue in discussions on pedagogy. This book addresses these debates through a creative development of the concept of productive uncertainty.

Using case studies focusing on teachers working with children with autism, a particularly fertile crucible for considering uncertainty, the book explores how the radical twentieth-century psychoanalyst Wilfred Bion's epistemological approach to uncertainty can be used to reframe Donald Schön's concept of reflection in action, offering a new perspective on the practice of teachers and other caring professionals. Several areas of potential uncertainty are identified, including uncertainty relating to areas of practice including diagnosis, the relationship between expert knowledge and practice, the implications of autism for autonomy and agency and uncertainties in relation to the understanding of and use of new technologies. A strong argument is made, based on both theoretical and empirical grounds, that in juggling between theoretical and tacit knowledge in the classroom there is more to be gained by staying with the struggle with uncertainty than by fleeing from it too early, towards the promise of expert solutions. Consideration is also given to the relative importance of specific theoretical training for teachers, both in general and in relation to working with children with special educational needs, in the context of international and UK policy developments in this area.

This book will be of key value to researchers and postgraduates in the fields of education studies, teacher thinking and research and psychoanalytically informed psychosocial studies, as well as to practitioners working in special educational needs/autism education.

Joseph Mintz is Senior Lecturer in Education at the Institute of Education, University of London, UK. His interests include special educational needs, inclusion, autism education, mobile technology for special educational needs and the professional practice of teachers.

Routledge Research in Education

Professional Uncertainty, Knowledge and Relationship in the Classroom

A psychosocial perspective

Joseph Mintz

Routledge
Taylor & Francis Group

LONDON AND NEW YORK

First published 2014
by Routledge
2 Park Square, Milton Park, Abingdon, Oxon OX14 4RN

and by Routledge
711 Third Avenue, New York, NY 10017

Routledge is an imprint of the Taylor & Francis Group, an informa business

British Library Cataloguing in Publication Data
A catalogue record for this book is available from the British Library

Library of Congress Cataloging in Publication Data
Mintz, Joseph.
Professional uncertainty, knowledge, and relationship in the classroom:
a psychosocial perspective / Joseph Mintz.
  pages cm – (Routledge research in education)
  1. Autistic children–Education–Psychological aspects–Case studies.
  2. Teachers–Professional relationships. 3. Knowledge, Theory of.
  4. Uncertainty. 5. Bion, Wilfred R. (Wilfred Ruprecht), 1897–1979.
  6. Schön, Donald A. I. Title.
  LC4717.M56 2015
  371.9–dc23
                                        2014002018

ISBN: 978-0-415-82296-1 (hbk)
ISBN: 978-0-203-55246-9 (ebk)

Typeset in Galliard
by Sunrise Setting Ltd, Paignton, UK

Printed and bound in Great Britain by
TJ International Ltd, Padstow, Cornwall

For Eva, my wife

Contents

List of illustrations

Foreword

It is a privilege and a pleasure to write a foreword to this important, progressive and profoundly thoughtful book. Too much research and academic writing aimed at helping professionals with their day-to-day practice remains remote from the lived experience of the work, the minute-by-minute, hour-by-hour struggle to makes sense of what is happening for the practitioner and those with whom he or she is engaged. Joe Mintz knows his craft as a practising teacher from the inside, and in the research that informs this book spent many hours undertaking close observation and then systematic reflection upon his records of the emotional and practical transactions of a number of teachers with their students. In the resulting case studies which lie at the heart of the book, teachers everywhere will recognise themselves and the anxieties and uncertainties that attend their everyday classroom experience. The author's conviction is that 'uncertainty' – about what is happening in the minds and behaviours of students and teachers alike – is an experience we should not be afraid of or seek to eliminate, but should embrace in our search for an authentic pedagogic practice and philosophy.

What he terms 'productive uncertainty' is not the same as professional confusion or helplessness, although it may require us to traverse moments of this kind. Rather, it is a necessary precondition for genuine engagement and understanding – ultimately of *connection* with the student and the meaningfulness of learning, in the context of the student/teacher relationship. Here Joe Mintz is drawing on particular aspects of traditions of thinking about professional practice developed over many years at the Tavistock Clinic in north London. 'Learning from experience' is a central principle of this approach to professional development and of the key thinker with whom he engages, the radical and visionary psychoanalyst Wilfred Bion, who believed that 'emotional experience', as well as a capacity to reflect on such experience and give it shape and form through words and ideas, lay at the heart of all true 'thinking'. But our emotional experience in classroom or therapeutic encounters often overwhelms us and makes us anxious. 'Productive uncertainty' is the zone in which we first tolerate these uncomfortable moments rather than flee from them and then allow meaning and understanding to take shape, often with the aid of colleagues who are able to engage in a similar quest of their own.

Joe Mintz's engagement with Bion leads him into a profound and illuminating dialogue with the possibly more familiar work of Donald Schön, in search of a synthesis that seems to me to deepen our appreciation of the relevance of both for modern educational philosophy. So, this is a multi-layered book, and one which I believe will repay sustained engagement from the reader of the very kind which it proposes should lie at the heart of 'good teaching'. I was fortunate to play a small part in the process of the research which informs the book. But like all original and innovative thinkers, Joe has developed his work well beyond anything that I myself was able to offer him and, in his search for a properly psychosocial account of contemporary pedagogic practice, has also signalled new directions for the work of Tavistock theorists and teachers. I believe this book will make a lasting contribution to our thinking about what it is to teach, to be a teacher and to learn, and above all to the health and vitality of our struggle to sustain recognition of the subtlety, complexity and significance of the educational task.

Andrew Cooper
Professor of Social Work
The Tavistock Centre and
University of East London
December 2013

Acknowledgements

I would like to thank Heather Price and Andrew Cooper for their input to the theoretical developments on which this book is based, as well as Claudia Lapping and Dominic Wyse for commenting on drafts.

Chapter 1

Introduction

About uncertainty

Teaching is a difficult job. In no other profession does one need, for up to six hours a day, day in day out, to interact with and meet the varied learning, social and emotional needs of groups of young people who are daily changing, developing and negotiating their identities and the boundaries between themselves and the world. My interest in uncertainty arises from reflection on my experience of 'not knowing' when working as a class teacher. I understand the complexity of the task can often mean that teachers are unsettled, anxious and uncertain about the 'right' thing to do in any given teaching moment. Uncertainty is the anxiety and confusion linked to classroom situations in which one experiences a state of 'not knowing' which knowledge to make use of when deciding what to do with a child who misbehaves, a group that does not seem to understand or progress or a child who experiences difficulties with learning. For example, teachers may be uncertain as to whether to draw on explicit psychological theories about child development, past experiences of working with similar children or groups, advice from colleagues including specialists as educational psychologists or their ongoing tacit experience of working with that particular child. A particular question, both for teachers themselves and for those observing and thinking about their practice, is perhaps, 'What is the balance between the uses of explicit versus tacit knowledge?' As such, my framing of uncertainty is predicated on the work of Donald Schön (1983). Schön emphasized the importance for professionals of tacit as well as explicit knowledge. His concept of 'reflection-in-action' is based on the premise that all professionals make use of a combination of both types of knowledge when working 'in the moment' on solving professional problems. Schön's work has been hugely influential on how professional bodies, and professionals themselves, think about their practice, as well as on the academy's evaluation of such practice. Schön's work has also been much developed and critiqued, and I consider some of this exegesis on Schön's work in Chapter 2. However, my focus in this book is on Schön's consideration of what goes on 'in the moment'. My contention is that in

Schön's work, as in the work of many of his commentators, this consideration is both undertheorized and underexploited, particularly for professionals working in the caring services. I propose to make use of a psychoanalytic lens based on Wilfred Bion's epistemology of how knowledge arises in the intersubjective relationship between two people. Bion was one of the great psychoanalytic theorists of the twentieth century, who developed (or perhaps revolutionized) the ideas of Melanie Klein and the object-relations approach in psychoanalysis. His ideas continue to have a pervasive influence on psychoanalytic thinking. His intersubjective quasi-Kantian epistemology, with its dash of (not uncontroversial) mystical dualism, can, I propose, serve to illuminate what goes on in that 'uncertain moment' when teachers, and indeed other caring professionals, come to decisions about how to work with children. In particular, a Bionian lens suggests that there is something inherently uncertain in the 'moment' when teachers relate intersubjectively to their children, and that this uncertainty is a crucial part of – or even defines – the process of coming to know, in a truly useful sense, about the child.

Uncertainties are not just provoked by the inescapable demands that any group of thirty or so children would place on any adult tasked with working with them in the hope of bringing about learning and development. They are also produced in the context of the political, cultural and individual debates which influence the ways in which teachers think about the problems they need to solve in the classroom. Policy debates, as well as policy imperatives, serve to shape and constrain the ways in which teachers approach dealing with uncertainties in the classroom. In particular, how teachers conceptualize and make use of tacit versus expert knowledge is, to a significant – although by no means all-embracing – degree, influenced by policy strictures. In turn, such strictures are partially informed by an ongoing theoretical debate about the conceptualization of, relationship between and relative importance of expert versus tacit or experiential knowledge. Schön, in deriving his paradigm of the reflective practitioner, draws on Polanyi (1962), who considers tacit knowledge as knowledge which cannot be set down in mathematics or language and which is expressed through action. For Polanyi, it is an elusive, not easily tied-down knowledge that arises or comes into view when, for example, the violinist picks up his bow and starts to play. Although there may be a set of rules ('knowing that') which the violinist has learned, his performance is not defined by these, and Polanyi conceptualized the space between the rules and the performance as tacit knowledge. We might ask if teachers are similarly involved in an art whereby, having learned a basic set of rules, their 'performance' is based on tacit knowledge. Alternatively, are they quasi-scientists who work with a detailed evidence base and use a clear set of rules to decide what strategy is needed for each class and each child? The elucidation of this question is, of course, at the heart of Schön's enterprise, and much of his analysis is based on questioning the basis for such a clear-cut distinction in professional life – not just for teachers (and social workers and nurses), but in his view just as much for doctors and lawyers. Yet the reality of the distinction itself, as well as the putative balance of these two types of knowledge, remains a subject of intense debate in public policy as well as in academia. For example, in 2010, the newly in-post English Education Secretary, Michael Gove, declared that teaching was a 'craft' best learned on the job, and that as such English teacher training needed to have its centre of gravity shifted from universities to schools. Mirroring this, in 2013, English Health Secretary Jeremy Hunt unveiled requirements for those entering nurse training to have spent a year as a health care assistant, mucking in on the wards where the 'real learning' takes place. These political announcements in the UK in the second decade of the twenty-first century follow a variety of policy positions over many decades where different perspectives and emphasis have been applied to the importance of tacit versus expert knowledge in professional training in the caring services. In the USA there are similar ongoing policy debates about teacher education (Scheckel, 2009) and nurse education (Labaree, 2008).

In teaching, national and local approaches to curriculum and assessment also serve to constrain perspectives on the relationship between tacit and expert knowledge, and concomitantly the space available for uncertainty to play a role, productive or otherwise, in the thinking of teachers. Instrumentalist approaches to education, where curriculum objectives and assessment systems are tightly defined, tend to push schools and individual teachers towards a reliance on similarly well-defined bodies of knowledge, perhaps shifting the emphasis from tacit to expert knowledge. Surveillance systems linked to tightly defined curriculum and assessment, such as the English Office for Standards in Education (OFSTED), also serve as a constraint, further pushing the education system towards a reliance on a particular set of rules about how teaching should be performed. There is, of course, room for considerable debate about in what way such rules, largely derived from policy as opposed to a research programme, can be considered as expert knowledge. Notwithstanding this, from the perspective of many teachers, these rules are likely to at the very least have the appearance of a body of expert knowledge, representing the way in which things should be done. Returning to Polanyi, such pressures will tend to reduce the space available between the rules and the performance of teaching.

Productive uncertainty

My contention is that it is in the space between rules and performance that Polanyi maps out, which we might consider equivalent to Schön's idea of 'in the moment', that uncertainty can be thought to operate. Further, it is through grappling with this uncertainty that the teacher comes to know the child more fully. The uncertainty is productive. I will use the term 'productive uncertainty', not as a formal concept but, borrowing a term from Schön (1993), rather as something akin to a generative metaphor, which gives a new frame or emphasis for thinking about a problem.

It is of course the case that certain domains within the human sciences, including communications research and cognitive approaches to professional stress, have positioned uncertainty as a clear negative. Berger and Calabrese's (1975) influential uncertainty reduction theory posited that during social interaction, high levels of uncertainty tend to reduce levels of communication and thus the potential for learning. This reflects to some extent the common-sense view that uncertainty is undesirable, and that the more we can achieve certainty, or its close correlate expertise, the more effective we will be. In teaching, this might be seen in the common occurrence, as Hargreaves (1994) identifies, of feelings of guilt, failure, or lack of confidence in their professional abilities when teachers experience uncertainty.

Others have taken a more balanced approach to thinking about uncertainty. Helsing (2007), Wasserman (1993) and indeed the broader movement using concepts influenced by or derived from Schön's idea of the reflective practitioner as a lens for thinking about professional development (Kolb, 1984; Moon, 1999; Brookfield, 1995) suggest that it is only by engaging with uncertainty, by identifying critical incidents that are at least initially unclear to the professional, that professional development can come about. It is worth noting here that there is something of an implication that this involves a move from uncertainty to expertise.

My use of the term 'productive uncertainty' is very much one in which uncertainty is seen as a positive that leads to the learning of the professional. However, my development of the idea of uncertainty is based on concepts from psychoanalysis, in particular concepts from Bion's psychoanalytic epistemology. In this it has some significant similarities to Deborah Britzman's (1998, 2013) use of Bion's conceptualization of uncertainty in the teaching situation. However, Britzman both assumes Bion's epistemology and leaves its relationship to other frames for thinking about professional practice and development largely untouched. Here I go further – in fact, I would argue, much further – in working out how productive uncertainty relates to the theoretical and professional discussion about what might be meant when Schön and Polanyi refer to a space between expert and tacit or experiential knowledge. I will develop a theoretical argument based on the premise that this space has a particular quality that is to do with relationship, and that this is of particular relevance for professionals working in the caring services such as teachers. Although the vast majority of occupations involve interaction with others, it is reasonable to propose that in the caring professions there is a particular intensity about the relationship between teacher and child, or nurse and patient, or social worker and client. The problems with which these professionals are faced are problems about people, and the uncertainties that they experience involve, to a significant extent, the human mind; certainly an embodied mind, but nevertheless a complex mind that they can only come to know through relationship. Wilfred Bion (1963) formulates the term 'learning from experience', by which he means a particular type of learning in which we come to know – or even, in his epistemology, to have thoughts – through the relationships that we have with others, starting with our earliest relationship with our primary caregiver. The analyst – and Bion's focus was primarily on the work of the psychoanalyst – comes to learn about the patient, to know them, through their ongoing intersubjective relationship. This process is not, in Bion's worldview, an easy one. It is fraught with difficulty, with uncertainty. The therapist must shy away from the easy temptation of rushing to quick certainties, but rather grapple with the pain of 'not knowing', of being uncertain, and wait expectantly for the (still contingent) knowledge that arises through the intersubjective encounter. What this means might be further illuminated by a personal example. Psychoanalytic systems of thought and explication derive from the process of intersubjective encounter – the knowledge, which is often emotional knowledge, on which they are predicated is experientially derived, and derived in the first person. This is of course from some perspectives the great weakness of psychoanalysis – because of this many saw it, and see it still, as a sham masquerading as a science (Grunbaum, 1985). The reader will have to decide for themself, but I hope that this vignette from my experiences as a primary school teacher working with a child called Avi in a London Jewish school will perhaps show the potential power of such experiential accounts and, concomitantly, what Bion was getting at:

> It was my fifth year as a teacher. I was teaching a Year 3 (ages 7–8) class. They were a 'nice' class, many of whom were good-natured and eager to learn, although the class was not without children who had particular difficulties and needs. One of these was Avi. He was bilingual, coming from an Israeli family of Iraqi origin. Although generally fluent in English, his reading and writing skills were a bit behind those of his classmates. He was quite a sparky child, often pleasant and enthusiastic, but also quite emotionally immature for his age. He would quite frequently, and often for no clearly obvious reason, get quite strongly upset in class. He would screw up his face, sometimes stamp his feet, and quite frequently burst into tears. Usually during these episodes, if given some attention and left for a while, he tended to calm down. He also had a tendency to be quite clingy, and developed a strong attachment to me as his teacher over the course of the year. One interaction with him, eight years ago at the time of writing, has stuck very strongly in my memory. There was a whole-school activity taking place – a dreidel competition. Dreidels

are four-sided spinning tops with a particular letter on each side, which are used for a game associated with the Jewish festival of Chanukah. Two classes together were given a time to work in the hall on making dreidels and to practise spinning them. During our time in the hall, most of the children were getting on fine with their dreidels, but Avi was finding it hard. I can't remember the precise problem he was having – it might have been getting his dreidel to spin properly. He was quite frustrated by this and starting to get upset. I do remember quite strongly noticing this from across the room and coming to work with him. I made some suggestions as to what he might do. He looked up at me, but didn't take any notice of what I had said, and carried on not managing the task. I remember having a strong feeling, and it was more of a feeling than a precise thought, that what he needed was just for me to be there with him and not necessarily to say anything. I also remember that it was quite an effort to concentrate on him – the hall was very noisy and there was lots of movement from excited children and spinning dreidels. But I managed to do just that, crouching down near him, watching him use the dreidel. On the surface he didn't seem obviously to react to me in any particularly strong way, although he glanced momentarily up at me every so often. But I had a strong sense of communicating with him in some way, of being alert to what he needed, and of it being somehow important for me to be there and alert with him, even though I didn't have anything specific to say or do. He just carried on playing with the dreidel, noticeably more calmly now, glancing up at me every so often.

My recounting of this vignette here introduces several ideas, all of which will be further explored and illustrated in subsequent chapters. First, it gives some very initial idea of what I mean when I talk about intersubjective encounter as a way of coming to know. Thus I report my emotional state and how that, in some way, was a bellwether for what was going on for Avi or what it might be that he needed at that particular moment. It also serves to give an initial introduction to the idea of using emotional states as a way of finding out about what is going on in a field of study or professional practice. In this case, the conclusion that I drew after this incident, based on my observation, if you will, of my own emotional state, is that it was difficult for me to 'stick' with Avi and his possibly quite difficult work with the dreidels. I identify difficulty with concentrating on Avi in the bustling hall, but part of this difficulty may also have been that of engaging with 'not knowing', of being in a state of uncertainty about what it was that Avi needed. It would have been much easier to dive in quickly and help Avi with the dreidel, or to offer him advice about what he should be doing – much easier than staying with the difficult task of being uncertain, and of entering into intersubjective relationship with him.

Bion's concept of productive uncertainty also implies, in my view, a particular position on agency; this can be applied at the level of the analyst and the patient (or analysand), and potentially by extension – although not without controversy – to the teacher and the child. For the professional, the existence of a productive uncertainty which sits between rules and performance must on the face of it be predicated on an 'I' that chooses, that moves from uncertainty to decision. For the child, or the teacher–child dyad, if knowledge arises from intersubjective relationship this implies two agentic subjects, for otherwise what is it knowledge of? Just as Buber's 'I–Thou' encounter is predicated on a knowing mind with intrinsic value encountering another of intrinsic value, Bion's focus on the intersubjective relationship implies a similar encounter of knowing, relating minds. Bion's philosophy could be considered as 'I relate, therefore I am' (Andrew Cooper, personal communication). I see Bion's account of thinking as an agentic account of both the therapist and the patient. Partly as a consequence of this, the perspective on Schön and professional thinking that I will develop in Chapter 2 will also place agency at its centre, and in doing so I explicitly enter into contention with determinist accounts of the human subject, particularly in terms of their relevance for how we think about professional practice in the caring services.

Deterministic accounts arising from the Enlightenment, spanning Comte, Spinoza, Marx, Freud and Darwin, can be seen as having devalued the currency of the idea of a freely choosing agentic subject whose future is at least to a significant degree undetermined by genes or by social background. As Jonathan Sacks writes, 'what makes human action free is that it is future orientated [...] freedom is written in the future tense' (2007, p. 59). What profession could be more future-orientated than teaching? Whatever view you take of the purposes of education, it has to have something to do with creating the future through the development of the child. Deterministic accounts of human nature, which sometimes interpenetrate with public policy, also tend towards the specification of tightly defined sets of rules about professional practice. This can be seen particularly in relation to the work of teachers with children with special educational needs (SEN). Psychiatry and cognitive psychology – clear products of the Enlightenment – in applying a scientific lens to the human subject tend towards the specification of rules and procedures for particular diagnostic categories. Of course, sociological critiques of the role of psychology in special education, based to a significant extent on Foucault – such as Henriques *et al.* (1988) and Barton (1988) – have highlighted the dangers of scientism in this application of psychology, although, of course, such critiques are themselves predicated on another sort of deterministic account about human action.

The dangers of determinism could be considered to have increased in recent decades, with the rise in the influence on education of evolutionary psychology and neuroscience influenced by genetics. Exaggeration notwithstanding, if the teacher sees the child as an agglomeration of genes – of which some are 'faulty' – and it is the phenotypic expression of these which determines both their present capacities and future abilities, it is not a very large step to the allure of a set of scientifically derived procedures for dealing with this particular phenotype. The influence of such a mindset on teachers working with children with SEN in particular, even if only partial, will tend to further reduce the space available between the rules and the performance, where productive uncertainty based on intersubjective relationship between agentic subjects could also lead to the derivation of a valuable type of knowledge. As an example, in the case of my encounter with Avi, I might have grasped for a theoretical construct about attention deficit hyperactivity disorder, rather than staying with him 'in the moment'.

Clearly, there are elements of exaggeration in my account and it should not be taken to suggest that I am embarking on an anti-Enlightenment, anti-scientific enterprise, nor one that ignores the legitimate and complex debates about accounts of consciousness and free will in metaphysical naturalism, as well as the nature of agency going back to Kant. As will become evident, my position is that psychology, neuroscience and even evolutionary biology have much to tell us about how children, including children like Avi, learn in ways that can productively inform the practice of teaching. The same applies to the other caring professions. The question is how professionals make use of them in practice now, and how they should make use of them in the future. My argument in this book is that idea of productive uncertainty, rooted in a psychoanalytic perspective on professional practice based on Bion's epistemology, offers a powerful frame for thinking about this question.

Uncertainty and autism

Dealing with children with special educational needs raises particular areas of uncertainty for teachers, of which agency is one dimension. Children with difficulties with learning, often with diagnostic labels attached to those difficulties, can add an additional layer of complexity and uncertainty to the experience of being a teacher in the classroom. In particular, children with SEN in schools often have diagnostic categories applied to them that come with associated cognitive accounts and bodies of expert knowledge. This leads to potential uncertainty about how to make use of this expert knowledge and brings more explicitly to the fore the question of how this is balanced with their ongoing experiential or tacit knowledge gained from working with other similar children or from working with the same child over time. One condition in particular, namely autism or, more commonly, autism spectrum disorders (ASD), raises significant questions in the minds of caring professionals – specifically around issues of agency, autonomy and independence – because its impairments strike at the heart of what we often take to be a given in human experience, namely the ability to engage in social communication. The empirical study from which this book emerged concerns an investigation of the ways in which five teachers experience and deal with uncertainty when working with children with ASD. The teachers, all working at Randall School – a special school for children and young people with ASD between the ages of 11 and 18 in the north of England were involved in a project in which a new smartphone app designed to develop social and life skills was introduced into the classroom.[1] The context of working with children with autism can be thought of as representing a fertile crucible for the exploration of teacher uncertainty. It will, as I hope to demonstrate, illuminate what I mean by productive uncertainty. However, this illumination is not, I contend, restricted to just this context. It is a special case of a linked set of phenomena that are present in many teaching situations, with 'normal' children and groups, in mainstream settings where children with SEN are included and, by extension, to other professionals working in the caring services. I hope to show how productive uncertainty is an idea that has relevance in all of these contexts, with particular implications for both professional practice and public policy.

Note

1   All names, including that of the school, have been changed to preserve anonymity.

Chapter 2

A view of professional thinking
Combining Schön and Bion

Floating around in the mix so far when considering professional thinking are expert knowledge, tacit knowledge, theoretical knowledge and craft knowledge. There are a number of perspectives on how to think about these but, drawing on Schön (1983), Higgs (2008), Kemmis (2005) and Sternberg and Horvath (1999), I argue as follows:

1   Polanyi (1958), drawing on Ryle (1945), considers *tacit knowledge* to be those things we know how to do, but cannot easily put into language. It is close to Higgs' concept of professional *craft knowledge*, which means knowing how to do something as opposed to 'knowing that'.
2   *Theoretical knowledge* – 'knowing that', equating to Higgs' *propositional knowledge* – is knowledge that, in Schön's terms, is developed in the university, and that professionals then make use of in their practice.
3   Kemmis discusses *practical reasoning*, which is reasoning about uncertain practical situations. As Kemmis puts it, experienced professionals 'also rely on their capacity to "read" situations in the light of what has happened in other situations' (op. cit., p. 405). This is something like Schön's concept of reflection 'in the moment', whereby there is a fuzzy internal dialogue between propositional knowledge, craft knowledge and the actualities of the specific situation or problem. Kemmis' take on this is framed more discursively, i.e. historical and social processes which are extra-individual are as much at play as individual processes in the embodiment of such practical reasoning. As will become clearer in this chapter, I am more interested in the 'in-the-moment' aspects of practical reasoning than the discursive aspects.

It is probably fairly self-evident that these are messy categories, with no very clear delineation between them. For example, I left out *expert knowledge*. Is this derived from theoretical knowledge, or are they the same thing? Or is expert knowledge a mixture of theoretical and tacit knowledge together. If so, is this the same as 'in-the-moment' thinking or is it something altogether different? For now, these terms are a useful heuristic as we start to explore Schön and his problems in a bit more detail.

Schön – reflection-in-action

In *The Reflective Practitioner*, Schön (1983) identifies the growth in the influence of the professions and professionals since World War II and the dominance of science and positivism in determining their prominent role both in technological societies and in conceptualizing their activities. Schön describes this as the 'technical rational' model, in which privileged major professions (medicine, law, etc.) take a body of scientifically derived knowledge (propositional or theoretical knowledge) and then apply this to solve clearly defined and delimited problems. Further, in this model, a second class of minor professions, including teachers and social workers, are as a corollary thought of as having an ill-defined knowledge base and competing sets of theoretical explanations which are ineffectually targeted at fuzzy real-world problems. Schön criticizes this model on a number of grounds. One of his key points is that the technical rational model does not work in many cases and that, increasingly, the recipients of the professional services and the professionals themselves realize this. The growth of the expert patient movement might be an example. Specifically, the technical rational model only works for 'convergent cases' which fit the textbook parameters; yet Schön proposes that in fact in many (or most) cases, the textbook does not or does not quite fit, and the professional needs to use both propositional knowledge and 'in-the-moment' thinking to find the solution to the problem. Further, Schön points out that these messy problems are actually quite common in both the major and the minor professions, and that the distinction between the professions on those grounds is really a false one. Schön denotes the process of thinking about problems 'in the moment' as 'reflection-in-action'. For Schön, it is 'in the moment' when tacit and theoretical knowledge come together somehow and are translated into or effect decision and action. However, there is significant debate and, I would suggest, a certain lack of clarity about the following:

1 What Schön actually means by 'reflection-in-action' and what he is actually suggesting goes on 'in the moment' when professionals come up with solutions to professional problems.
2 Concomitantly, how Schön sees professionals integrating theoretical knowledge that is expressed in language and tacit knowledge gained from experience 'in the moment'.

There are two generally accepted ways of answering these questions: via a turn to either cognitive or sociocultural approaches to thinking about professional practice.

The cognitive turn

The teacher thinking literature of the 1980s and early 1990s can be considered as a cognitively orientated attempt to think about how teachers come to decisions in the classroom. Researchers such as Clark and Lampert (1986), Clark (2005), Clark and Petersen (1986), Brown and McIntyre (1993) and Shulman (1987) all had a working assumption that all thinking can at least in principle be related to particular mental functions, and that these can be described and delimited in language. In a sense, they implicitly concurred with Jerry Fodor's (1981) critique of the very idea of tacit knowledge, in that surely it just represents a set of mental functions that we have not yet been able to describe or put into language.

Polanyi (1958) considers tacit knowledge to be those things that we know how to do (knowledge how) but can't put into language. Fodor notes that we differentiate between tasks done and tasks done well based on tacit knowledge. A concert performance can be sublime or a noisy mess; how, asks Fodor, can we make such a differentiation based on an assessment of competency, and such variation in competency (and assessment of varied competency), without instantiating these judgements in mental operations? In other words, using the term tacit knowledge is simply a way of avoiding the acknowledgement that there are mental operations going on that we don't yet understand. Fodor wrote this in 1981 in the context of the 'New Synthesis' in which, based on Turing's work on formalizing computer operations, thoughts in the mind are seen as being syntactical operations which (again in principle at least) could be represented in some sort of very advanced Turing machine. In other words, human thoughts are syntactical and as such can be represented as syntactic operations in a computer, and therefore this gives a good working model of how the mind works.

Simplifying Fodor's critique, his main point is that the distinction between 'knowing how' and 'knowing that' is a false one. Cognitivist accounts of professional practice, such as the teacher thinking literature, implicitly assume that if you dig deep enough, you can get the teacher to consciously describe what went on when they were making a decision 'in the moment' in the classroom. Of course, it is also possible to argue, as Fodor recognizes, that the efficacy of such (in principle) discoverable mental operations for the mind in question might possibly depend on them remaining consciously unknown to that mind. Notwithstanding this point, elucidation of teacher reflection on this directly after a lesson observation was felt to be the most effective way of digging deep to uncover the teacher's hidden mental processes. For example, Shulman (1987) proposes, in his categorization of the teacher 'knowledge base', a type of knowledge denoted as 'pedagogical content knowledge', which is a type of craft knowledge relating to teaching specific subject areas. So, for example, a science teacher would have particular working theories about how best to explain or demonstrate key concepts such as transpiration or the structure of the atom. This is partially derived from training or reference to, say, schemes of work, but also partially derived from their experience of what works in explaining things to children. This concept could usefully be extended to craft knowledge associated with working with particular groups of children. So, for example, we could posit the existence of pedagogical content knowledge about how to work with children with autism. In Shulman's account, as in much of the teacher thinking literature, there is an underlying assumption that this type of pedagogical content knowledge could at least in principle be captured and described – the teacher's working theories could, with sufficient powers of mental recall and enough prompting, be put into language. In Fodor's terms, what first seems tacit can in fact, with sufficient digging, be uncovered as theoretical.

Thus, in the cognitive turn, the answer to what Schön means by 'in the moment' is to say that it is simply a set of mental operations that has not yet been put into language, but in principle could be, with enough digging.

It is worth noting that Fodor is a metaphysical naturalist through and through, and certainly in 1981 he writes from a perspective in which such representations of tacit thinking are at least in principle discoverable. These supposedly tacit mental operations will one day be fitted into his then over-arching theory of how the mind works as a Turing machine. Clearly this implies a nativist conception of the human mind as supervening (corresponding via instantiation) on a physical substrate. It fits very nicely, and to some extent persuasively, therefore, with Fodor's naturalist metaphysics. For me, though, this then raises the issue of agency – how can we conceive of the human subject as an autonomous choosing agent, whose actions are at least to some extent undetermined, if the human mind does in fact supervene on the physical? This is both an old and a much discussed question, and I discuss it in more depth below. For now, suffice it to say that such a cognitive account of Schön inescapably raises the issues of agency and determinism, which, as I set out in the introduction, is in my mind problematic when we are considering the work of professionals in the caring services.

It is also interesting to note that as teacher thinking studies accumulated, it became more clear just how difficult it was to get teachers to talk explicitly about what had gone on implicitly in the classroom (Denicolo and Kompf, 2005). This observation was in fact quite important in pushing researchers away from cognitivist accounts of teacher thinking, and implicitly towards the alternative position that the mental operations underlying tacit knowledge are in fact either in principle or in practice immune to categorization or delimitation in language. Coupled with this was a growing realization that knowledge and practice are, when we look at how people learn and work, not as clearly split as a cognitive account suggests. This was of course one of Schön's key observations about the technical rational model. This brings us on to the sociocultural turn in interpreting Schön.

A sociocultural Schön?

Schön's rejection of a technical rational model of professional, and an extreme split between knowledge and practice, does tend to imply that there is a type of tacit knowledge that plays a part in the work of professionals that is just as important as theoretical knowledge. It is not a major jump from this position to considering process and product in professional thinking as intertwined and even indistinguishable. Thus a common reading of Schön is that he is adopting a sociocultural position (Cobb and Yackel, 1996; Kelly, 2006, Lave and Wenger, 1991).

As Erlandson and Beach (2008) point out, for these theorists' interpretation of Schön, acquisition of the skill and engagement in the process are indistinguishable; knowing-how and knowing-that are intertwined. The knowledge or skills gained cannot be considered as separate from the embodied practical engagement with the process. Process and product are the same and, further, it makes no sense to think about a wholly separate individual cognition that is distinct from the tool-supported interpersonal interactions from which the mind emerges. In proposing that in reflection-in-action knowledge arises from engagement with professional practice, Schön could be seen as advocating such as a sociocultural position. Erlandson and Beach identify the following conclusions which can and have been drawn if Schön is read like this:

> for practice-oriented professions that rely on tacit knowledge, such as those of architects, psychotherapists, nurses and teachers, there is a special kind of epistemology that differs from epistemology in the classical sense; that this epistemology is situated such that questions of epistemology have to involve questions concerning situated practice; these practice-oriented professions involve a special kind of situated thinking and this 'situational thinking' is what being a professional is all about.
>
> (Erlandson and Beach ibid., p. 411)

However, Erlandson and Beach (2008) and, prior to that, Erlandson (2007) remind us that an alternative position to the sociocultural – namely cognitivism – does very much hold to the idea of a de-situated mind that is separate in many ways from the world that it acts upon. Erlandson (2007) terms this the 'control matrix', the Cartesian mind which is split from the body (and also split from action). Erlandson and Beach (2008) argue that Schön is, in fact, quite closely aligned with this cognitive position and that for Schön, reflection-in-action implies that there is an active construction of an abstract concept that then drives action. This might happen very quickly – 'in the moment' – but it still happens in that order: abstract thought and then action. Kemmis (2005) makes a similar although perhaps less polarized critique of Schön, noting his focus on the individual practitioner at the expense of the surrounding social field (a discursive reading of community of practice), arguing Schön's individual focus meant that, perhaps unwittingly, 'he fell prey to the danger of reasserting the primacy of thought over action (the rationalistic conception of action), of theory over practice, and of the university over the professions' (ibid., p. 408), even when his over-arching intention was to point out that such dichotomies were false.

Schön lies accused, in actuality, of failing in the project to successfully integrate 'knowing that' and 'knowing how', and of simply ending back where he started. Indeed, if Schön has failed in this way then it would, of course, be something of a vindication of Fodor's cognitivist argument that the differentiation between tacit and theoretical knowledge is false.

In my view, the sociocultural turn takes us back to the issue of agency and determinism. My interpretation of Schön is that he responds, perhaps implicitly but in my view inescapably, to the significant problems that many people have with many sociocultural accounts which position the individual mind as a false construction. They are the flip side of cognitive determinism, removing – or, to be fair, in Kemmis' case, shrinking – the space available for the exercise of individual agency. So to my mind, Erlandson and Beach and Kemmis are correct in their critique of Schön, but for those – such as myself – who think that more rather than less emphasis needs to be given to individual agency in accounts of professional thinking, the response to this critique would be that Schön is in fact right in leaving space, even if only unwittingly, for the individual control matrix.

Does this then leave us with a return to the cognitivist approach, and the extreme split between knowledge and practice present in the technical rational model? Schön, and his commentators, are rightly preoccupied with the way this model does not fit with what actually goes on in professional practice. If a sociocultural reading of professional practice is rejected, as I reject it, based on concerns to preserve more of a space for conceptualizing individual agency, then where does that leave us in thinking about how theoretical and tacit knowledge are applied 'in the moment' by professionals in action? My solution is the idea of productive uncertainty, based on the work of Wilfred Bion.

A psychodynamic approach – Bion and uncertainty

Tracing a path to Bion

The key argument I develop in positing the idea of productive uncertainty is that my understanding of Bion potentially gives a new frame for looking at professional practice, for thinking about the relationship between theoretical and tacit knowledge in teaching and other caring professions. The key elements that I derive from the analyst–analysand context and extend to other professionals focus on Bion's concept of 'O', and his theory of epistemology, in which when the analyst moves from not knowing to knowing in the analytic encounter, the 'conceptions' that arise can be kept unsaturated and flexibly integrated with existing theoretical concepts to allow the analysand to 'become', to develop their autonomous potential. In doing this, I mark out Bion starkly as no metaphysical naturalist and interpret his work as being incompatible with a determinist naturalist account of how professionals in the caring service should approach their practice.

Understanding Bion's ideas is difficult and his writing, although sublime in its formulation and ambition, cries out for interpretation. In coming to know Bion, as well as Bion's books and papers, directly – fermenting my understanding of them over a period of a number of years – I have also made use of several commentaries on his work by Bion scholars – particularly Symington and Symington (1996), Bleandonu (1999) and Grotstein (2007). However, in order to understand Bion properly we need to place him in the context of the development of psychoanalytic theory.

In a common characterization, Grotstein (ibid., p. 37) describes Freud as 'steeped in positivism'. Just as Darwin had worked out the mechanical processes of the derivation of the body, so Freud had set out the mechanical processes of the mind, both mirroring the triumphant mechanisms of the industrial revolution. Freud's psychosexual theory of development, his emphasis on the structural model (id, ego, superego), his presentation of the pleasure principle and the reality principle and the drive-related conflict between these does, it is hard to deny, have mechanistic aspects to it. However, this view of Freud is a matter of some debate. Shuttleworth (1997) argues that although Freud could be thought of as characterizing the pleasure principle as a drive originating in the id, he also placed the reality principle in the ego; Shuttleworth sees this as part of Freud's overall project to bring the unseen drives of the unconscious into conscious perception. This means that the conscious mind can have control of them, and become healthy. This may be a mechanistic account, but I agree with Shuttleworth in saying that it is not necessarily a deterministic one.

Connecting Freud and Bion is Melanie Klein, with whom Bion was in psychoanalysis. Unlike Freud, the focus of Klein's work was on children. Her clinical work can be seen as confirming, at least in her own terms, the reality of Freud's discoveries based on his clinical work with adults, identifying the existence of infantile sexuality and aggression. For Klein, the young child is a cauldron of hate and fear and anger, with these emotions being played out unconsciously in phantasy. By phantasy, Klein means that the anger or hate is associated with internal (unconscious) images of external players. This internal reality, which in Klein's scheme may be only loosely based on external reality, is where the crux of emotional life takes place. Yet it is not only negativity, her extension of Freud's death instinct in the id, that Klein identifies; through her clinical observation of young children she also saw guilt, the desire for reparation and love. Both may be entertained by the infant about the same person, most importantly the mother, in phantasy. Klein theorized that for the infant to experience the good, loving mother as also possibly hateful was overwhelming, and that instead – again in phantasy – the infant would 'split' the mother into a good, loving mother and a bad, persecutory mother. This process of splitting becomes a fundamental process of the unconscious mind. Klein denotes the mind, in the process of defensive splitting of aspects of the world into idealized good and hateful, persecutory bad parts, as being in the 'paranoid–schizoid' position. This idea resonates with most of us in some way. I was recently flashed by a speed camera whilst going just slightly over the speed limit. At that moment, as I seethed with anger and fear, the government was a persecutory body that I hated intensely. Klein's theory is that these mechanisms, which start in the very early life of the child, set down a psychodynamic pattern which persists into adult life. However, Klein, again from her clinical observations of young children, observed that sometimes an object that was regarded as hateful might also be treated differently. The rag doll that was bitten and thrown away might be picked up and caressed. The baby that at one minute bites the mother, in the next smiles and attempts to caress. Klein argues that at least partly, the infant in phantasy feels guilt and the desire for reparation. The dislocation between phantasy and reality may also be quite stark – Klein argues that in phantasy the infant may have killed or severely damaged the mother, meaning that the feeling of guilt and desire for reparation may be very strong. Associated with these feelings of guilt and the act of reparation is also a growing understanding in the mind that perhaps the split between the good and bad objects can be somewhat reconciled. A minute after the speed camera flashed, I may still have been hoping not to get a ticket, but I might also have been more able to entertain positive feelings for my local council, and some understanding that following the rules of the road has benefits for everyone (or perhaps not). Klein denotes the mind, in this process of guilt, reparation and reconciliation, as being in the depressive position (a rather different usage from our common use of the word depression). It is also in this process of reconciliation that, as with Freud, the agentic function of the ego can be seen at play. Waddell 1998, p. 19) notes that the oscillation between paranoid–schizoid and depressive positions, which she describes as 'varying states of mind', is something that persists throughout the life course. It is developmentally appropriate for infants to be consistently more in the paranoid–schizoid position, and adults more in the depressive position. Yet at all ages we can and do oscillate between the two positions.

There are a number of opinions on how to think about Bion in relation to Klein and Freud. For Bleandonu, Bion is a Kleinian and his ideas are a natural extension of Klein; for others, such as the Symingtons (Symington and Symington, 1996), he is an innovator who creates a brash caesura between himself and what came before in psychoanalysis. Alternatively, O'Shaughnessy (2005) thinks of Bion as transforming Klein and Freud. I like this way of thinking about it. Bion was quite clear in linking his work to that of Freud, and particularly to the ideas expressed in Freud's paper 'Formulations Regarding the Two Principles of Mental Functioning' (1911), in which Freud lays out the pleasure principle and the reality principle. The id desires pleasure and seeks it immediately, and later the reality principle, identified with the ego, introduces the possibility of waiting, delaying the pleasure in the furtherance of other goals. For Bion, the gap that exists between the pleasure principle and the reality principle, in other words our ability to tolerate frustration (or uncertainty), was particularly important. Bion was, as O'Shaughnessy points out, particularly interested in how we come to know, how thinking arises:

> [...] Bion's ever present concern is with the instinct to know—the K link, as he calls it, and I think this is also the main reason why Bion's writings are of such notable psychoanalytic significance. From the start, K was—and so it has remained—at the very centre of psychoanalysis. Freud wrote in 1919, for instance, 'we have formulated our tasks as physicians thus: to bring to the patient's knowledge the unconscious, repressed impulses existing in him, and, for that purpose, to uncover the resistances that oppose this extension of his knowledge about himself' (Freud, p. 159). Bion's wide-ranging work advanced our understanding of K in clinical practice, and furthermore brought about an overall shift in psychoanalytic theory by placing K in a new position where it has the same pre-eminence as the instincts of love and hate, so that instead of a duality there is posited a trio of interacting human instincts: love, hate and trying to know—L, H and K.
>
> (O'Shaughnessy, 2005, p. 1523)

Klein also was interested in the desire to know, but she conceived of the epistemophilic instinct, the infant's desire to find out about the world, as being initiated by the infant's desire to know what was inside the mother and their phantasy that perhaps the mother was filled with lots of little persecutory infants. There is, as Grotstein points out about both Freud and Klein, something mechanistic and instinctual here. Yet in Bion's formulation there is a shift away from instinct and mechanism – although I do think these are only part of the story of both Freud and Klein – towards a more nuanced, alive and genuine view of the human mind. For me, following Grotstein, it is here that Bion's influence on psychoanalysis, particularly in his later quasi-mystical work, is most importantly felt. His shifting of the psychoanalytic enterprise towards the generative, agentic aspects of Freud's original work is what is of most significance. In Grotstein's words, Bion recharacterized psychoanalysis as concerned with 'emotions and infinite imagination' (op. cit., p. 37).

This shift can also be seen in how Bion approaches Klein's process of projective identification. Linked to her theoretical development on splitting, Klein posits that in phantasy the infant splits off parts of the self that are felt to be negative or hateful. These split-off parts are then projected out on to an external person. There is then an unconscious identification with this split-off element of the self residing in this external person. This may be associated with unconscious evocative behaviour designed to make the recipient of the projection behave in accordance with the projective phantasy. It is also possible that both good and bad elements of the self can be the subject of this process of projective identification, although as O'Shaughnessy (op. cit., p. 1525) points out, Klein's formulation was very much of projective identification as a defensive mechanism. Bion extended – or, perhaps better, transformed – Klein's concept, reconceptualizing it not just as a defensive mechanism, a way of evacuating painful aspects of the self, but as a mode of primitive communication.

Bion also extends (or transforms) Klein's theory of the paranoid–schizoid and depressive positions. Klein, and following her Segal (1957), had already considered that the ability to split was in fact a fundamental aspect of being able to understand. It is only by splitting the world into categories that we can come to know it. Bion focuses on the oscillation between the two positions and places this oscillation at the centre of his epistemology, in which emotions, relationship and thinking are bound up together.

Bion developed his system of epistemology based on Klein, proposing that the process of coming to know depends on the development of the ability to tolerate the frustration of uncertainty – of 'not knowing'. In *Learning from Experience* (1962), he proposes that it is the growing toleration of frustration signified by the development of the depressive position that allows 'thinking' to develop. Thinking and/or thoughts are what happens in the space where the infant can tolerate the non-appearance of the breast or other part-object, as opposed to evacuating it in paranoid–schizoid mode. For Bion, the process of thinking and learning is rooted in the developing ability of humans to tolerate uncertainty and unknowing. As such, relationship is at the centre of Bion's epistemology. Normal projective identification from the baby to the mother, which the mother recognizes and can process with her free-floating benign attention (reverie), is the central aspect of knowing someone else (the K link). Bion (1962, p. 91) suggests that the baby has a preconception of the mother's breast. The exact meaning of 'preconception' is somewhat unclear. My initial reading of *Learning from Experience* suggests to me that it means something like an instinct in its first instantiation. When the breast is absent, so that this preconception cannot be realized, the baby feels that it is going to die. In normal development, according to Bion, the baby uses projective identification to communicate with the mother. In this case, the baby cries, with the intention of provoking in the mother the same feelings that the baby is having – that is, 'I'm going to die' – thus projecting its feelings of annihilation onto the mother. The mother, again in the course of normal development, uses her maternal reverie to process these feelings. The mother can, in a process that at least initially occurs to a significant extent in the unconscious, recognize the communication contained in the projection, and her response to this communication models for the baby that such communication is real and possible. This establishes or represents a constant pattern of communicative interaction between mother and baby. We can see here in more detail Bion's broadening of Klein's idea of projective identification as a pathological process to one of normal infantile intersubjective communication.

Thus the mother can tolerate both this projection of anxiety from the baby and her frustration in not knowing what it is that the baby wants. In this gap of toleration, thoughts arise and the mother then thinks the baby is not going to die and in fact needs a feed, or investigates what the baby might need. The baby receives unconsciously this communication of the message 'you are not going to die' from the mother. The baby is then able itself to tolerate the frustration of waiting for the breast; so when the baby then receives the breast, its preconception is met with realization, leading to a conception. The initial development of the thought of the breast becomes possible. For Bion, the development of thought is rooted in the ability to tolerate frustration, or – to put it another way – to be able to tolerate not knowing whether the breast will return. Perhaps the next time the baby feels the absence of the breast, due to its new ability to begin to formulate the thought of the breast, it will be able to wait a little longer before the mother reacts, and in that space where the baby is tolerating frustration, it can think about what is not there. Thus the baby can create a mental representation of the absent breast, which is a thought.

Further, Bion considers the formation of a conception to be part of an ongoing cycle. He proposes that when a conception is formed, part of it remains 'unsaturated'; that is, part of its meaning or the understanding it represents is not fully formed. In this space of 'not knowing', the search for the next realization and the formation of higher concepts can take place. In simpler terms, every piece of understanding that we attain has within it the seeds of further questions which we go on to (painfully) explore.

A Bionian lens on professional practice

Bion proposes that these processes do not just occur during infancy but are in fact the underpinning of human thought at all stages of human development. It is a theory of epistemology and not just of mother–infant communication. Extending this epistemological approach to the classroom, teachers might – similarly to the mother in infancy – act as a container for the child's frustration extant in the process of learning, and thus allow 'thinking' to develop. Making such a leap from consulting room to classroom involves grappling with some significant epistemological issues. However, in this book I go further than that and propose that not only can concepts from psychoanalysis be applied to the classroom, giving us a powerful lens to think about professional practice from a relational perspective, but we can also develop appropriate emotionally and relationally 'tuned-in' research tools for exploring professional practice based on psychoanalytic technique. Making such a move is not, however, novel, and it locates the study reported in this book in the developing field of psychoanalytically informed psychosocial studies. It is, though, both complex and contentious, and I give a full treatment of the issues involved in Chapter 4 on methodology.

One of the key features of such a psychosocial approach is an appreciation that it is possible to make use of the phenomenon of countertransference when observing a research field. The precise definition of countertransference in the psychoanalytic community is a matter of some debate, but it is generally taken to mean the emotional reaction that an analyst feels when with a patient, which serves as a clue to what the patient is feeling. In one sense, it is the counterpart to projective identification. In this process, the patient has an intolerable feeling and projects that externally, lodging it in another person, who holds that feeling for the patient. In this unconscious communication, by gesture or wording, the patient makes the other person feel something. This is something that we all experience: the friend or colleague who, without you being able to put your finger on exactly why, makes you feel angry or incompetent (or, conversely, happy or powerful). For the analyst, being able to notice these unexpected feelings due to countertransference, and then to reflect on what unconscious communication they represent, provides a window to the emotionality of the patient. This is something that is inherently experiential – an analyst could report to you what feelings they had, but the actual veracity of the experience only exists 'in the moment' between analyst and patient.

In the study reported on in this book, countertransference is used both as a way of explaining part of what might be going on when a caring professional engages with a client, or child, or patient, and as a research tool whereby an observing researcher uses countertransference responses to work out what is going on emotionally and relationally in the field of study. In a book, the closest we can come to illuminating this idea, and indeed properly arguing in favour of its application to thinking about professional practice, is via a detailed vignette which makes genuine reference to the feelings engendered in the observer.

We can see a putative example of this in the following classroom observation of Mandy at Randall School – one of the teachers in the empirical study – working with her class of eight 13 and 14-year-old boys, including Angus, Steven and Piers, all with a diagnosis of high-functioning autism or Asperger's syndrome. The observation took place in March 2010.

> I come in to the classroom a few minutes early. Mandy is not there, nor are the children, but Dougal and one of the other teaching assistants are sitting at the computer. We chat about the weather – it was raining heavily after a few days of sunshine, so I say, 'It's been too hot really the last few days'. After a few minutes, Mandy comes in. She says 'Morning, Joe' quite loudly and warmly, and I say 'Hello Mandy'. Mandy sits down at the central table and I go over and sit at the end of that table. Mandy's demeanour is bright and energetic – she seems to be in a very good mood. Then Angus comes in and Mandy says 'good morning' to him and he says hello back. Then he comes over to where I am sitting to get his things and says, 'Hello Joseph'. I say hello back and smile and ask him, 'Have you had a haircut?' He nods. He smiles a bit nervously. Angus then goes over to Mandy and she looks at his contact book. There seems to be an issue over missing information – I miss the first bit but it is something to do with missing information – 'she thought I lost it but...'. Mandy interrupts him, clearly not understanding what he is trying to say, and says, 'Angus, Angus start again'. Angus does and gives a long, list-like explanation of what had happened. It appears to be about some information on a form or piece of paper – 'I put it by the printer, then my mum started looking round for it and in the end we both forgot about it'. Mandy listens patiently; this list of what happened carries on for a while, and finally Mandy says that she will give his mum a ring tomorrow to sort it out.

On the face of it, this is an exchange not particularly worthy of comment. However, I had on several occasions been on the receiving end of what felt like long, boring monologues from Angus just like this one. During these, a part of me honestly felt like I would rather be dead than carry on listening. Working out how to let Angus both get over the relevant information and feel that he had been listened to, without taking up the whole morning, required considerable judgement on Mandy's side about when and how to intervene.

> Then Steven comes in, looking out the window, and says, 'Mandy we can't do the low ropes today?' His voice is rather monotone and he has quite a marked American accent. Mandy puts her hands down square on the table, sits up and says, very pleasantly, and smiling broadly, 'Yes you can! – you were told you were going to do low ropes whatever the

weather, so I trust you've brought your dirty clothes that you don't mind getting dirty'. Steven doesn't seem sure what to say for a moment and then continues to argue the point, asking if they can do low ropes inside. Mandy says, more stridently, 'of course you're not doing low ropes inside, it's an *outside* assault course ... outdoor adventure activities happen whatever the weather, Steven' (the last part said in a softer, slightly mischievous tone). Then, more conciliatorily, 'it's going to stop raining soon anyhow'. At this point Steven seems to give up and goes off, saying, in something of a non-sequitur, 'Never believe the weather, people ... never believe the weather'.

Mandy sets clear expectations and boundaries for Steven and the rest of the class. Yet she carefully modulates her tone, using humour and an expression of compromise and amelioration – 'it's going to stop raining soon anyhow' – which both binds Steven to her and allows him a measure of face-saving. Her approach may also have served to help Steven and the rest of the class deal with latent anxiety associated with leaving the safety of the classroom. One can imagine another teacher whose responses were not so closely attuned to the emotional state of her students perhaps tipping Steven and the class into a heightened state of anxiety and overt rebellion.

There is a huge range of complex interactions and task activities going on for Mandy in these five minutes. Although Mandy has a significantly smaller number of children here than in mainstream school classes, they are children whose sense of emotional and sometimes physical integration is significantly impaired, and who are likely to be in a continuous state of potential anxiety about their ability to function in the world in terms of both social interaction and organization. Compared to typical teenagers, their ability to think of themselves as people growing towards adulthood and independence is, for them, all very much in question. Yet Mandy offers the right word, the right tone of voice, the right look; she knows when to take notice and when to ignore. In Bion's terms, we could say that she can tolerate the considerable frustration that must be associated with working with these children, with their frequent communication of their anxieties and uncertainties about their experiences in the world. For Mandy, uncertainty is not something that needs to be run away from, but something that can be experienced. She can tolerate the frustration of uncertainty, containing and interpreting the children's difficult projections and offering them back to the children in a modulated, more manageable form, which allows them to develop their capacity to think as agentic human subjects.

This observational record also provides an initial example of what I mean by an observer making use of countertransference responses to the emotional experience of the actors in a research field.

Bion: a Kantian perspective

Bion peppered his writings with references to philosophers, particularly Kant. Bion's writings are famously pithy, and sometimes imprecise; I would argue that an example of this is how he made use of Kant's ideas in his epistemology. However, I will argue, and I think demonstrate fairly clearly, that his use of Kant clearly positions Bion not as a metaphysical naturalist but rather as a psychoanalyst who gave primacy to human agency, and in particular a human agency that is most fully realized in the intersubjective encounter between one person and another. I will also argue that it is not tenable to suggest that Bion – or, indeed, any theorist – could hold such a position and at the same time hold to a naïve metaphysical naturalism which sees the human subject as prey to the determinism of genetics or psychology.

I will first consider Kant's formulations and then discuss how Bion makes use of them. In doing so, I am cognizant of the fact that neither Bion in his writings, nor any of the major commentators on Bion – particularly Grotstein – have attempted to do this in any systematic way.

Kant's formulation is that causation is an a priori synthetic, resulting or consequent on the way the human sense apparatus perceives the world. As such, we cannot, in the phenomenal world, have any actual knowledge of 'things in themselves'; nor can we have any definite knowledge of how 'things in themselves' (the noumenal world) relate to objects that we perceive (the phenomenal world). Further, as Ward (2006, p. 10) points out, in Kant's transcendental idealism, space, time and causation are products of our sensible minds; they cannot be said to subsist in themselves independently of human sensibility. In this 'two-objects' interpretation of Kant (Rohlfe, 2010), the noumenal and phenomenal worlds are separate. A key critique of Kant, put forward for example by Russell (1946), amongst many others, is that he makes a very fine demarcation between on the one hand stating that we can have no knowledge of things in themselves, that they cannot be considered to subsist in space and time in the noumenal world, and on the other insisting that things in themselves are in some way the cause of appearances in the phenomenal world (even though his defence against Hume's views on causation is that causation is also a product of our sensible minds). Such critique leads to the alternative 'two-aspects' interpretation of Kant which argues what he really means is not that there are two separate type of objects – noumenal and phenomenal – but rather that transcendental idealism has a more limited scope, and is better interpreted as meaning that objects have two aspects (Allison, 2004). One aspect is presented to the cognitive faculties of human beings, the a priori forms of our sensible apparatus. Another aspect is hidden, and cannot be perceived by us – the 'thing in itself'. However, as Ward (op. cit.) points out, this latter interpretation is problematic in that it less well supports the key aim of Kant's Copernican revolution in the three critiques in relation to what is its key aim, the moral justification of free will and the (possibility of) the existence of God. Kant's argument is that our awareness of the imperative of necessary and universal moral laws can only be explained by the existence of a noumenal world which in some unknown way acts as a first cause for our action in the phenomenal world, allowing us to act as autonomous agents. It is worth noting, as Ward (op. cit., p. 152) points out that for Kant, autonomy of will is in relation to natural moral law; that the act of autonomy is in suppressing our base desires in relation to law. Autonomy is the autonomy not to do anything, but to do what is right.

Bion's epistemology

Edna O'Shaughnessy (2005) splits Bion's work into two phases. The first phase of writing covers the 1950s and the beginning of the 1960s. Bion, as we have seen, develops Freud and Klein's ideas, introducing in particular a theory of thinking and approaches to practice for the psychoanalyst. He also makes a very significant contribution to psychoanalytic theory on the working of groups. In this phase, Bion sees himself as being in search – perhaps similarly to Freud – of a scientific approach to psychoanalysis. For example, he introduces the grid (Table 2.1) associated with his theory of thinking. This is intended as both a system of notation useful to the analyst when reflecting on the analytical session and an outline for how thoughts and concepts emerge.

There is a mathematical flavour to this approach which can also be seen in the use of innovative notations introduced in his theory of thinking and the use of mathematical notation in the *Elements of Psycho-Analysis* (1963), *Attention and Interpretation* (1970) and *Transformations* (1965) to denote how the analyst transforms what the analysand has been saying. Bion (1965) uses the term 'transformation' analogously to the idea of a mathematic transformation, where for example a shape is transformed in size. Just as in the mathematical transformation, when the analyst transforms what the analysand

Table 2.1 Extract from Bion's grid

		Definitory hypotheses	Psi	Notation	Attention	Inquiry	Action
A	Beta elements	A1	A2				A6
B	Alpha elements	B1	B2	B3	B4	B5	B6
C	Dream thoughts	C1	C2	C3	C4	C5	C6
D	Pre-conception	D1	D2	D3	D4	D5	D6
E	Conception	E1	E2	E3	E4	E5	E6
F	Concept	F1	F2	F3	F4	F5	F6
G	Scientific deductive system		G2				
H	Algebraic calculus						

Source: Adapted from *Learning from Experience* (Bion, 1962).

has presented, certain invariants remain. For the shape, the ratio of the length of the sides is invariant, whereas for the analyst–analysand it may be something of the key emotional content of what was said that remains invariant.

Bion's use of mathematical notation is partly rooted in his desire to avoid the use of existing language terms which have associations of meaning attached to them, this being the rationale for his use of the terms α and β elements. Bion uses β elements as 'things in themselves', in Kantian terms; a sort of unprocessed sense data. These elements are then acted on by alpha function, a function deliberately undefined by Bion which 'operates on the sense impressions, wherever they are, and on the emotions, whatever they are, of which the patient is aware' (1962, p. 6). This process transforms the β elements into α elements, which are then available to the unconscious mind for mental work. Bion also uses this abstract undefined terminology because he wants these terms to remain 'unsaturated', and thus open for continuing development and interpretation by the reader. It is also the case, as O'Shaughnessy (2005) markedly points out, that this potentially leaves some of Bion's writing open to misinterpretation.

The use of such terms also reflects the side of Bion's writings, most marked in this initial phase, which sees the practice of psychoanalysis as part of a wider scientific enterprise. Bion hopes to develop a set of tools which will, if properly used, help analysts to categorize, in a scientific way, their experience of the application of psychoanalysis. One might think that what Bion was hoping to achieve was a bit like the process of clinical audit in medicine, the aim being to identify 'invariant' features of psychoanalysis across different contexts that analysts can use both in reflecting on their own practice and in discussions with other analysts.

However, as O'Shaughnessy (op. cit.) indicates, in the second phase of Bion's writing, from the 1970s onwards, an element of mysticism enters his writing, introducing scope for accusations of imprecision. O'Shaughnessy identifies in particular his introduction of mystical associations into the concept of 'O'. She quotes Bion in *Attention and Interpretation* (p. 27) – 'I shall use the sign *O* to denote that which is the ultimate reality represented by terms such as ultimate reality, absolute truth, the godhead, the infinite, the thing in-itself' – and goes on to comment:

> This statement mixes the psychoanalytic idea for which the sign *O* was originally introduced with the vast 'penumbra of associations' of an assortment of philosophical ideas. Earlier, in *Learning from Experience* (1962), *O*, as part of his exploration of *K*, denotes the process and experience of getting to know—in opposition to the static state of possessing knowledge. Later, as *O* mingles with 'ultimate reality, absolute truth, the godhead, the infinite, the thing-in-itself', Bion's earlier work rather than being developed, in my opinion, is confused...
>
> (op. cit., p. 1524)

I strongly disagree with the thrust of this assertion that Bion's overall enterprise is confused, although, as I will argue, it is clear that some elements of
Bion's use of Kant are indeed imprecise. More critically, O'Shaughnessy's
statement reflects a commonly held reaction to Bion's work in this second
phase, where much of the psychoanalytic community felt that Bion had
crossed the line from the generation of evolutionary extensions of Kleinian
thinking and technique to mystical irrelevance (Grotstein 2007, p. 21).

In his *Notes on Memory and Desire* (1967), Bion recommends – or, if we
stay true to the language of the paper more closely, directs – that the analyst
working with the patient should suspend memory and desire. With regard to
the former, Bion specified this as desire derived from the senses – memories
triggered by sight, sound and smell – referring back to previous experiences
with this patient. Desire in this case relates partly to the desire for knowledge
or certainty:

> What is 'known' about the patient is of no further consequence: it is
> either false or irrelevant. If it is 'known' by patient and analyst, it is obso-
> lete. If it is 'known' by the one but not the other, a defence is operating.
> The only point of importance in any session is the unknown. Nothing
> must be allowed to distract from intuiting that.
>
> (ibid., p. 272).

In his chapter on the 'Opacity of Memory in Desire' in *Attention and Interpretation*, Bion (1970, p. 71) similarly points out, when referring to the irrelevance of referring to notes between one session and the next, that 'it ceased
to be of importance when it was formulated ... the attempt to remember or
record destroys the capacity for ... observation of psycho-analytically significant events'. In discussing this statement, Bion does differentiate between
remembering points such as the analysand's name and the day and time of the
next appointment and remembering what they said or your interpretations,
in the sense that they could still be relevant for what you will observe in the
consulting room in the next session. Mysticism notwithstanding, it was and
is a revolutionary statement – not one that can be imagined from Freud or
Klein, however much Bion acknowledges his allegiance to them.

What, though, does Bion actually mean by this? As O'Shaughnessy has
pointed out, there is something imprecise here. Did Bion mean that the
analyst should never think about 'what is known about the patient'? This
question of imprecision parallels our discussion of Schön. Bion seems to be
suggesting that theoretical knowledge has no place in the analytic consulting room, and that there is certainly no room for expert or craft knowledge
derived from previous experiences.

The original 1967 paper is presented in dialectic form, with Bion's paper
followed by responses from several discussants, and a final response by
Bion himself. It could be, as several of the discussants suggest, that Bion is

saying the analyst should not project, based on his sense-activated memories or theoretical constructs, into the developing thoughts of the patient. If you do, you run the risk that your desire for an outcome, a cure or an end to the session, or your desire to neatly fit the patient in to an existing theory rather than struggle with the unknown, will deflect you and the patient from what is really going on. How then will you actually get to know what is really going on? For Bion, the answer is bound up with 'O'. Grotstein (op. cit., p. 68), following Bion in imprecision, describes 'O' as 'Absolute Truth, Ultimate Reality, infinity, godhead'. This obviously relates somehow to Kantian ideas – including, I think clearly in Grotstein's view, Kant's privileging of free will, God and the immortality of the soul within his Copernican revolution – but quite how is not very clear.

In the 1967 paper, Bion goes on to say:

> In any session, evolution takes place. Out of the darkness and formlessness something evolves. That evolution can bear a superficial resemblance to memory, but once it has been experienced, it can never be confounded with memory. It shares with dreams the quality of being wholly present or unaccountably and suddenly absent. This evolution is what the psychoanalyst must be ready to interpret.
>
> (op. cit., p. 272)

Something evolving out of the darkness and formlessness is Bion's idea of 'O', the reality of 'things in themselves', that the analyst comes to most effectively by focusing on his responses to the patient's projective identifications. To achieve this focus, memory of past sessions and desire for knowledge must be minimized.

So where is theoretical knowledge when the analyst is without memory and desire? Bleandonu (1999) suggests that Bion implies a temporary exclusion, to be followed by a renaissance of the conscious, directed development of concepts, based on psychoanalytic theory. But this is to be based on a reading of the theory which is attuned to the intuited reality of the patient, rather than a reading which starts from the theory and fits or squeezes the patient into its constraints. Given the detailed, laboured development of psychoanalytic theory that Bion presents in his writings, this seems to make sense.

Grotstein, who is much more drawn to the mystical side of Bion, presents what is essentially the same argument, but with a more detailed treatment of Bion's mysticism. He sees Bion as describing an unending dialectic between conscious and unconscious thought, which is mediated through 'O'. In the analytic session, the analyst's task is to become

> intuitively responsive to [...] his waveband of O, which then resonates with the analysand's psychoanalytic object, his own O, which is

characterized by his Ultimate Reality. [...] Thus the analyst's O becomes resonant on that ineffable waveband with the O of the analysand, which the former must then transduces or transform for the analysand in K as symbols in the form of interpretation; if accepted, it then becomes transformed into the analysand's personal O.

(op. cit., p.117)

When this happens, a pattern, picked up via this process of unconscious communication, emerges in the conscious mind of the analyst. Bion terms this the 'selected fact' (1967, p. 48), whereby a 'constant conjunction' of emotional communication becomes clear or saturated enough that it can be given a tentative label by the conscious mind.

My earlier observation of Mandy's interactions with her class also resonates with Grotstein's (op. cit.) interpretation of Bion's directive to be 'without memory or desire'. Mandy is in intersubjective relationship with the child; something about their reality is created (transformation of 'O'), the selected fact arises and Mandy acts.

However, 'O' is always in flux and there is an ongoing dialectic between cognitive verbal 'interpretations' in 'K' and the ineffable 'O'. In Grotstein's interpretation, they never come to an end point, but continue in an iterative reflexive relationship.

Bion's use of Kant

Bion says nothing really definitive about how he interprets Kant or uses the term 'things in themselves'. Echoing O'Shaughnessy, I think this imprecision is not helpful to his readers. As such, Bion's metaphysical position, and in particular whether he is using 'O' as a mystical device, is open to debate. Grotstein says yes. Others, such as Mawson (2010), say no, he just uses it as a heuristic device with regard to the limits of knowledge about the other in the consulting room. Still others, such as O'Shaughnessy, think his later use of the term is imprecise and confused. For example, O'Shaughnessy quite reasonably asks if the concept of β element is equivalent to 'O'. Is Bion using one or other or both as equivalent to Kant's idea of the 'thing in itself?' Grotstein (op. cit., p. 58) suggests that the β element is the 'emotional sense impression of O'. In this reading, the β element is analogous to Kant's sensuous data, but one could not honestly say that Bion makes it easy for the reader to work it out. However, I do think that when we look more broadly at Bion's arguments and use of wider theory, particularly his use of Christian mysticism, there is in fact a fairly clear answer to the question of whether Bion is using a naturalist or mystical interpretation of Kant.

We can posit that the two trends in interpreting Bion revolve around different interpretations of what Kant means by 'things in themselves'.

When Mawson and O'Shaughnessy consider 'O' as a marker for the limitations for the knowledge of the analysand that we can hope to derive in the analytic session, they seem to argue, albeit implicitly, for a two-aspects interpretation of Kant, where there is no linked Copernican revolution in the mind of Bion about metaphysics, no project to rescue the soul from the jaws of the Enlightenment. Alternatively, Grotstein, as well as other recent commentators on Bion such as Civitarese (2012) and possibly Reiner (2012), see 'O' as a marker for the mystical noumenal world. This take on Bion's Kant is a 'two-objects' interpretation, where the personal godhead, the noumenic soul, is alive and well.

However, it is worth noting that in the 'two-objects' interpretation of Kant, and Bion, the major difficulty lies in how the noumena can influence the phenomenal world. Bion clearly posits that 'O' influences what goes on in the psychoanalytic consulting room, but never visibly notices the obvious objection to using Kantian 'things in themselves' in this way, and I think this is an undeniable – although certainly far from fatal – omission in his application of Kant's ideas to his epistemology.

I think there is a very significant trend in Bion's writings which supports the argument that Bion makes use of Kant's ideas precisely because he is making the argument for a view of the human subject as autonomously agentic and one who truly 'becomes', reaches their potential, in intersubjective relationship with the other – and that something unknowable, indefinable in purely physical terms, takes place when this encounter occurs. I will now go on to hopefully substantiate this contention.

Godhead or God dead?

In developing his idea of 'O' and the relationship between noumena and phenomena, Bion makes significant use of Christian mysticism, particularly the work of Meister Eckhart, a fourteenth-century Dominican monk. Eckhart differentiates between God, who operates actively in the world, and godhead, which is the irreducible, unknowable power of the Trinity. Eckhart, in common with Maimonides, feels the only way we can come to know the unknowable Trinity in any sense is through a series of negations (the godhead is not this, not this, etc.) Bleandonu (op. cit., p. 211) suggests that Bion parallels the K link with the active God – knowledge which causes (and perhaps also arises from) action in the world – and 'O' with the godhead, as a form of knowledge that arises from being; that is, something irreducible that is a property of human existence. This irreducible being might be equated with the soul, which might further be considered an emanation of the godhead. If this is the case, then 'O' is the personal godhead – the divine soul of the analysand – that the analyst comes to know in the session, and the link between 'K' and 'O' is based on a mystical metaphysical perspective.

Grotstein does point out (op. cit., p. 120) that Bion is sometimes inconsistent on the point of whether 'O' is in fact a universal or personal god-head. However, Bion's reference to mystical traditions does point towards a personal 'O' which, in some way, is the manifestation of a universal 'O'. This, it seems to me, must parallel the Judaeo-Christian idea of a transcendental G–d, a part of whom, the soul, is instantiated in the human person.

A further aspect or extension of Bion's perspective is his use of the term 'becoming'. Grotstein (op. cit., p. 305) notes that this derives from Plato's idea of 'that which is always becoming'. This applies to the analyst who, through his reverie, the resonance of his 'O' with the 'O' of the analysand, 'becomes' the analysand. This does not suggest a merger, but rather a deep intersubjective meeting in relationship. At the same time the analysand, through the transformative experience of having his being recognized by another, is able to come into contact with his own 'O', and thus to 'become' himself. This might be considered as happening on a prosaic or even cognitive level in that the analysand comes in to contact with his emotions, embraces and interprets them. This has echoes of Freud's hope that the process of psychoanalysis would allow the analysand to take control of their unconscious so that they could work and love productively. On the mystical metaphysical level, however, 'becoming' has more to do with a productive encounter that the analysand has with his own essence, the 'O' of the Godhead, the soul that derives from God. On either level, this is, for sure, an uncertain process for the analyst and for the analysand. Bion's clinical accounts reflect the difficulty in maintaining emotional contact long enough for this type of intersubjective encounter to occur. Yet if the difficulty of this uncertain encounter can be battled, then the productive process of 'becoming' could occur.

In *Attention and Interpretation*, Bion considers the role of the mystic in religion and society. Mirroring the process of communication between analyst and analysand in the consulting room, which leads to the emergence of the selected fact, he posits the mystic as being the conduit for the development of revolutionary ideas in society. He sees Jesus as the archetypal mystic and notes how, in his view, the 'ossified' 'rabbinical directorate' reacted to him. He contrasts this to the development of the Kabbalah.

> The rabbinical directorate learned caution, so that when it had to adjust to the Lurianic doctrine, and to the injuries that the Lurianic doctrine was alleged by its opponents to have inflicted in Judaism, it did not contribute to an explosion.
>
> (1970, p. 115)

To modern ears, post-Vatican II, it is hard to not to identify something of an echo of Christian prejudice against Judaism. More generously, the echo of

Buber, who clearly influenced Bion, is probably stronger. In the introduction to his 1977 paper 'Caesura' he opens with a quotation from Buber's *I and Thou*: 'From the glowing darkness of the chaos he has stepped into the cool and light creation without immediately possessing it...' (Buber, 1956, cited by Bion, 1977, p. 38).

Bion also refers to Buber several times throughout the paper. Buber's fascination with Hasidism and its disruptive effect on Judaism, which Buber parallels with the effect of Jesus, is, I think, what drives Bion's reference to Isaac Luria, whose championing of the mystical Kaballah was a significant influence on the rise of Hasidism.

When a revolutionary idea arises in the mystic on behalf of the group, the group needs both to name it and to allow it flexibility. It needs to avoid the desire to murder the idea, or to reify it as a set of rules. Or by extension, I might suggest, when a new theoretical idea arises related to professional practice in the caring services, the profession and the professional similarly need to both name it and allow it flexibility.

Michael Eigen (1998, p. 15) says of Bion that he 'paid homage to the mysticism of old', and notes that in a personal communication to him, Bion noted his interest in and debt to the Kaballah. It is also interesting that two important books about Bion were written by Jewish authors, Michael Eigen and James Grotstein, who both reflect on the resonance between the experience of reading Bion and their Jewish experiences of faith. It is probably worth noting that I am in the same category.

His use of Buber and Meister Eckhart, his interest in the Kaballah, all I think make Mawson's contention that Bion is a naturalist who sees 'O' as denoting what remains unknown when the analyst works with the analysand, seeing Bion's thought as a two-aspects version of Kant, rather unsustainable.

Nevertheless, there remain questions about exactly how Bion conceptualized 'O', and how he relates it to religious thought. Reiner (op. cit.) suggests that he is arguing for an impersonal God or spiritual force, closer to the Eastern traditions. It is entirely possible, and indeed right, to interpret what Bion is saying without recourse to any belief whatsoever in a personal God, just as it is similarly possible to do so for Kant, in that the Copernican revolution points towards a noumenal world but transcendental idealism by definition says nothing about the attributes of such a world.

I think it is very hard when one looks at Bion's broader writing to classify him glibly, as Mawson and others clearly want to, as a metaphysical naturalist. His view of what goes on in the psychoanalytic session, as I think is very clear from what he wrote, just does not fit easily with such an ontological position.

Metaphysics, agency and professional practice

Now Jonathan Sacks, as well as myself, might rail eloquently against the 'evils' of determinism, particularly the determinism of genetics and evolutionary psychology, but railing against something and not liking it is not the same as having a reason to dismiss it. To theorists such as Dennett, Dawkins, Grayling and the many influenced by them, Bion's apparent inclusion of mysticism in his epistemology is open to rebuttal. Rather than accept that psychology in any form can be about the godhead, they would simply argue back that God is dead.

John Zammitto, in his 2008 paper on Kant and naturalism in which he comes down firmly in favour of naturalism, quotes Barry Stroud's analogy: 'Naturalism seems to me ... rather like "World Peace" (p. 534). In other words, everyone nowadays is for it. So is it possible to maintain an idealist mystical position in psychoanalysis or psychology? In exploring this I come back to Jerry Fodor. For Fodor, the 'hard problem' for psychology is consciousness. This is how he puts it:

> it is widely supposed that the world is made entirely of mere matter, but how could mere matter be conscious? How, in particular, could a couple of pounds of grey tissue have experiences?
>
> (Fodor, 2007, p. 9)

Going back to Kant and transcendental idealism, answering this question was at the heart of the Copernican revolution; we can also ask, by extension, how could mere matter have agency? As Fodor points out, there are two traditional approaches to this – either consciousness is an illusion or it emerges when matter reaches a certain level of complexity, such as the human brain. Magee (2000) points out, in discussion of Kant, that when you see how much of human interaction is predicated on the idea of agentic consciousness, the suggestion that it is an illusion is difficult to argue for. The 'emergent properties' argument is more compelling. For example, Cilliers and DeVilliers (2000) point out that developmental and evolutionary accounts of the human brain point towards a plausible idea of emergent complexity. Thus the agentic self and consciousness is something that arises when the brain reaches a certain level of complexity, although, as Fodor also stresses, as an emergent property it is not reducible to its simpler constituent parts. Social realists such as Margaret Archer make similar arguments that we can maintain a (limited) space for a human agency that arises out of our biological nature. Archer (2000), drawing on Callincos and Rorty amongst others, argues that our biological background gives rise to a continuing mental self of sense, which translates into agency.

This is a strong argument, and it is precisely arguments such as these, based on this evidence base, that for many make the idea of a mystical psychology even more difficult to swallow in the twenty-first century than it was thirty years ago, at the time of Bion's later, most influential writings.

However, as Strawson and Freeman (2006) point out, there is a bit of a conceptual problem with the idea of emergent consciousness. Strawson posits that 'For any feature Y of anything that is correctly considered to be emergent from X, there must be something about X and X alone in virtue of which Y emerges, and which is sufficient for Y' (2006, p. 18). Yet, as Strawson argues, how could anything 'about' inanimate matter be related to consciousness? In order to escape from this and still retain a commitment to metaphysical naturalism, Strawson resorts to panpsychism – that is, the idea that all matter is in fact conscious in some way. Fodor, in his review of Strawson, demurs on the basis that panpsychism does not really get around the hard problem, as it is not still not clear how concatenating lots of little of individually conscious bits of matter would lead to the human 'I' with agentic self-consciousness. Instead, Fodor argues that perhaps there are basic laws of the universe apart from the laws of physics, that mean 'Consciousness might emerge from matter because matter is the sort of stuff from which consciousness emerges' (Fodor, 2007, p. 10). But Fodor is not really happy with this, as he concedes that in effect this would mean giving up on metaphysical naturalism as we normally understand it. Fodor is something of a troubled metaphysical naturalist.

There are also reasons to be suspicious of reductionist evolutionary accounts of the mind and of interpersonal processes. Fodor (2007) points out that most current models of the mind tend to be computational in nature in some way, and thus by implication predicated on a reductionist view of what the mind is. Putting it glibly, neurons equal silicon chips. Thomas Nagel, in his famous paper 'What is it like to be a bat?' (1974), asks whether, if we knew everything there was to know about a bat's brain and its sensing organs, we would be able to say we know what it is like to be a bat? Given the considerable strides that science has made in understanding the operation of echolocation in bats since the paper was published, the question has perhaps even more force in the twenty-first century. Nagel suggests that we could not really hope to know what it is phenomenologically to be a bat unless we actually were one, even if we had a perfect technical description of what a bat is. There is something irreducible about being a bat. This is of course, if you like, the flip side of the hard question of consciousness and emergent properties – if it's difficult to conceive how mind can emerge from matter, then you can't reducibly define mind in term of matter.

Fodor, with Piattelli-Palmarini (2011), makes somewhat parallel – although in their case naturalist – arguments about evolutionary biology and agency. Drawing on Gould and Lewontin's (1979) critique of naïve and unsupported adaptationist arguments, they point out that many arguments about evolutionary biology and psychology are post hoc circular arguments. I should say

I do not agree with Fodor that the lack of counterfactuals is a good argument against natural selection, and I do think that non-circular, albeit still post hoc, arguments can be made for evolutionary psychology, even if this does not happen very often; however, Fodor's substantive point is that even if all of our traits could be explained instrumentally, doing so is a complex task that takes more than glib assertions, unsupported by evidence, of post hoc explanations of the history and teleology of current functions.

One (potential) way out of the problems involved in a computational account of human consciousness, and in particular the problem of how humans appear to relate to each other as agentic subjects, is to make use of a sociocultural (sometimes called interpersonal) turn in psychology. A number of developmental psychologists, including Aitken and Trevarthen (1997), Fonagy and Target (2007) and Neisser (1993), make use of this. Fonagy and Target (2007) in fact suggest that the idea of the human mind as a big computer is Cartesian in both origin and sympathy. One could argue, in this vein, that a privileging of functional cognitive processes in considering what the mind is and does has been the dominant mode in western thought since Descartes.

The interpersonal or sociocultural turn, influenced very much by Soviet psychology, sees the mind not as something independent, approaching the social from a cognitive perspective, but rather as something that in essence arises from or is created from the social. In Vygotskian terms, the intrapersonal mind can only be conceived as coming into being when a person encounters the social interpersonal, and in particular when it encounters language.

This turn within psychology, exemplified in the writings of Trevarthen, Fonagy and Neisser, makes significant use of evidence from developmental psychology, neuroscience and evolutionary psychology. Neisser uses the term 'the interpersonal self' to refer to the development of a perceived self based on patterns of reciprocated, instantly graspable communication behaviours between people. In common with Neisser, both Trevarthen and Fonagy see such communications as instantly graspable because they are instinctual patterns which have an evolutionary origin (an argument somewhat similar to that of the social realists). They also rely on a very significant body of work on the neurological and behavioural study of developing infants. This research (Trevarthen and Aitken, 2001; Csibra, 2010; Lee and Siegle, 2012) provides persuasive evidence to support two contentions: first, that from birth (as well as before), human infants have the ability to engage in mutual relational communication with other humans, and this communication forms the bedrock of the development of the mind and the personality; second, that the development of the brain is intertwined with and dependent on the presence of such relational communication with adult caregivers.

Trevarthen and Aitken (op. cit.) are particularly taken with studies which use conversational analysis techniques to show that there is a statistical identity between the expression and timing of informal adult conversations and typical interactions between caregivers and infants in the first few months of life. Following Bateson (1979), they term these 'proto-conversations' and use this in combination with evidence from neuroscience to postulate the existence of an 'Intrinsic Motivation Formation', an as yet undefined function in the brain that facilitates and regulates this intersubjective communication between infant and the other.

Thus in the sociocultural/interpersonal turn, the mind is conceived, in contrast to the supposedly computational Cartesian view, as both physically instantiated in the brain and socially situated, where relational functions precede cognitive functions, and where the brain has evolved to innately possess the capacity for primary intersubjectivity.

Now, we might think that this developmental and evolutionary account has a significant degree of resonance with Bion's ideas about how thinking arises from relationship. In particular, in his call to the analyst to work 'without memory or desire', Bion similarly foregrounds a type of person-to-person communication in which formal cognitive processes play, at the very least, a background role. Yet does Trevarthen and Aitken's account suffice to encapsulate the mystical metaphysics of Bion's writing? I do not think so, and I do not think it even manages to come up with a sufficiently complete naturalist explanation of intersubjectivity. Partly this is because, as I have indicated, I don't think the sociocultural approach in the end succeeds as a materialist project, any more than Marxism does. More important, however, is that an interpersonal account rooted in developmental and evolutionary biology has a big gap – precisely the one that Fodor identifies. For Fogarty and Trevarthen – as well as, I might add, for the social realists such as Archer who rely on their biological analysis for their account of agency – the interpersonal turn in the development and working of the brain would need some working theory to fill the enormous gap between neuroscientific accounts of what a neuron does and our conceptualization of how thoughts come about or thinking occurs (that is, to actually find the Intrinsic Motivation Formation), as well as overcoming Fodor and Nagler's ontological objections about the irreducibility of emergent properties of consciousness to physical components.

Now, none of this should be taken to mean either that neuroscience or developmental and cognitive psychology have nothing useful to tell us about human behaviour. They clearly do. And just because we can't do better than the New Synthesis model right now, this does not mean that we won't do so at some point; we might also be able to describe neuronally what the IMF is. It is certainly the case, as Andrew Melnyk (2012) points out, that so far all identifiable neural events supervene on physical events. So nothing in neuroscience, particularly work on connecting mental events to neuronal events via functional Magnetic Resonance Imaging, suggests anything other than a physical basis for what happens in our minds, even if at this stage we have no particularly detailed idea about how the brain works or how in practice the mind might supervene on it.

So, even if we can poke holes in metaphysical naturalism and thus at least open an intelligently reasonable space for Bion's metaphysical mysticism in thinking about professional practice, it still must be the case that to a very great degree, minds are instantiated in physical brains. When you see what happens to a mind when a brain is damaged by Parkinson's or Alzheimer's, or indeed autism, then it is really impossible to rationally believe otherwise. So it is reasonable to suggest that science of the mind and science of the brain can tell us lots of useful things, which of course they do; however, in my view, they tell us something quite different from what Bion – and, I would argue, much of psychoanalysis post-Bion – is telling us about the mind, something more than statements about the equivalence of human relationships with neuronal structures. This 'something more' is akin, although not identical, to Buber's idea of the 'I–Thou' relationship. It is about the unknowable noumenal reality of the human subject that somehow becomes known to the analyst in the mystery of the intersubjective encounter, an encounter in which the analysand is helped to 'become'. It is the space within that encounter of productive uncertainty, where one autonomous agentic human grapples with the difficulty of coming to know the other and, through that difficult encounter, facilitates the growth of another autonomous agentic human subject.

This is not a religious position. Bion was clearly not making an argument for a Judaeo-Christian view of reality; he was not interested in talking about God. It is, though, a position in which the human subject in its core remains unknowable, and it is in the space of this 'unknowability', and only in that space, that productive encounter takes place. It is hard to argue that Bion would disagree with Nagel's contention that what it is to be another human is ultimately unknowable. It also seems quite likely that Bion would agree with Fodor that when complex mind emerges out of matter, the emergent properties are ontologically not traceable back to simpler components. Whether, in the end, Bion would align himself with Nagel's metaphysical mysticism or Fodor's troubled version of metaphysical naturalism is not something we can fully determine from his writings. What is clear is that Bion teaches us it is only in the encounter with the unknowable that learning and growth takes place.

Does it make a difference to professional practice?

One could very well argue, well, so what? No one really thinks that it is selfish genes that make us love our children. As Magee (2000) has noted, even the most hardened positivist thinks you have agentic consciousness when you stamp on his foot. This is certainly true up to a point; however, I really think that Sacks is on to something when he points to the dangers of a modern *weltanschauung* which is overly influenced by determinism. Sacks argues that societies dominated by this view will tend to be backward rather than forward-facing, and will downplay the place of responsibilities over rights. This has an effect on how individuals approach thinking about their lives and about problems in their lives. I would argue further that the social realists, such as Archer, aim to recover a space for agency which is too limited, and whose defence against naturalistic determinism is too weak.

There is a fairly close parallel to be made between these arguments at the macro level and, at the micro level, the way in which teachers and other professionals think about agency – both their own and, even more importantly, that of their students or clients. There are dangers involved in teachers thinking that a child's capabilities are defined by a naturalist account. Of course, no real, living, breathing teacher that I have ever met thinks that their students are wholly defined by a naturalist account, any more than any living, breathing foot-stampee thinks that foot-stampers are just agglomerations of genes. The danger, more precisely, is that teachers influenced by deterministic accounts may place too high a premium on what a naturalist conception of the world can tell us about the human other, particularly the role of psychology, in coming to decisions about how to work with the children they care for. Putting it another way, the space for productive uncertainty, where their 'O' can resonate with the 'O' of the child, can be significantly and unnecessarily reduced – and what I mean is a mystical, or at least a non-simplistic, naturalist resonance. This is why the argument matters. As I have shown, *untroubled* metaphysical naturalistic accounts, particularly under argued varieties such as those based on selfish genes, cannot really claim to capture what human nature is and why humans behave as they do. In my view, this has important consequences for how we conceptualize professional practice, particularly in relation to agency.

Consider the secondary school teacher looking at the Standard Assessment Test scores that a child brings with them from primary school, or the similar scenario when a university professor looks at the scores a student brings with them from high school. In either scenario, the teacher has to decide how much weight to give to the 'scientific' picture of the student. Do they ignore it, treat it as background information whilst they wait to see how the student does in the first term, or does it inform their view of the student from the outset? This is perhaps an eternal question in the practice of education. However, the way in which we treat eternal questions tends to depend on how we view the world. Too much determinism might mean that as teachers we fail the children we are working with. Bion's mystical metaphysics points towards the need for teachers to maintain the space for a productive uncertainty based on relationship, on knowing the child. The productive capacity of this space should have at least as much to tell teachers about what their performance in the classroom should be about as the very necessary knowledge they derive from the scientific view of the child.

Moving towards the psychosocial

In order to investigate this putative phenomenon of productive uncertainty empirically (and I do think it can be so investigated), we need to have a set of tools to do so. I have already referred to the empirical study around which this book is based and begun to consider the particular methodology used in the study, which – perhaps unsurprisingly – shares many features of Bion's epistemology. Putting it another way, in order to uncover the operation of productive uncertainty in professionals working in the classroom, the researcher must also adopt something of an open stance, to be without memory and desire, to allow their 'O' to resonate with the 'O' of the subject. So what might be otherwise a social science investigation of the classroom needs to have the psychoanalytic inserted into it, taking us towards a psychosocial account. Achieving this does, as already noted, mean engaging with a significant number of methodological issues, and I intend to unpack these in Chapter 4. Before doing so, however, I want to present a more detailed justification for why special educational needs has been chosen as the focus area for thinking about productive uncertainty, which I will attempt in Chapter 3.

Chapter 3

Uncertainty and special educational needs

Introduction to the study

I am going to assert, and I hope reasonably demonstrate, that the concept of productive uncertainty has wide application to teaching in a range of situations – mainstream and special schools, 'normal' children, children with emotional and behavioural problems, children with problems learning or paying attention, and so on. In fact, I go further, and in Chapter 7 I discuss the potential application of productive uncertainty for the work of other caring professionals. However, in arguing this case I make use of an empirical study focused on teachers working with autism. I contend that this is a particularly apposite context because issues of uncertainty are thrown into relief so starkly for these teachers.

The empirical study around which this book is built concerns an investigation of the ways in which five teachers experience and deal with uncertainty when working with children with autism. The teachers, all working at Randall School – a special school for children and young people with autism between the ages of 11 and 18 – were involved in a project in which a new smartphone app was introduced into the classroom. The app allows teachers to flexibly develop interventions which support children with autism with social skills and life-skills functioning.

The software provides a web-based toolkit for teachers that allows them to develop both diary functions and specific support and intervention sequences ('personal trainer' function) to meet the needs of individual children. These are then loaded, via a synchronization function, onto the app on the child's smartphone. The sequences consist of a series of linked screens, each of which can include customizable text, images, video and sound. The diary function allows for the creation of appointments, reminders and prompts, which can be directly linked to personal trainer functions. Implementation took place at Randall School with five teachers and ten children working with the technology tool in the 2009/2010 academic year.

Randall School is located in a rural part of the UK and has around ninety children and twelve teachers, as well as a large number of support workers who act in what is essentially a teaching assistant role. All children admitted to the school need to have a psychiatric diagnosis that places them on the autism spectrum. Most of the children are higher functioning, with most having an IQ on the Weschler Intelligence Scale for Children fourth version (WISC-IV) of over 70.

The principal focus for the software was developing social and life-skill functions. Social skills functions included prompts to support children in remembering to consider other people's perspectives and short personal trainer sequences to help children calm down in situations likely to lead to emotional outbursts. Teachers also used the personal trainer function to adapt 'social stories' (Gray, 2007) presenting a narrative about a situation, skill or concept, in terms of relevant social cues, perspectives and common responses, to an electronic platform. The life-skills interventions developed included managing money, dealing more effectively with time management, managing public transport and aiding self-monitoring of medication administration.

As will be shown later in this chapter and in Chapter 5, the teachers in this study experienced considerable levels of uncertainty. Work with children with special educational needs – with its inevitable conflation with controversies regarding integration and inclusion, as well as on capability and agency –is a contested area, where wide-ranging debates on policy and practice penetrate into the classroom. As such, special educational needs is a particularly relevant context to think about teacher uncertainty.

It is also, as a widely contested area, appropriate for considering how the issue of the balance between theoretical and tacit knowledge in teacher practice is considered from a policy perspective. There is considerable international debate about this issue, particularly in relation to teacher education policy. In this book I will, based on my development of the idea of productive uncertainty, make recommendations about policy and practice in relation to teacher practice and teacher education, as well as to the caring professions more broadly.

Uncertainty about special educational needs

In both mainstream and special schools, teachers work with children who have the label 'special educational needs'. Some might argue that recent developments in the sociology of childhood mean we have moved past arid debates about inclusion. In particular, sociologists such as James and Prout (2004) have suggested that we should see childhood not as developmentally driven, given the experiences that children's biology pushes them through, but rather as a socially constructed phenomenon that places particular cultural and historical valences on children's biological selves. At the same time, they place a greater emphasis on children as social actors who exist at the intersection of many possible aspects of childhood – 'childhoods', rather than a unitary childhood. In the context of disability studies, this means a notion of the child that, in common with Burman's (2008) critique of developmental psychology, less jettisons psychology than reframes its role in defining developmental paths for children not as undisputable norms but rather as reflecting particular cultural practices that may well have significance for both individuals and society – but that can also be challenged and disrupted, as much by children as actors themselves as by the adults around them.

Some might see this as a bold re-framing that makes the social versus medical model debate obsolete. I would tend to disagree. Although it might be the case that many cognitive and developmental psychologists appear to have taken on board Burman's critique, this is often in the form of lip service – a gloss on an underlying commitment to the objective justification of categories and comparisons. The recent debates on DSM-V, the 2013 update of the American Psychiatric Association's Diagnostic and Statistical Manual of Mental Disorders (Davies, 2013; Carey, 2012), I think quite clearly show that the debate between the social and medical models, between Barton's psychological and sociological positions on special educational needs (Barton, 1988), is alive and well. Putting it another way, attempts in the sociology of education to reframe the debate on their own terms have largely failed in the real world. Teachers have to work within a context in which the very use of the term SEN reflects an underlying political, cultural and individual debate which is often translated into tensions and uncertainty in the classroom, reflecting debates about policy and practice which are very much live in the first decades of the twenty-first century. In the arena of policy and practice we remain, on the one hand, with cognitive and developmental psychology and psychiatry, intimately involved with the diagnosis and treatment of conditions given diagnostic labels. In this psychological position, SEN is seen as a fixed, unchanging quality located within the child. On the other hand, in the sociological position, the special needs of individual children are seen as arising mainly as a result of the social and educational environment's response to an impairment whose expression can vary and develop depending on the effectiveness of that response. If you think that such debates have been superseded by debates in the academy on the sociology of education, then just attend any conference about autism, ADHD (Attention Deficit Hyperactivity Disorder), inclusion in schools, etc., and you will see quite clearly, in the range of presentations, this same debate going on about how best to conceptualize SEN, with the split most commonly following a rough fault line with clinical and cognitive psychologists on one side and teachers, parents and sociologists on the other.

In fact, one could consider that for teachers, uncertainty and confusion are in fact the rule when they think about SEN and inclusion. For example, some of the children with whom they are working will have a diagnosis such as Asperger's syndrome (again a matter of definitional controversy in DSM-V) or ADHD. Such a diagnosis is, in a real sense, a medical categorization. Other children may have been diagnosed as having dyslexia or dyscalculia by an external professional such as an educational psychologist. Yet at least some of local school policy, and much of the 'meat' of the discourse about inclusion in the classroom in many countries, including the UK, is based on a sociological position whereby talking about the existence of real deficits inherent in the child is thought somehow suspect – with the emphasis in practice being on how teachers can meet the needs of all children, all of whom are seen as lying on a spectrum of qualitatively similar need, as in Florian and Black-Hawkins' concept of inclusive pedagogy (2011). It is the case, therefore, that teachers are faced with the inherent tension involved in the political and cultural imperative of looking at children's needs as part of a social model of disability whilst at the same time having often to rely on a medical concept of diagnosis. This split mirrors, to a significant degree, the tension between the focus on tacit knowledge about the child which is implicit in an inclusive pedagogy approach, and the focus on theoretical knowledge which is explicit in a diagnostic approach to special educational needs.

Autism: even more uncertainty

Most clinical and cognitive psychologists regard autism as primarily a developmental disorder of the human nervous system which is characterized by mild to severe impairments in reciprocal social engagement, reciprocal communication and flexible regulation of self, behaviour and interest (see the 'autism triad', e.g. Wing and Gould, 1979). Although DSM-V has specified two core impairments for autism – social communication and repetitive behaviours and restricted interests – the triad of impairments is still a widely used and accepted conceptual model for understanding the condition (Wing *et al.*, 2011). Such psychological definitions of autism are clearly located firmly within the medical model, and have unsurprisingly been subjected to sociological critiques which note that 'normal' modes of social and emotional communication can be thought of as socially constructed and that greater recognition needs to be given, in the educational setting in particular, to seeing this as difference rather than deficit. Such critiques add that as such the diagnostic labels themselves are suspect, serving only to negatively pathologize groups of children (Molloy and Vasil, 2002; Bogdashina, 2006). At the same time, essentialist accounts of autism contend that the biological, genetic and clinical evidence, indicating a variation from the norm, is clear in pointing towards the psychological definition of autism as the key starting point for thinking about this condition. Such accounts have significant force in schools, as they tend to be the ones which are directly operationalized by the educational and clinical psychologists alongside whom teachers of children with autism often closely work. For teachers working with children with autism, the competing psychological and sociological positions tend to foreground the issue of capability. This leads to questions extant in teachers' minds as to whether, for example, it is possible to change the classroom (or society) to meet the children's needs given the extent of their social impairment. Other associated questions also arise, including whether special or mainstream placements are appropriate for individual children (this can often be a significant issue for teachers working in both mainstream and special school settings). There are also questions of agency, often focused on the tension between allowing children with autism to stay in their social 'shells' as opposed to encouraging them to engage in greater encounter with the social, educational and economic world as it is. The underlying issue of whether individual children with autism are able and willing to take decisions for themselves, to express themselves as rational choosing agents as opposed to being forever in a dependent role in which decisions are made for them, is a live one for all teachers working with children with autism in the classroom.

Uncertainty can also arise about the implication for practice of specific diagnostic labels within the spectrum, or of the autistic spectrum in general. Autism is a syndrome and, as such, it has a very broad range of expression. In a sense, then, the use of the term 'autism' can be even more of an abstraction than the use of terms for other conditions. This can make it more difficult for teachers to balance the significance of an autism diagnosis with the specific knowledge of and relationship with the individual child that they know. The tension between these two aspects is a potential source of considerable uncertainty for teachers working with children with autism. Teachers can also be uncertain about their level of knowledge and understanding of the autism spectrum, as well as being uncertain as to the significance of this in relation to their effectiveness as teachers.

It is worth noting that there is a partial mapping between questions of agency and independence and the psychological and social positions on autism, although it is far from straightforward. Psychologists who take an essentialist position often tend to see children's attributes as fixed – they can't do it now, they won't ever be able to do it. However, those taking the sociological position, such as Barton (1988), by underplaying the role of the individual/self can also – perhaps unintentionally – lessen the focus on the development of individual agency.

As I will discuss further, such theoretical tensions – around capability and agency, sociological and psychological positions on SEN and the balance between theoretical and tacit knowledge – tend to be played out in public debates about SEN policy. Such policy debates interpenetrate with teachers' ongoing thinking and can be a significant source of uncertainty in terms of their day-to-day practice. For example, they might feel a general commitment to developing the autonomy of a child but also wonder if there is not some truth to an essentialist position – that is, if they can't do it now, they might never be able to – and encouraging them might be setting them up to fail.

Working with uncertainty about SEN in the classroom

A good example of how uncertainty is a real presence in the classrooms of teachers working with children with SEN can be seen in the following extract from the empirical study around which this book is based. This is an interview with teacher Penny, originally from Brazil, who is talking about her class of 13–14-year-olds with ASD diagnoses. She focuses on one boy in particular, Oscar.

In the previous interview, Penny had given me some quite detailed answers about her thinking in relation to working with children with autism, uncertainty and the sources on which she draws in coming to a decision about what to do in the classroom. In the second interview, Penny had told me in quite a bit of detail about her concerns for Oscar. Whilst generally, in the observations, he had presented as a personable, very polite boy, Penny noted that he tended to have an air of superiority which led to conflicts with the other children. In this extract, Penny describes her considerable ongoing uncertainty about how to approach Oscar's social problems.

Penny: Yeah we discuss it with … obviously the psychologist department … we have this meeting … every time I think I don't know how to manage something I go to them …

Joe: Does that help?

Penny: Well, unfortunately I don't think we have much idea how to … apart from talking to him … because when we try things, for example writing a social story or having some special sessions with him and stuff like that, he becomes very stressed and goes home and then Mum becomes very stressed and then calls us and say, 'Why?'… in a certain way … Mum, yes encourage us and wanted for us to encourage Oscar's social independence … to be … independent life, independent skills … like he will be able to manage his own things … waking up, making his breakfast and these kinds of things … be responsible of his own items and all these kinds of things … yes mother is very happy with all this kind of things. … I'm not sure it's because she wanted [it] really or she wants to do less work … [so that] Oscar would manage his own … the problem with Oscar is … the only way we can really go to him is we speak to him but when we speak to him we try to explain to him very clearly … he interpretate *(sic)* things in the wrong way … you know, I cannot remember … and now …

something he wanted to go from beginning of September ... 'I want to go mainstream school', when we said the school said that mainstream school is no option for Oscar because [of] his social difficulties ...

[...]

Oscar ... He'd never recognize he does anything wrong... mmm... and then you can... you try to put things in place for him um but he feels that you are thinking that he's less able and this is why he'd need maybe social stories or needs to practise certain skills because definitely he's no good in them. Um he feels we're treating him like a, you know, like a less able student ... mmm ... because he is very clear that he is in the top, you know, he's the cleverest one in the whole of school and obviously Mum encourages those kind of thoughts ... mmm um and then um many times um social stories and stuff like that ... because you know he [feels that he] doesn't need that. He is above all these things.

Joe: Well it seems generally um I mean it seems generally it's kind of difficult to know what to...

Penny: Yeah, yeah, yeah it is, it is.

Joe: So just thinking about that for a minute cos I, you know, obv ... difficult thing about what to do as in generally difficult ... what's gonna help him. So when you're in that kind of situation, with Oscar but with other children as well, what, what do you kind of draw on, what do you use to help you to work out when you're, when you're, you know when it's ... you're thinking about ... I'm not quite sure what to do, it's difficult, what shall I do with him? What, what do you, what do you draw on ... is it experience with other children, is it...

Penny: Well it's experience [with] the kids and obviously um this is what I try to put in place as I said before I think, I'm sure I just said it before, or I was talking to somebody ... then it's very difficult to know how much you can push or how much they're going to understand that, what you're trying to explain, talking about social er interaction or social um or independence, all this area you know. This [makes] it very difficult ... Like in many other kids, well you know we have Nancy from the speech therapy department or Donald they, they want, they can suggest the strategies of things we can put in place to help them but I have to say the majority of the staff here in the school we are quite lost [laughter] about how to help them, how we can...

It is striking how uncertain Penny sounds in this extract, and how her uncertainty about how she should work with Oscar has been sustained over a long period. A key question both here and in later interview material with Penny (see Chapter 5) is whether he is a boy whose autism makes it difficult for him to engage in social interaction or is just, as with many children in early adolescence, quite narcissistic and unable to admit there could be anything wrong with being like that.

In this extract, Penny also seems to be quite unclear about the place of theoretical and expert knowledge in her work with Oscar.

Policy tensions about special educational needs

I have identified significant theoretical tensions between sociological and psychological positions, and the balance between a focus on theoretical as opposed to tacit knowledge. Such tensions have been amply reflected in trends in policy development. In England and Wales the ideological move towards inclusion heralded by Warnock, and to a significant extent supported by the Labour government of 1997–2010, has to some extent been reversed by the Conservative–Liberal coalition government in place since 2010. Their reversal of the Labour government's programme of special school closures is a case in point. The Children and Families Bill (2012–2014) and subsequent Act (2014) also heralded greater emphasis on the role of specialist skills and knowledge for teachers and other care professionals working with children with SEN. In the US, although there is a much more clearly embedded tradition of specialist training for special educators, since the passing of the Individuals with Difficulties Education Act (IDEA) in 1997 there has also been growing debate about mainstreaming (Kavale, 2002) and the extent to which specialist knowledge, restricted to special education teachers, is the best way to achieve good outcomes across different groups of children (Brownell *et al.*, 2005; Jones and West, 2009).

This policy question is linked to an ongoing debate as to whether developing specific understanding about particular diagnostic categories and associated specific teaching strategies makes teachers more effective practitioners. As I have noted previously, there is often an implicit view – from authors writing from a sociological perspective – that professional development which promotes an overall positive disposition and attitude towards inclusion is far more important than specific knowledge about specific conditions (see for example Leatherman and Niemeyer, 2005; Avramidis and Kalyva, 2007). Lewis and Norwich (2005), writing from such a perspective, reviewed teacher effectiveness studies to consider whether or not there should be a specific SEN pedagogy. They conclude that for moderate learning difficulties and conditions such as dyslexia, there is no clearly identifiable specific pedagogy. Children may need more repetition, over-learning or attention to detail, but they characterize this as a change in emphasis, not a qualitatively different pedagogy. Simpson *et al.* (2004) identify a parallel trend in the US towards more generalist rather than condition-specific SEN training courses for pre-service teachers, as well as, in some states, a limited move away from a workforce split between special and mainstream educators towards a more unified profession in which all teachers have expertise in working with children with SEN.

Other authors, who perhaps have been able to maintain a perspective based more on evidence than on ideology, have adopted a different position. Osler and Osler (2002) presented data to indicate that, particularly for some impairments, the level of understanding about those conditions and what implications they can have for teaching strategies makes a significant difference to the teacher's effectiveness in meeting the needs of those children. Wedell (2008), drawing on government statistics on academic outcomes for children with SEN, argues that student teachers in England and Wales are generally unprepared to meet the needs of those with SEN and concludes that emphasis in teacher education on subject knowledge, rather than on child development and the psychology of learning, meant that teachers were not well equipped to support children with SEN.

The debate about the balance between theoretical and tacit knowledge in the work of teachers working with children with special educational needs, and in their training, is very much a live and contentious one. For many of those adopting a sociological position, autism might sometimes seem to be something of a problem. On first inspection, the typical social functioning of children with autism seems to be so much at variance with a school environment designed for 'neurotypical' children that the challenge of developing an inclusive school environment that can meet the needs of both groups simultaneously seems to be a bridge too far. So the sociologists, such as Lewis and Norwich (2005, pp. 207–11), accept that autism might be a bit different, but do so begrudgingly. It is difficult, though, to follow Lewis and Norwich in their tendency to just ignore the combined clinical, qualitative and quantitative research indicating the efficacy of long-standing specialized educational programmes for autism such as TEACCH (see Mesibov and Shea, 1996; Mesibov, 1997; Howlin, 2004; Rogers and Vismara, 2008). Further, many other academics and clinicians with extensive experience in the field – Rita Jordan (2005) is a noteworthy example – have written extensively on the issue of specialized approaches in autism education, arguing forcefully for the need for an autism-specific pedagogy in schools.

Yet, when you look more closely at this literature on evidence-based practice in autism in school settings, it is not quite so clear-cut. For example, in a later paper considering the evidence for TEACCH, Mesibov and Shea (2010) – respected and influential researchers whose work is quite explicitly located within a psychological discourse – reflect on the American Psychological Association's adoption of Evidence-Based Practice in Psychology (EBPP), defined as 'the integration of the best available research and clinical expertise within the context of patient characteristics, culture, values, and preferences' (APA, 2006, p. 273). Mesibov and Shea, in their review of field scale studies on TEACCH, note that what seems to work well in 'close to lab' small-scale tests tends to be much less effective in wider-scale evaluations of use in the field. They argue strongly, therefore, for the integration of clinical evaluations of effectiveness, based on the clinician's knowledge of the individual child and using quasi-randomized controlled trial data, in coming to an overall evaluation of autism-specific interventions.

Mesibov and Shea are quite clearly not arguing, as Lewis and Norwich do, that there only *may* be a basis for an autism-specific pedagogy. They would regard the premise inherent in Lewis and Norwich's argument that one might question the need for such a pedagogy as nonsensical. Yet there is, nevertheless, an element of agreement, in that both sets of authors are accepting that what we can know about children with autism and how to work with them cannot be defined solely by the definitions attached to a clinical diagnosis. Further, the appropriate use of this clinical definition, and any specific pedagogies attached to it, has to be considered in the context of what we also know about the individual child and their specific needs.

If we adopt this more nuanced position, somewhere in between the polarities of the psychological and sociological, this might suggest that what teachers need to know about autism is derived from a mixture of both their understanding of individual children and their needs and knowledge about the significance of diagnostic terms and associated specific pedagogies. Stating this so glibly, however, still leaves unanswered the question of how this tacit and theoretical knowledge might intercalate. One way of thinking about the answer to this question might be through the lens of productive uncertainty.

Issues with teacher training

Thinking about these issues related to how teachers should make use of theoretical and expert knowledge in working with children with SEN through the lens of productive uncertainty will lead to some recommendations for teachers and policy-makers in the concluding chapter of this book. The preceding discussion indicates that the issue of what teachers should know about theory is a live political debate internationally, which also relates, quite clearly, to the issue of the structure and curriculum of initial teacher education courses. Any recommendations about policy will need to refer to this. As Wedell (2008) argues, what teachers learn about SEN and related issues as part of their initial teacher training may have a significant level of influence on their understanding and thinking in this area. Indeed, one could argue that some of the uncertainty that teachers feel in relation to working with children with SEN would be founded on their experiences as student teachers. This is potentially arguable independent of whether one takes a psychological or sociological position on SEN. Garner (1996a) reports on the levels of dissatisfaction with training provider teaching in this area and (1996b) the lack of relative emphasis on special educational needs by training providers in the UK. Hodkinson (2009) identifies this tendency towards dissatisfaction as a historical trend going back to the 1960s. It is important to highlight the historical differences between the training approach taken in the UK as compared to other countries. As noted, both the US and many European countries have a tradition of specialist initial teacher training for SEN teachers, who would in the past go on to teach in specialist provisions for children with SEN, although there is an increasing trend for such teachers to start and continue their careers in mainstream settings as well (Hodkinson, 2009; Hegarty, 1998). In contrast, there has never been any established tradition of specialist education for teachers of SEN, at least in initial teacher training, in the UK. The historical reasons for this approach are not very clear. In a useful historical review, Hodkinson (2009) describes the development of SEN training in initial teacher education since the 1960s, but doesn't provide a rationale for this overall difference in approach in the UK. It could be that since 1980, UK education policy has been very heavily influenced by the social model of disability and sociological discourses of SEN. However, I have not identified any clear evidence to link this to policy decisions on teacher training. It seems possible that the relatively low levels of funding for initial teacher training in the UK may equally be implicated.

Whatever the historical forces at play, there is currently concern amongst UK policy-makers that there is not enough emphasis on SEN in initial teacher training in the UK (which, although it is a gross generalization, mirrors – as I have described – something of an opposite trend in the US). Particularly influential in this regard has been the report by the UK House of Commons Education and Skills Select Committee (2006), which undertook an in-depth review of SEN provision in schools and received representations from a range of stakeholders, including teachers, parents, other professionals and special interest groups. The Committee concluded that there was a lack of emphasis on training in SEN in both initial teacher education and Continuing Professional Development (CPD) frameworks and recommended that 'SEN training should become a core, compulsory part of initial teacher training for all teachers' (p. 70).

No doubt partly in response to this report – and other policy reports that reached similar conclusions, such as the Lamb Enquiry (Lamb, 2009) – government policy in the UK since 2008 has placed more emphasis recently on special educational needs training for teachers, with a range of (albeit patchily implemented) initiatives, including a national training programme for special educational needs coordinators (Training and Development Agency for Schools, 2010a) and a proposed greater emphasis on SEN in initial teacher training in the Children and Families Act (Department of Education 2010; 2013).

There is also debate as to how teachers should be prepared for working with children in specific diagnostic categories, such as autism. As noted, Simpson *et al.* (2004) identify a trend in the US towards non-categorical and cross-categorical special education initial teacher education programmes; that is to say that many training providers are moving towards programmes which focus on SEN in general, without a specific focus on any one diagnostic category. That is *not* to say, however, that US programmes do not have specific content on particular diagnostic categories. For example, Barnhill *et al.* (2010) undertook a postal questionnaire of 185 HE institutions across the US, focusing on the level of autism-specific content offered in their special education programmes; 59 per cent indicated that they offered courses with significant levels of autism-specific content. This is a very stark contrast from the situation in the UK, where there is little current emphasis in initial teacher training on any category-specific, SEN-specific training, let alone on specific training related to autism. Some online resources have been developed by central government, such as the Inclusion Development Programme, a series of online e-learning resources designed to be used as a CPD resource by teachers (Department for Children, Families and Skills, 2008), and in 2010 these were complemented by advanced training materials for several diagnostic categories, including autism (Training and Development Agency for Schools, 2010b), although these materials' impact on pre-service and in-service teachers is questionable. Again, the Children and Families Act proposes a greater emphasis on explicit expert knowledge for teachers working with children with SEN generally, although how this is to be achieved is unclear. As such, teachers working with children with autism in mainstream and special school settings have little specific training, at least initially, in theory related to cognition, development or intervention in autism. One of the aims of this book, therefore – as it is predicated on a study focusing on the professional practice of teachers working specifically with children with autism – is to consider, through the lens of productive uncertainty, if and how such teachers should balance theoretical and tacit knowledge in their work.

Back to uncertainty

To sum up, I am proposing that teachers working with children with SEN, in any context, do so in a climate that is inherently uncertain and likely to stimulate uncertainty, productive or non-productive, in the thinking of the teachers. To recap, this uncertainty can stem from a number of sources. Teachers can be uncertain as to whether they should be applying labels linked to SEN to children at all. Teachers operate within a 'mixed mode' environment, where the social model and medical model continue to uneasily coexist. School processes, deriving from policy structures, require teachers to work with diagnostic labels; yet the categorization of difficulties with learning that arise in the classroom is not straightforward. Educational diagnostic labels are abstractions which are applied to a complex reality that is formed from the interaction of teacher and child in a particular school at a particular time. As such, they always act to simplify the complex, and as such it is not surprising that teachers, in applying them to complex interactions which they are actually experiencing directly – particularly in the context of overarching policy and practice debates about inclusion – find themselves uncertain as to whether the label fits, or even makes sense at all.

Even if the complexities of the use of diagnostic terms in terms of theoretical debates could be surmounted, uncertainty may still arise from a lack of knowledge about a particular condition on the part of the teacher and other staff in the school, or because the difficulties are too nebulous to be given a label. In addition, the need to assign a diagnosis in order to obtain specialist resources or expertise input for a child, and/or in some instances parental desire to 'know what's wrong', can create a context where the teacher feels under pressure to find a label. It can also be the case that in their own mind there is a desire to assign a label in the hope that this will facilitate their understanding of the child's problems and help them work out the best strategies for the child. In such situations, the lack of a label can itself be a significant source of uncertainty for teachers. Finally, teachers working with children with SEN can often face ongoing uncertainty when strategies that they do employ – particularly if they have been recommended by specialists such as educational psychologists – then turn out not to be wholly effective. They are left with the question of how to make sense of theoretical knowledge in the context of their experiential encounter with the child. I hope here to provide a lens for thinking about this question, about the relationship between theoretical and tacit knowledge in the work of teachers, as I develop the idea of productive uncertainty.

There is another source of uncertainty involved in the empirical study that is the focus of this book. This is the introduction of a technological innovation, a smartphone app, into the classroom. Although it is not the purpose of this book to consider issues related to technology in any depth, it is nevertheless worth noting that the introduction of change in the classroom is also a potential source of uncertainty for teachers. The field of computer anxiety – see Chua et al. (1999) and Russell and Bradley (1997) – has some potential parallels with teacher uncertainty when working with children with SEN. In addition, smartphone technology is associated, for teenagers in particular, with new modes of communication around social networking and instant messaging, and as such is likely for some teachers and schools to throw into relief differences between adult and adolescent identities. This is likely to be a source of anxiety and uncertainty for teachers working with adolescents. They may experience uncertainties related to their ability to relate to young people who hold new technology as a sign of their youth, and anxiety about whether their 'old' knowledge still has any relevance in the face of new ways of deriving and developing learning.

Further, teachers working with young people with autism might also experience uncertainty as to whether these particular young people will join in with these new ways of communicating or, in contrast, wonder whether this technology offers new ways for them to join in with their 'normal' peers?

As interesting as these questions are, they are not the key focus of this book. In the empirical study the new technology tool is primarily regarded as a classroom innovation which acts as a 'change stimulus', if you like, increasing the likelihood that the teachers in the study will reflect on their existing practice, and thus throwing issues of uncertainty into starker relief. As such, any innovation, technological or not, could theoretically have acted as the context for the study.

Nevertheless, the technology tool's focus on social and life-skills development does raise some significant relevant questions when thinking about questions of uncertainty in relation to working with children with SEN, and autism in particular. Problems with life and social skills functioning are a central concern for teachers and other professionals working with children with autism, because they are linked particularly to issues of agency and autonomy. As such, introducing a technological innovation related to these domains is likely to have stimulated teacher reflection and uncertainty around questions regarding what these young people can in fact do by themselves, and whether they will ever be able to engage in autonomous social communication and interaction that will allow them to live as adults independently.

Chapter 4

Methodological issues
Psychoanalysis and sociological research

Towards a psychosocial research methodology

Investigating productive uncertainty in the work of teachers in the classroom requires a particular set of methodological tools whereby, in Grotstein's terms, in some way the 'O' of the researcher can resonate with the 'O' of the subject. In other words, the psychoanalytic needs to be inserted into the sociological, resulting in a 'psychosocial' approach. Others have preceded me in considering this, and in this chapter I consider some of the significant epistemological issues involved in attempting such an integration as well as locating my particular approach within the broader arena of the rapidly developing field of psychosocial studies, and the particular subset of this field which makes use of modified infant observation approaches (discussed in depth below) as a research tool. My approach is innovative when compared to most reported psychosocial studies, in that it uses a combination of observations and interviews as opposed to the typical use of observations alone, supplements narrative recording of observations with audio recording and uses a comparative category coding approach to interpreting case studies, which can enhance and extend the transparency and reach of psychosocial approaches. In the chapter following this, I use the case study material to illuminate how such an approach can be used to detect the presence of productive uncertainty in the classroom, demonstrating how countertransference responses can be helpful in developing, from observations and interviews, an interpretation of research data sensitive to intersubjective relationship.

Before considering the particular approach employed in the study in greater depth, I first want to consider some of the epistemological issues involved in inserting the 'psychoanalytic' into the social.

As Grotstein (2007) contends, Freud saw psychoanalysis as a science. His conceptualization was largely positivist. He believed he had, based on his experiences in the consulting room, been able to derive testable hypotheses about the inner drives of individuals that could be generalized to the whole population, and that further clinical work by himself and others would provide evidence to support these hypotheses and thus give them the status of facts. Although few in the past forty years would be as empirically gung-ho about psychoanalysis' status as science, it is still seen by many in the psychoanalytic community as a way of objectively establishing something about the emotional life of an individual. Thus Edna O'Shaughnessy (1994) attempts to write about the existence of 'clinical facts' in the consulting-room encounter. She defines a fact (including a clinical fact) as 'a truth claim which is not infallible or unique to the fact, and also a claim that must offer itself for verification' (p. 939). Although her discussions appropriately reflect the epistemological complexities, she essentially proposes that the knowledge gained in the clinical encounter based on an understanding of dynamic unconscious processes such as transference and countertransference can be communicated in an understandable form to others who understand these terms, and that what she has learned from one patient can be tested out in the context of other patients with other therapists.

Others have rejected this attempted classification, and have typified psychoanalysis more as hermeneutic exploration than as science. Frosh (1997) markedly points out that whereas in the classical scientific method the observer aims to be as independent as possible from the events under observation (significantly so that someone else acting as an observer could validly replicate the observation), in the therapeutic psychoanalytic encounter, the therapist is completely involved in the encounter. Further, the clinical facts of which therapists make use are often reflections on their own emotional state, and as such are inherently resistant to independent observation or verification. If psychoanalysis is clearly not a science in any straightforward sense, how then does it relate to sociology? In exploring this, some theorists (e.g. Rustin, 2006) have suggested that when modified infant observation approaches are used as research tools they have a number of parallels with ethnographic approaches, particularly those based on symbolic interactionism, which focus on the emotional experience of those participating in the study as observer and subjects. Considering where these approaches are similar and where they diverge, from an epistemological perspective, is one way of thinking about if and how we can in fact insert the psychoanalytic into the social. In order, however, to allow for such an analysis, I need first to introduce some of the history of infant observation and its subsequent development in modified form as a research tool.

The Tavistock method of infant observation (hereafter just 'infant observation') was originally developed by Esther Bick (1964) at the Tavistock Clinic. Her method was primarily designed as a preparatory phase in the training of psychoanalysts. Indeed, a period of infant observation remains today a mandatory part of many psychoanalytic training courses, both at the Tavistock and more widely. In the Tavistock method, an observer observes a baby and their family in the home setting, ideally once a week over two years, with the observations ideally starting very soon after the birth.

It is relevant to note that Bick's initial development of the method was more or less contemporaneous with Bion's publication of *Learning from Experience* (1962). Bion's ideas, although original in many ways (particularly his use of the Grid and 'O'), were nevertheless part of a process of theoretical development of Klein's work in the 1960s, including for example Hannah Segal and Herbert Rosenfeld, but as Rustin (op. cit.) suggests, Esther Bick could quite reasonably be added to this list. Certainly Bick, as with Bion, was keen to emphasize the need for infant observers to tolerate 'not knowing' and to avoid premature certainties.

Later developments of the Tavistock method have extended its use to post-qualification training in interventions both by those with training as psychoanalysts (who by definition have had a full analysis themselves) and, more widely, non-analysts, including teachers working in early years settings. In *Closely Observed Infants* (1997), Miller and colleagues recommend the use of largely free-floating attention which, although it is informed by a particular curiosity about intra- and interpsychic events, does not mentally foreground these – particularly from a theoretical perspective – in the process of observation. The rationale for this, drawing on Bick's original formulation, is that if they were in the foreground, they would potentially push the observer into premature conclusions about the true nature of the psychic events unfolding in the field of observation. This rationale, as well as a concern not to interfere with the free-floating attention of the observer, also leads to a general recommendation not to take notes during the observational session, and to adopt a non-participant stance in the observation. The similarity with Bion's warning to analysts to beware of memory and desire is quite clear.

Close attention is given to focusing on (and recording in the post-observation observational record) what goes on in the observational session – the use of language and tone by the mother, the physical and facial reactions of the baby, the close pattern of interaction between the mother and baby. Further, again in order to avoid coming to premature conclusions, the initial observational record is written up without detailed psychodynamically informed interpretations or reference to theory. Where there is a particular need to record these at the time, they are placed as footnotes outside the main narrative of the observation.

The observational record is then reviewed in a work study group. In Bick's original formulation, trainee analysts undertaking infant observation would meet frequently with a trained analyst as a facilitator. One trainee would present their observation notes, reading these out loud to the group, and the group would then consider their emotional reactions to the presented material. Miller's view, mirroring Bick, is that the emotional interaction between baby and mother is very strong and that, when exposed to these strong interpsychic communications, there is a significant chance of the observer initially repressing their countertransference reaction to them. Accordingly, Miller notes that trainees in infant observation often say they observed very little – 'the mother fed the baby and that was it'. Review in the work study group allows the observer to make use of colleagues as auxiliary egos and, by joint mindful attention to the written record, to uncover some of the interpsychic communication that occurred in the observation. Following Bion, the work study group can be seen as acting in a containing role, processing the initially difficult material presented so that the observer can begin to make sense of the material, identifying what may have initially been unprocessable, thus making effective use of their countertransference response to the material.

Infant observation as a research tool?

Both Bick and Bion see the toleration and working through of 'not knowing' as the path to coming to know the other. This Bionian lens on uncertainty is the facility to tolerate uncertainty and thereby gain understanding, based on intersubjective relatedness, of the baby and the baby–mother dyad or the analysand and the analyst–analysand dyad (although we should note both the symmetry and asymmetry between the two sets). In achieving this, the ability to detect unconscious communication (countertransference) based on projective identification allows the analyst to understand, at least to some extent, what might be going on 'in the moment' for the analysand; to derive a selected fact that can be a working hypothesis about this analysand in this moment and with this analyst, with its crucial unsaturated component, that can then be tentatively explored in the session. Working within a broadly similar conceptual framework, Bick applies a similar lens in the observation of the infant, albeit with the significant difference being that in the consulting session, the analysand can speak and respond to an interpretation. Nevertheless, the promise of infant observation is that it allows the observer, when supported by the auxiliary ego of the work study group, to come to know – by working through the difficulty of uncertainty – what the emotional experience of the baby and the mother–baby dyad is 'in the moment'.

We can argue then, by extension, that such a technique could potentially yield similar fruits where the observer is a researcher, not an analyst in training, and the actors in the observational field are not just infants, but others as well. This argument has been made in some of the literature in the field of psychosocial studies. For example, Price (2004) uses this approach to think about the emotional context of young children's literacy learning. Walker (2005) reports on her use of psychodynamically informed participant observation to consider the effect of latency as a developmental stage on reading progress with a group of primary-age boys. Cooper and Lousada (2005) consider the use of psychosocial approaches to thinking about social work practice. Bibby (2010) uses sensitivity to countertransference in a study of children's identities of learners of mathematics. Finally, Sclater *et al.* (2009) review several examples of the use of a psychosocial approach in fields including mental health, criminology, teaching and social work, including instances of the use of such a modified infant observation approach.

It is, of course, quite a step to take infant observation – a clinical method designed to uncover the workings of the dynamic unconscious and emotions, even one that might be used by teachers in some form as part of their educational practice – and to make use of it as a research tool. In judging the permissibility of such a move, as I have indicated, it is useful to consider strands of interpretivist research which have put a greater emphasis on uncovering emotions. For example, Woods (1996) has considered that the emotional life of the subject will be a significant part of the 'thick description' that uncovers the meaning of symbols for the subjects, and additionally that the way in which the researcher understands such meanings will inevitably be mediated by their own emotional history. Woods considers a case study of a school undergoing a public inspection. One of the researchers writes a reflective journal about his observations of the experiences of staff during these inspections, in which the researcher focuses on their emotional experiences as well as on how his life experiences have, in his perception, allowed him to be more attuned to their experiences, as in this extract:

> It might be the case that my strong connection to these teachers is an empathetic one based on my own history. I failed the eleven plus, taught in the same area for twenty years… and I am of the same educational generation as many of them […]
>
> (ibid., p. 104)

Woods, commenting on the journal entries presented, points out that in more scientifically orientated strands within sociology such a focus by the researcher on their own background and emotions would be regarded as unwarranted interference in the research process. In sociological approaches influenced by feminism and postmodernism, the background of the researcher is seen as inescapable, and the research findings inevitably constitute a production based on the interplay between the researcher's perspective and those of the subjects. Yet Woods – in the same way as Hammersley – ultimately adopts a realist conceptualization of interpretivist research in which there is some possibility, even if limited, of discovering some essential truths about the experience of the subjects independent of the position of the researcher. The focus on emotions is then for Woods an additional tool that can be used as part of the discovery process. Woods even extends this to reflection on emotions outside of the research setting. Thus Woods reports the researcher reflecting in his journal on his feelings whilst going to the ballet after a day of observation during the inspection:

> As I enjoyed the invigorating and joyous music […] with its party atmosphere, I began to feel quite close to the Tafflon teachers and felt angry that they were not part of this very jolly and uplifting environment.
>
> (ibid., p. 98)

Woods, analysing the journal, suggests that the researcher's emotional reaction during the ballet indicates an empathy with the teachers – that is, his continued thinking about the school in his leisure time mirrors the experiences reported to him by the teachers of being unable to switch off from the ever-present inspection presence. For Woods, this increased attunement means that the researcher is better able to pick up on these aspects of the teachers' experience and thus better able to interpret the meaning of symbols for them.

Such an emotion-orientated interpretivist approach does have a number of striking parallels with infant observation. Indeed, Hinshelwood and Skogstad (2000) specifically compare the use of psychoanalytic observation to naturalistic research practice in fieldwork in sociology and anthropology. What is less clear is how the consideration of the unconscious is to be incorporated into such a marriage of approaches. These authors were working as researchers, using institutional observation, which was informed by aspects of infant observation as well as by organizational consultancy. In the case of Woods, he describes how symbolic interactionism is based on the experience of self from two viewpoints – that of 'I' and 'Me' – which has some (perhaps obvious) echoes of Freud's structural model of id, ego and superego, with the 'I' corresponding to the ego and the 'Me' sharing some features with the superego. Of course, what is clearly missing in the analogy is the id; this is absent from the symbolic interactionist account, which is explicit in holding mental processes about the self to be conscious.

Hinshelwood and Skogstad consider the 'research' methods used by the therapist in a clinical setting. Viewing the therapist as a participant observer, they list these faculties:

- Observes with evenly hovering attention
- Employs their subjective experience, filtered by personal analysis
- Has capacity to think and reflect about experience as a whole
- Recognizes unconscious dimension
- Applies interventions to verify their interpretations of events

(ibid., p. 17)

The authors suggest that all but the last point can be applied to psychoanalytic research in a non-clinical setting, yet the glaring mismatch is with 'recognizing the unconscious dimension'. One approach would be to treat it as a development or an extension of Wood's focus on emotional life. Indeed, the ballet episode discussed above seems to come very close to a consideration of countertransference. However, some theorists have questioned the epistemological assumption underlying the move of infant observation from clinical to social research purposes – that is, that the glaring mismatch cannot be overcome – arguing instead that the psychoanalytic needs to stay in the consulting room. Frosh and Baraitser (2008), in a special edition on psychosocial research methods of the journal *Psychoanalysis, Culture and Society*, strongly criticize the validity of the use of transference/countertransference outside of the consulting-room context. However, on closer inspection their critique, in common with Walkerdine *et al.* (2001), Reay and Lucey (2010) and Lapping (2007), focuses on what they see as the modernist and mechanistic approach of Kleinian object-relations. They are partially willing to admit that the inherent split (according to their interpretation) in Kleinian and, in their view, to a lesser degree (although still present) in Bionian thought between a knowing therapist and a not-knowing patient can be relevant to the consulting room. But their critical position leads them to be suspicious of the stretching of these ideas, based as they see them on a split between the individual and society, to the broader field of qualitative research outside the consulting room. Their solution is an appeal to a reflexive Lacanian psychoanalysis, where 'psychoanalysis has more to offer when its disruptive and performative elements are placed in the foreground, that is, when the kind of reflexivity it advances is one that acknowledges the way the phenomena of the psychosocial are produced through the actions of analyst and analysand, researcher and researched' (Frosh and Baraitser, 2008, p. 363). Hoggett (2008), in his response to their paper in the same journal issue, points out that Frosh and Baraitser's critique of the possibility of a unique claim to knowledge inevitably tends to undermine the clinical recognition of real difficulties and of clinical work that can lead to promising outcomes.

There are, though, much more fundamental concerns. Many social scientists would be deeply concerned about the use of countertransference as a research method. Rustin (op. cit.) has noted the ongoing concerns about validity, or trustworthiness, in relation to the use of countertransference in this way. There remain troubling questions as to how we can put sufficient warrant on the emotional reactions of an observer as a way of telling us about a social research field. This question is particularly relevant when coming from such researchers adopting a realist position, as then issues of validity and reliability become even more important. Surprisingly, there seems to be very little, if any, direct consideration of this particular issue in the current psychosocial literature. Although a small number of papers on the application of psychoanalysis to wider professional issues regularly appear (see for example Rustin, 2006; Shuttleworth, 2010), I have not been able to locate significant detailed consideration of, for example, the issue of respondent validation; however, as noted above, Hinshelwood and Skogstad (2002) do point out that the therapist's undertaking of interventions in the clinical setting is not typically something in which a researcher can engage. The use of countertransference in all forms of Kleinian technique is based on validation of interpretations by the patient. The therapist suggests an interpretation, in the ongoing context of the consultation, and the patient gives a response. Whether or not they agree with the interpretation, their response gives a significant amount of additional information to the therapist and thus their use of the countertransference is grounded, so to speak, in an ongoing intersubjective dialogue between therapist and patient. This is also true of Bion, although in his epistemology the focus on the unsaturated element of a preconception or conception introduces a good deal more uncertainty into both the interpretation given by the analyst and the use made of the analysand's response. Nevertheless, both elements are very much part of the process of how the analyst comes to know in the session. Such an open, ongoing dialogue, which takes place simultaneously with the interaction between the actors, is not possible in either typical infant observation or its application to qualitative research. How, then, can we have confidence, even with the use of auxiliary egos of the work study group (none of whom, it will be noted, were even there with the research subjects or the infant) and/or in my case with follow-up interviews, that the conclusions drawn from the use of countertransference are reliable?

An additional challenge, particularly for those adopting infant observation from a realist perspective – about which, again, there seems very much an absence of debate in the psychosocial literature – is the place of memory; that is, is it possible to accurately recall what went on in a lesson one hour or more later? If realism attempts at least to identify the traces of an independent reality, then most realist interpretivist researchers would consider that it has a better chance of doing so if its methods of data collection can be regarded as having a significant degree of validity and reliability (that is, correspondence with that reality).

This does not mean that we need to go back, in respect of classroom research, to the educational research 'paradigm wars' (see Gage, 2007) where, from a quantitative perspective, only structured classroom observations amenable to regression and correlation techniques can be considered as having reliability. Rather we can, from a realist perspective, suggest that there can be an intermediate position in which we do not rely on the function of memory recall at a distance. It is also relevant to note here that such critiques about the use of memory-based recall could also be applied to ethnography and anthropology more widely.

Critical ethnography and infant observation make a broadly similar response to this challenge, although for the latter it tends to be implicitly assumed rather than formally stated. In essence, they return to Frosh and Baraitser's (op. cit.) analysis, in which there is no normative independent truth about the interaction between observer and researcher or therapist and client, and what exists (and can only be said to exist) is, respectively, the construction or co-construction of a particular interpretation. However, from an infant observation perspective this argument seems weak, particularly if we admit Rustin's response to Frosh and Baraitser and do sign up to the existence of real problems and real therapeutic interventions based on psychoanalytic theory and technique. If psychoanalysis is based on a realist perspective, as Rustin suggests, then how can infant observation rely on an argument which sounds very much like a critical perspective when arguing for the use of data collection methods?

I propose that it cannot – but, at the same time, it needs to take more account of concerns about validity in the use of countertransference as a research tool. My response to these concerns in the study was to employ particular variations to the modified infant observation technique, specifically the use of audio recording in observations and the use of a comparative coding approach. I will consider the latter later in this chapter, but for now will concentrate on the use of audio recording.

With the innovation in the methods that I employ in the study, particularly with regard to the use of audio recording and comparative category coding, I hope – at least to some extent – to see how far these concerns can and should be addressed.

Use of audio recording in modified infant observation

An Olympus voice data recorder with a tie-clip microphone was used to record classroom observations. After the initial write-up of the observation following the observation itself, the observational record was reviewed with the audio recording. In this review, the audio recording was listened to at the same time as viewing the initial observational record. The intention was not to produce a verbatim transcript of the recording, but rather to amend the observational record for accuracy. Thus, events which were initially recorded in the wrong sequence would be repositioned, and dialogue which was paraphrased or inaccurate in the initial observational record was similarly updated. Verbal sequences in the audio recording which were relevant to the narrative of the observational record were written down in detail, although in some cases, either due to lack of strong relevance or time constraints, the record was left in its initial summary form.

Of course, a key argument against the use of audio recording in infant observation, and the main reason why audio or video recording has not been commonly used in psychosocial studies to date, is the concern that the introduction of recording equipment distracts the observer from properly applying free-floating attention. Bion admonished analysts not to make or substantively rely on notes during sessions. He feared the analyst's premature desire to crystallize concepts with the certainty of words, or to run after words on the page as an easy alternative to encountering the analysand anew in each new session. However, my experience in using an essentially hidden audio recorder was that there was relatively little, if any, of such interference with the field of study. Once I had put the recorder on, it just sat there in my pocket and I could largely forget about it. Would Bion have made a similar argument about the dangers of memory and desire in relation to an audio recording? Perhaps. The significant discrepancies between my initial observational record and the audio recording, however, indicate that the reliance on memory alone in modified infant observation techniques is likely to lead to the introduction of significant distortions. It seems hard to argue that these distortions are irrelevant. This is particularly the case in work study, where colleagues rely to a large degree on the written observational record in making sense of what went on in the classroom. Much significance can be attached to the use of a single word in work study review. Surely it makes a difference if, potentially, that word was never said or another word entirely was used?

Countertransference and validity

The analysis of the data from the study presented fully in the forthcoming chapters also threw light on the validity, from a realist perspective, of using a privileged knowledge about the dynamic unconscious which cannot be separated out from an ongoing intersubjective experience between therapist and client. In other words, if realism is seen as essentially disagreeing with Marxist and Foucauldian false consciousness, then how can it admit psychoanalytic 'un- consciousness'? In terms of realist interpretivist research, this question comes to the fore when using countertransference to make judgements about the motivations and actions of actors in the field of study. The answer might be that we can legitimately regard the psychoanalytic lens, as Freud did, as simply another way of finding out about the reality of the world. Even in purely symbolic interactionist accounts, it is never possible to take everything that the actors say at face value. Conflicting accounts, both by the same actor and between actors, and multiple motivations all need to be resolved in any interpretivist analysis. In fact, on a number of occasions in the data analysis, it became clear that the application of a psychoanalytic lens was allowing me to uncover hidden motivations and desires which, it could be argued, were more closely aligned to the real experience of the actors than the initial accounts given in surface interview responses. Further, when this was linked to my countertransference response to what went on 'in the moment' of the observation, then it laid some claim to be able to reveal, through the process of grappling with uncertainty – particularly through the use of the auxiliary ego in the work study group – something of what went on in the intersubjective encounter between teacher and child 'in the moment'. This is of course, from a methodological perspective, the nub of the matter. The productive uncertainty (or lack of it) inherent in the encounter between teacher and child was uncoverable (at least partially) by my own process of productive uncertain encounter with the actors in the field of study. At the same time, I would contend, the use of audio recording in particular rooted the analysis more closely in reality, and in realism. It helped to avoid the dangers of 'wild analysis' that Joanne Brown (2006) warns can be an ever-present danger in psychosocial studies. In this sense, I think it can also be reasonably aligned with Bion, in that I think he may well have recognized the dangers inherent in transposing psychoanalysis from consulting room to research field. Putting it another way, in psychoanalysis as a research tool we lose both the immediacy of intersubjective encounter in the consulting room, and the immediacy of ongoing (verbal and non-verbal) dialogue between analyst and analysand. Such a loss introduces more of a risk of a flight to memory and desire, particularly the desire to come up with a wild analysis that might fit the limited information we have. A verbal recording acts as something of a bulwark against this flight to the wild which, it can be argued, outweighs the risk of flight to desire to use the words on the tape as a prematurely crystallized version of the actors' reality.

Bion's overarching aim was to come to know the other in intersubjective relationship. Yet he recognized, most strikingly in *Attention and Interpretation*, that knowledge which just sits between the analyst and analysand is not enough. He recognized the need for categorization, and language, in order that communication across a community could take place, whilst at the same time – echoing Lacan in some ways – recognizing the dangers of premature ossification and misunderstanding inherent in this process of turning the intersubjective moment into words. Productive uncertainty that just stays 'in the moment' between teacher and child has, in the end, limited value. Bion's writing can in a sense be viewed as a struggle between a categorical mathematical view of psychoanalysis on the one hand, and on the other a reaching out to the ineffable unknowable other in intersubjective relationship. In the end, Bion came out largely on the side of the latter, although he was always cognizant of the need to take account of the former.

This tension between the categorical and the individual also rears its head in the analysis of the data. In a sense, it partially mirrors the tension between deductive and inductive approaches in the analysis of qualitative data. However, in this study, the introduction of the psychoanalytic into the sociological and how this impinges on the data analysis, particularly in regard to validity, needs further consideration. Before undertaking this, however,

I will present more detail on how the data collection methods were employed in the study.

Interviews and observations

There were two key data collection methods used: observations and interviews. For each teacher, the pattern was a series of five classroom observations spread out over the academic year, with a follow-up interview scheduled shortly after each observation. The application of these methods intertwined two orientations. From the perspective of an interpretivist approach to teacher thinking and teacher research (Hammersley and Atkinson, 2007), classroom observations allowed for the identification of events in the classroom that could serve to elicit discussion of what was going on for the teacher in follow-up interviews. From the perspective of a psycho-dynamically informed infant observation approach applied to researching professional practice, the transference and countertransference experienced by myself as a researcher in the field of activity provided an important additional tool in understanding the teacher's emotional experience of working with children with autism.

An infant observation approach was adopted in my classroom observations. I adopted a non-participant observer stance where I gave free-floating attention to the interactions between teacher and focus child – with, however, the overall objectives for observation listed above the 'background' of my mind. Sketch notes were also made during observations, including noting physical positioning of actors in the classroom. A detailed observational record, modelled on infant observation recording, was made as soon as possible after the end of the observation, usually within two hours and at most within twelve hours. The narrative of the observational record did not focus on interpretations or theory, and instances of particularly strong emotional register and any initial theoretical considerations were recorded as footnotes.

Although it was not possible to schedule work study group reviews of all of the material, at least one observation from each teacher was brought to a work study group. The experience of working through this material did demonstrate the efficacy of the infant observation approach in considering professional practice. Material which on my first analysis seemed either uneventful or difficult to interpret was rendered more potent and understandable through the process of a work study review. In particular, my strong identification with the success of the app project, and its potential interference with my interpretation of the material, was revealed in the process. In several work study sessions, colleagues noted how material suggested significant negative feelings about the project. It was also interesting to observe, in the work study sessions, my initial strong negative reaction to these comments from colleagues. However, during the sessions it became clear that my role as an academic partly involved in the implementation of the app at the school had led me to be overly identified with a positive outcome, making me (unconsciously) resistant to the negative messages from the teachers present in the observational record.

Emotional register in interviews

Interviews were semi-structured in that a flexible interview guide was developed for each interview stage, matching the outlined areas of focus. Questions were phrased in an open, exploratory manner, and respondents were given a significant degree of leeway in interpreting the questions in their own frame of reference. Frequent use was made of follow-up probing questions depending on the response given. Certain topics, particularly ongoing uncertainty and their conceptualization of autism, were approached obliquely rather than directly, although a more explicit approach was taken if it was felt appropriate in the later interviews.

I set out to pay attention to relevant feelings that arose during interviews, including potential countertransference responses. Where such responses came to conscious awareness, they were noted in interview field notes. Some accompanying interview material was also brought to work study review sessions. Colleagues in the work study review gave some useful insights into some of the positions adopted by teachers in the interview records, particularly where I had again, due to my dual role, been resistant to some of the negative messages being presented.

Relatively few instances of strong emotional or countertransference responses were noted in respect of the interviews; however, in one informal conversational interaction with the school educational psychologist directly after an interview, a very strong emotional response related to an incident in the observation was noted. It may be that the need to follow an interview guide, with a concomitant requirement for quite strong cognitive attention to particular lines of thought, may have interfered with the ability to be properly attentive to emotional interactions in the interview. It could be that an unstructured interview format, perhaps more closely following the pattern of a clinical psychoanalytic session, may be more successful in allowing for sensitivity to the emotional register of the interview material.

Constructing cases: a psychoanalytic approach

I have argued that we can view the application of a psychodynamic lens to interpretivist research, specifically the use of a modified infant observation approach, as a method to help find out more about the emotional experience of the actors in the field of study. As such, arguments about case study development, as well as about deductive and inductive approaches in interpretivist data analysis, could be considered to apply equally well. Yin argues that when comparing across cases (1981, p. 62), cross-case surveys, in which particular factors are cross-tabulated across cases, are problematic. They are undesirable for Yin because the extraction of single factors from the case unduly simplifies the phenomenon being studied, and further treats cases as data points when really they are better thought of as coherent explanatory things in themselves (ibid., p. 62). In contrast, Yin prefers a cross-comparison approach. He uses a detective example to illustrate this. The detective has one initial crime for which he has an explanation. He then comes across a second, somewhat similar crime. He applies his explanation from the first case, but of course modifying (or discarding it) it to fit the specifics of the second case. This leads to theory generation (ibid., p. 63). However, Yin's point about the problem of treating cases as data points rather than explanatory things in themselves needs particular consideration from a psychodynamic perspective. It is relevant in this context to consider extant debates about validity in research on psychoanalysis, by which I mean studies designed to demonstrate the efficacy of the application of psychoanalysis in bringing about positive treatment outcomes. Rustin (2006) refers to Fonagy's (2003) call for the application of more standardized scientific approaches commonly used in clinical and cognitive psychology, such as treatment outcome studies, to psychoanalysis. Fonagy notes that quantitative (deductive) research techniques are viewed with suspicion by psychoanalysts because 'Those who work at close quarters with the human mind will inevitably have an impression of reductionism when they see the full complexity of an individual's struggle with internal and external experience reduced to a single 100-point scale' (ibid., p. 131).

As both Fonagy and Rustin recognize, a possible solution to this impasse in psychoanalytic research runs as follows:

1   To, despite the reservations of analysts, make greater use of treatment outcome studies which can demonstrate the overall efficacy of psychoanalytic treatment when compared to other forms of intervention. There does in fact seem to be an increase in studies such as this. For example, Deakin and Tiellet Nunes (2009) report on a twelve-month study of the use of psychoanalysis with children in a clinical setting, using the Rorschach, Bender and WISC-III tests, which demonstrated statistically significant improvements in anxiety problems and school relationships.
2   To place a greater emphasis on qualitative methods in assessing, from a technical point of view, what works and what does not work in the consulting room.

Importantly, in respect of the latter, both authors recognize that something more is needed than just the typical clinical case study report, which is perhaps rightly open to criticism as methodologically underpowered, in that it is very often hard to see how information presented about one case might be usefully generalized across to other clinical contexts. In this respect, Fonagy highlights the significant need for a screening process that would help identify which patients are likely to benefit from treatment. It is hard to see how isolated psychoanalytical clinical case studies could usefully address this.

There is some resonance between the argument for greater rigour in case analysis in psychoanalysis that Rustin and Fonagy construct, and Bion's ideas. As I have noted, Bion was very interested, particularly in *Attention and Interpretation*, in what to do with the theories that are developed in psychoanalysis. This applied both to theories that arise about the analysand in an individual session and the use of more general theory, particularly the myth-based theories of psychoanalysis, as well as the interplay between general theory and individual theory-making about the analysand in the session. He writes (p. 83) that psychoanalysis, paradoxically, cannot escape from ideas of 'care, treatment and illness'; yet he warns against both a general theoretical structure that is too rigid and limited to permit development and one that is too flexible, because before long the 'members of the psychoanalytic movement [would] not understand each other'. Bion recognizes the paradox that psychoanalysis needs a 'vertex of medicine' that has ideas of disease, treatment, prognosis, pathology and cure as invariants. Both these and the knowing that comes from unconscious communication, that arising from 'O', are needed, and they somehow, paradoxically, need to meet. Both Fonagy and Rustin's ideas on case analysis – and, I would argue, my use of audio recording and category coding – could be viewed as a legitimately Bionian way of approaching the introduction of the paradoxically inescapable rigour of categorization into psychosocial research.

Comparative category coding

Carlberg (2010) reports on the use of a systematic case study approach, in which turning points in therapy are used as an interactional sequence to identify similarities in conditions, activities and consequences across cases. Carlberg's studies involved the use of semi-structured interviews of therapists, questionnaires provided to clients and reference to process notes.

This systematic case study approach serves to maintain the integrity of the single case, with its complexity specific to the experience of the individual therapist and patient. At the same time, using thinking similar to Yin's (op. cit.), it opens up the possibility of identifying common process themes across cases. Clearly, Carlberg's cases are about psychoanalysis. However, it does not seem too far a leap to propose that this systematic approach could also be applied to the use of a modified infant observation approach to researching professional practice. It allows the single case, with its complex situational emotional field, to be preserved, as the same time as allowing comparisons in respect of key processes across cases.

Thus, following Yin (op. cit.) and Carlberg (op. cit.), I adopted an approach where the essential unit of analysis in the study was the case of each individual teacher. The field of study in respect of the case extends out primarily to the focus children. In particular, in work study group review, although it was not possible to look at all textual material relating to each teacher case, the unit of analysis was nevertheless the teacher as a case. Tentative interpretations about psychodynamic processes going on in the observational material reviewed in the work study group were then further 'tested' out by me against the other observational and interview material. It would have been possible to have stopped there. As with many clinical case studies, a narrative record of my impressions of the teacher case could have been constructed based on the observational material and the work study review interpretations. Although this certainly involves a mixture of deductive and inductive reasoning from the data, the use of a detailed coding structure, as is commonly used in qualitative research, could have been avoided. The cases would have been presented as a series of phenomenological gestalts.

However, following Yin and Carlberg, as well as the influence of Fonagy, I considered this to be insufficient. Similar to my arguments about audio recording, this was partly due to issues of reliability when aiming to present this as a psychosocial study legitimately located within interpretivist realist social research. Putting it another way, when intertwining the psycho and the social, the latter social *science* part, when conceived of from a realist perspective, seemed to demand more reliability than was offered by the former psychodynamic part. Qualitative research involves the generation of large amounts of text, as was the case in this study. Human processing limitations make it difficult to absorb all this in one go, and if it is presented as a gestalt the conclusions are rightly open to criticism in terms of how the material was filtered in reaching those conclusions. Although coding approaches certainly do not remove this filtering problem, they at least make it more transparent and open to external review.

The second issue is that of comparison across cases. A descriptive followed by axial-coding approach allows for the identification of key themes across cases, which can allow the development of explanatory and causal mechanisms. It also, by identifying the number of instances in which a category type occurs, again allows for increased confidence in the conclusions that are made when considering the relevance of phenomena both within and between cases. Of course, this brings us back to the Bionian paradox. The process of categorization does represent the danger of premature flight to memory and desire – the desire, for example, to code a piece of text quickly because thinking about it carefully would be too difficult or painful. However, I do think it is possible to argue that the other side of the Bionian paradox is that without categorization the different aspects of the research study, the different pieces of text, will start to fly away from each other in to unintelligibility.

Accordingly, use was made of both descriptive and axial coding in relation to psychodynamically informed concepts. For example, the psychoanalytic concept of adhesive identification, to the smartphone app, was used as a coding category.

In summary, there is a twin-track presentation: a 'gestalt' of the overall case and, simultaneously, a between-cases comparison using descriptive and axial coding.

In developing a coding structure, a mixed deductive/inductive approach was used, but with a greater emphasis on the deductive. An inductive approach was used in particular to help, similarly to Fereday and Muir-Cochrane (2006), in building an initial coding manual. Thus an initial selection of text sources across cases was subject to a line-by-line 'grounded' microanalysis. In undertaking this analysis I tried to free my mind, at least to some extent, of the stated research questions, and to be open to associations and interpretations that arose from the text directly. This resulted in an inductive coding structure. In tandem with this, based on the research questions and my understanding of the relevant literature, a deductive coding structure was also developed. These two structures were then integrated and applied to the data sources. The coding process involved a repeated deductive/inductive iteration leading to the review of the codes, to check for ongoing logical consistency and consistency with the text data itself. All data sources for all five teachers, including observations and interviews, were coded using the integrated coding structure.

The Nvivo 8 software package was used for the data analysis. Memos and active notations in Nvivo were used extensively to aid the thinking process during coding. Process notes from the work study group review were included as memos on the system. Not all data nodes created, particularly some of those from the deductive exercise, were made extensive use of, or 'saturated'. Further, some codes were found to duplicate content meaning – two rationalization exercises were carried out during the ongoing data analysis, in which redundant codes were removed and duplicate codes merged. The query function in Nvivo was also used to quickly derive comparisons across descriptive codes by case. An example is the derivation of instances of sub-codes per teacher case for the high-level data node 'Teacher conceptualization of and ways of working with autism'. An extract from the coding structure is shown in Table 4.1.

Table 4.1 Extract from coding structure

High level code	Sub-codes
Child states	
	Adhesive identification
	Bereavement or life change
	Child identification with phone/app
	Child enthusiastic/engaged
	Child resistant/unengaged
	Child obsessional interest
	Manic states
Teacher conceptualization of and ways of working with autism	
	Children with ASD are just normal
	Lack of transferable skills
	Cannot see beyond today
	Stuck in rigid thinking
	Does not agree to social rules
	Problems with sequencing/executive function
	They need time to process
	Every child with autism is different
	Labelling is part of the problem
	Meeting in the middle re autonomy
	Reach out and draw them in
Teacher states	
	Could be closer to the action
	Responds to needs/individualizes
	Focus on the kids and relating to them
	Anxious state
	Crossing boundaries
	Containment
	Enthusiasm
Teacher focus autonomy	
	Structural arrangements prevent autonomy
	Aspires to develop autonomy
	Focus on independence and life skills now

Outcomes from the data analysis

Descriptive coding generally worked as planned, particularly with regard to what might be termed non-psychodynamic phenomena. For example, the high-level data node 'Teacher conceptualization of autism and ways of working with children with autism' and its sub-nodes worked straightforwardly, as shown in Table 4.1. However, when it came to axial coding – that is, constructing causal/explanatory frameworks based on the descriptive coding – the analysis did not follow what might be considered a typical pattern for an interpretivist study, in that with the introduction of the psychoanalytic component, the move from descriptive to axial coding was less clear-cut. Psychodynamic interpretations were successfully applied to the actors – both teachers and children – in the context of the introduction of the app, but these did not, as was expected, mainly derive from the descriptive codes. Rather, the interpretations made in the work study review were applied to the range of the source material for each case, and a broad 'gestalt' narrative based on these interpretations formed the main basis for psychodynamic conclusions about the case. Having said this, the Nvivo software itself proved a highly efficient tool in supporting this process, as it easily allowed for reference back to the source texts (and in particular the observation annotations), as well as for cross-referencing to both the memo notes from the work study review and more general memos on emerging psychodynamic interpretations also created during the coding process.

However, in some cases, the descriptive coding further supported the search across source material when considering interpretations from the work study review and the collation of instances where psychodynamic interpretations applied in one case were also potentially seen (whether in similarity or in contrast) in another case. For example, as indicated, at one stage my over-identification with the app was commented on at one stage in the work study review. The data node 'Observer stance conflict', in which I had collated a range of source references where I had felt conflicts between my positions as researcher and as someone involved to some extent in implementing the project, was helpful in allowing the review and identification of other instances where this over-identification may also have been operating, thus allowing me to consider if I felt the interpretation from the work study review had broader application beyond the observation material looked at in the work study review session. However, in many cases, psychodynamic conclusions about cases were often made without direct reference to the descriptive codes. Whether initially related to interpretations made in the work study review or not, they often just emerged when looking across the range of the data sources for a particular case. When this happened, it frequently had no link back to the original descriptive coding. It could be argued that this is what one might in fact expect from a modified infant observation approach. As I noted, Bion's paradox warns the use of codes per se may also potentially interfere with free-floating attention. It is only when, the codes, in a sense, are forgotten about – or at least pushed to the back of the mind – and there is open attention to the intersubjective emotional tone brought by the material that the relevant 'selected fact' can emerge. So we are brought back to the original concerns of the psychoanalytic body about the use of deductive approaches in psychoanalytic research. However, once interpretations were made, it was possible to operationalize them by assigning a metacode (or axial code) to relevant source references. This coding was then helpful in facilitating looking across cases to determine whether the phenomenon was present or absent in other cases. In this sense, Fonagy's and Rustin's argument about the potential benefits of categorization had some weight.

Category coding might, then, be a useful and indeed necessary tool for effective analysis of data in psychosocial research, but its overuse may lead us to lose the essential quality that gives the psychosocial method its inherent power. Categorization is a necessary evil, but we should be always on our guard for the dangers it poses in encouraging a flight to memory and desire.

This danger in the use of categorization when psychoanalysis is used as a social research tool parallels its dangers in the traditional use of psychoanalysis in the consulting room. Productive uncertainty means staying in a state of not knowing long enough to recognize and come to know, intersubjectively, the other in front of us. The extension of this lesson to the work of the teacher in the classroom, particularly in the context of working with children with SEN, an area so replete with categories, will I hope be further illuminated by the cases deriving from the empirical study in the next chapter.

Summary

In this chapter, I have considered how the idea of productive uncertainty, a particular lens for thinking about professional practice based on Bion's epistemology, can be brought to life by the use of a modified infant observation approach sensitized to picking up on the 'in-the-moment' emotional state of actors in a research field. As well as introducing the data collection methods used to achieve this, I have explored some of the issues involved in introducing psychoanalysis, particularly the use of countertransference as an investigative tool, into realist interpretivist research. Such a move raises epistemological concerns related to validity and I have detailed my response to these concerns, namely the innovative use of audio recording in data collection and a comparative category coding approach in data analysis. I have also highlighted how these concerns, and my responses, mirror Bion's own recognition of the inherent tension between the individuality of coming to know the other 'in the moment', in intersubjective relationship, and the need to use categories for language and theory development. This tension mirrors, and serves to further illuminate, the central concern of this book – namely how caring professionals experience the dialectic between theoretical and tacit knowledge about the other, and how a better understanding of this might be achieved through the lens of productive uncertainty.

Chapter 5

Case studies of teacher uncertainty

Introduction to the cases

A total of five teachers are presented: Lynne, Kathy, John, Mandy and Penny. We have met some of them already in material presented in earlier chapters. They have rich, complex and varying experiences of working with children with autism. The cases are presented roughly in the following pattern:

1   Their background, teaching history and role in the school.
2   An overview of the children with whom they are working in the context of the smartphone app.
3   The teacher's experience of working with the children.

The cases serve to illuminate a range of themes, including: the teachers' experience of uncertainty when working with children with ASD, including uncertainty about diagnosis and its implications; the ways in which teachers do (or do not) tolerate uncertainty in working with children with ASD; and their ability to tolerate frustration and to come into intersubjective contact in the teacher–child dyad. There is also considerable material on the interplay between theoretical and tacit knowledge in the teachers' work with children with autism, and how they deal with issues of autonomy and agency in relation to working with these children.

As such, they serve to demonstrate how Bion's emotional epistemology provides a different way of looking at the relationship between theoretical and tacit knowledge in the work of these teachers. Uncertainty is threaded throughout the cases as an overarching theme, and the psychoanalytic part of the psychosocial approach is used to further illuminate this. There is also considerable uncertainty, from my perspective as a researcher, about the cases. The meaning, particularly the emotional meaning, of utterances and events is often uncertain; however, following Bion, I hope that I have been able to tolerate the uncertainty at least sufficiently to be able to allow some plausible and productive accounts of the teachers' experiences of uncertainty itself to arise.

The cases also highlight methodological considerations, including the way in which a modified infant observation approach makes use of countertransference responses as a research tool, and the ways in which the use of audio recording and comparative category coding make a difference to the data produced.

Lynne – getting there

Current role and career background

Lynne works as a teacher with older children (16–18) at the Post-16 Further Education (FE) site, which is a short distance away from the main school site. Her students follow a mainly life skills-based curriculum designed to develop independence. Lynne has been working at the school in various roles for fifteen years; before this she worked in early years. She used to run her own nursery; when her children reached secondary school age she did an HND in early years education and then started working at Randall School as a support worker. After that she did a part-time post-compulsory teaching qualification. Lynne previously taught predominantly at the main school site, only working at Post-16 once a week, but two years ago she took on her current post of further education coordinator. In her words, this means 'I'm the coordinator of Post-16 rather than the teacher', and she now works fully at Post-16.

Lynne's background in special needs education, and autism more specifically, was limited before she arrived at Randall School. Her reported motivation for coming to work at the school was that she had a friend with a child with autism, and thought the job at Randall School sounded interesting.

Although Lynne is often positive about her experience of her role and of working with children with autism, she refers on a number of occasions to a feeling of isolation linked to the separate location of the Post-16 unit. She feels that she misses out on things going on at the main site, and that often her needs are often overlooked. She also feels that people on the main site forget about her, so she sometimes misses out on important news and events.

Key information sources for Lynne

Interviews and observations were undertaken with Lynne as follows:

> First interview 7 October 2009
> First observation 4 December 2009
> Second observation 25 March 2010
> Second interview 25 March 2010
> Third observation 28 May 2010
> Third interview 28 May 2010
> Fourth observation 2 July 2010
> Fourth interview 2 July 2010.

Lynne's children

Lynne has three children using the app: Tom, Patrick and Alan. The focus of the observations and interviews was mainly on Tom. Although there was some observation and interview review of Patrick and Alan, this was more limited in scope, and in the analysis presented here the emphasis is accordingly on Tom.

Tom was born in 1992, making him 17/18 during the 2009/10 app implementation period. He had a full IQ measured on WISC-IV of 89, a VQ of 87, and a clinical psychiatric diagnosis of autism on entry to the school. He had no co-morbid factors.

Tom lives at home with his parents and attends the school on weekdays. Classroom observation data, teacher, child and parent interviews, informal visits to the school and the baseline dataset combine to form initial impressions of Tom, in the school environment, as a generally polite and reasonably intelligent young man. He is good at using technology, likes using it in his free time and is able to pick things up quickly. He is well liked by other students and often friendly and sociable with classmates. Academically Lynne places him around three years below the average level expected for his age in English and maths. His communication skills are well developed and he can hold mature and sensible conversations. Due to difficulties in representing and planning time, Tom struggles to organize himself and finds it difficult to do things like get ready for lunch, transition between lessons and pack a lunchbox in the morning. He also finds it hard to discuss and understand his feelings and emotions and tends, according to reports by Lynne, to be typically quite lethargic and unmotivated – independently of issues of lack of sleep – typified by an 'I don't really know' attitude.

Working with Tom

On a number of occasions Lynne noted her concern over what will happen in the future to Tom and the other young people with whom she is working. This is exemplified in the following extract from the third interview with Lynne, where she discusses her anxieties:

> [...] I think Tom ... I don't know. He wants to stay at home with Mum and Dad and never wants to leave. Don't see the point of work ... there is no ambition there to do anything or ... I really don't know with Tom and I mean, he'll only have one more year with me after this year ... and he's been ... because of his ability he's not going to get any support when he leaves us anyway because he won't come under ... I don't know if you know how it works with adult services ... but because he hasn't got a learning disability he won't be accepted by them, so basically he won't get any help when he leaves us anyway. It's all going to be down

to the parents fighting for stuff for him. Tom does worry me because I just think what is he going to do with his life? Okay, he could go out independently but he wouldn't ... he's too set in his own ways to change at all. Say if you was interviewing him and you actually said something that he didn't like he'd argue with you and get annoyed and sort of like if you're in a workplace or whatever he's not going to be able to act like that is he? But I don't know with Tom. One day ... I mean some days he comes in as bright as anything and he says, 'Can we go and do this, can we do that?' and you think, 'Oh maybe he could!' and then another day he'll sit there and he'll fall asleep!

Lynne is conflicted about Tom. She wants to promote his independence; she has belief on one level about what he can do and could achieve; yet at the same time she is beset by doubts about whether there are in fact capability limitations deriving from his autism that will prevent him becoming independent in the future. Although she doesn't state it explicitly, it is reasonable to infer that she considers his inflexibility in thinking – 'he's too set in his own ways to change at all' – to be atypical, something resulting from this autism impairment. The phrasing is reminiscent of language more commonly used to describe middle-aged or older adults, not 17-year-old labile adolescents. For Lynne, it seems difficult to think of Tom as a typical adolescent boy.

This difficulty, or uncertainty, in how to think about Tom is further illustrated in the third classroom observation which took place at the end of May 2010, before the summer half-term break. One of the technical issues with the implementation of the app was that for a time the internet connection on the smartphones was lost. This was a significant area of concern for Tom, which is evidenced in the material.

In this extract from the observation, Lynne has been reviewing the use of the tool with Tom. Much of this has centred on a 'personal trainer' intervention that Lynne developed on the app in conjunction with Tom's dad, which is designed to remind Tom to go to bed and therefore stop him being so tired the following day. Up to this point it has proved rather ineffective and, as becomes evident in other data, this is largely because Tom doesn't understand why he needs to go to bed earlier:

As Lynne starts to talk to Tom ... he interrupts and starts asking when the internet is going to be put back on the phone. He has [his] face resting on both his hands, which are close together in front of him with his elbows on the desk – his fists are tightly clenched and he has an angry expression. He looks angry as he asks about this. His voice tone is slightly whiny, although generally not very expressive. Lynne stays very calm – she has her chin in her hand and one arm outstretched openly on the table in front of her. Lynne explains, in the lilting tone that I noted in previous observations, the reasons why the internet is not there. Tom continues to complain, although he gradually unclenches his fists and makes more and more eye contact with Lynne. She tells him that he will be getting the SIM card back, but that it will initially only be for phone calls and texts, not for internet. He looks very unhappy at this.

After this observation, I noted how this exchange made me feel somewhat uncomfortable. There was something that struck me as strange, but I could not quite put my finger on it. Later, during the review and coding of the data, whilst re-reading the section and listening to the audio, it struck me that what was making me uncomfortable was the lilting tone, which was rather reminiscent of how primary teachers talk to 8-year-olds and atypical of how teachers talk to 17-year-old young adults. I also noted that Tom's demeanour has something 'baby-like' about it, and there is a certain dependent, helpless quality in his interaction with her. However, in the immediately subsequent section of the observation there is a striking change:

Eventually Lynne tells him that he can discuss it with Donald (the school's educational psychologist and the school's lead for the technology project) if he likes and that Donald will be able to discuss it with him. Tom relaxes when Lynne says this and nods; Lynne moves on, rapidly moving to discussing the calendar function and the appointments that she has set up on the phone (mirroring his timetable). I observe that Tom now has his hands on his head, and his face looks more relaxed – he seems to have cheered up a bit. Lynne moves slightly closer to him, shifting her body forward slightly in her chair. Her voice becomes more lilting in tone and she asks him to show her how to get on to the intervention activity that she has set up on the smartphone. Tom takes the phone, still with Lynne close in and looking over with him. He navigates the phone with the stylus quite fluently and activates the personal trainer intervention. He runs through the intervention, which has a series of images with text at the bottom, with some sounds.

As soon as speaking to Donald is mentioned – a very adult approach to thinking about this technical issue with the technology – Tom relaxes. It is also relevant to note that Lynne moves on rapidly. On reading the transcript as a whole, my sense was that this vignette exemplified the tension, for both Lynne and Tom, between his desire to be treated like an adult and his inability to act independently. It also seems that when Lynne 'moves on rapidly' it may be hard, in Bionian terms, to stick with the uncertainty – that is, it may be difficult to tolerate the in many ways massive tension of not knowing and not really being sure what to do. For Lynne, the ever-present question is: what can Tom really do? Is he a middle-aged man stuck in the body of a teenager – unable, as Alvarez (1992) contends, to shift himself out of 'stuck' ways of thinking – who has no future as an independent adult? Is he a little boy incapable or terrified of making decisions for himself, who needs adult lullabies to soothe and persuade him to do what's best for him, or is he a teenager who can in fact introject a nascent adult, autonomous function, and who could even derive satisfaction from exercising that function? This is illustrated in the immediately subsequent section of the observation.

> Lynne asks him how he can see all the writing on the screen [if the text is too long, just the first two sentences show initially]. Tom says, looking rather unsure, 'Scroll it?' Lynne takes the phone and shows him: 'you just push it up like this'. Tom nods in understanding – Lynne passes back the phone and he has a go himself. Lynne then moves on to adding appointments. She says that she asked Dad to show him how to add an appointment – 'Dad showed you that, didn't he?' but Tom shakes his head and says 'No idea'. He is quite unresponsive – he just shakes his head slightly when saying this, but sounds rather uninterested – as though this is nothing to do with him.

It's quite striking here how as soon as Tom's dad is mentioned, and his dad's agenda, Tom's whole attitude and demeanour – previously more engaged and interested – becomes negative, 'as though this is nothing to do with him'. For a short period Tom had sustained, albeit with Lynne's facilitation, a lively autonomous interest, in this case in relation to the app. It seems, though, that the introduction of Dad's interest in the activity punctures this transient sense of independent thought and action.

It is important to note that of course the tension between adult and child-like states is typical of adolescence in general, as indeed are ambivalences about parental authority. Yet for Lynne, and probably on some level for Tom as well, autism complicates things considerably. Whether because of its intrinsic effect on Tom's capability, or due to how Lynne and the school position him because of what they believe about what it means for Tom, or both, the autism diagnosis aggravates the already significant uncertainties that adolescence invokes. In particular, anxieties loom large about whether Tom can ever really become truly adult in the future.

It is also relevant to note that the entire analysis of Lynne and her interaction with Tom was predicated on an uncomfortable feeling I had when I listened to that exchange. I propose that this is an example of countertransference at work in the observation. Lynne's uncertainty about how to work with Tom in that moment, with all its underlying complexities of issues of capability and the meaning of the diagnosis, was picked up by me as an uncomfortable feeling. As is commonly the case with countertransference in infant observation, as Margaret Rustin (2006) warns, it is not always obvious what the communication represented by the feeling engendered by countertransference is about. A process of reflection, in this research context the review of the transcript and re-listening to the audio tape (in this case without the assistance of the auxiliary ego of the work study group), is needed to unpick what the emotional communication was about.

Coming back to the content of this vignette, and my commentary on it, I certainly do not raise it in order to suggest that an autism diagnosis has no meaning and has nothing useful to say for teachers in how they work with young people with an autism diagnosis. Far from it. Rather, the tension Lynne experiences about the significance of the autism diagnosis serves to illustrate how deciding between scientifically (that is, psychologically) derived determinist accounts of a student's behaviour and what is known from the intersubjective relationship is a real live issue in the classroom.

Not tolerating uncertainty?

We saw above how Lynne uses the app to set up reminders for Tom to go to bed, which fail to be effective. It seems fairly clear that the app does not play a determining role here – these extant issues about autism, capability, autonomy and independence and the relationships between teachers, parents and child are there already. However, it is certainly the case that the introduction of this new app, designated as something that will help develop social and life skills, has seemed to activate Lynne's thinking (at least on an implicit level) about these issues, and illuminated the considerable uncertainty which they provoke.

Some aspects of this thinking as to how Lynne positions the technology bear further scrutiny. It is in fact rather strange that Lynne would think putting a reminder on an app would make Tom want to go to bed if, as Lynne knew, he doesn't see why he should go to bed earlier. It is possible that Lynne, at least in this instance, positions the app from a perspective of idealization – as though this new piece of technology is going to 'magically' make Tom become an adult, and in a way provide a short-cut that will avoid the need to grapple with all the sometimes unbearable uncertainties about him.

A similar reluctance to recognize the obvious about Tom and the going-to-bed reminders on the tool is seen in the fourth observation in July, towards the end of the summer term:

> Lynne then asks if the things she has put on, like the reminder to go to bed, help? Tom says, slightly more energetically, 'Well they do help'. Tom then says that when he goes to use it, it's 'always at low charge'. Lynne has a discussion with Tom about charging the mobile device – she has previously told him that he should put it on charge in his bedroom when he goes to bed. Lynne goes over this, and cajoles Tom into agreeing that

he'll try and do this. I observe Tom – he yawns quite a bit, his eyes are cast down and seem to sometimes flutter almost closed – he seems quite tired. Lynne changes tack and, referring to his earlier comment, says, 'so you think some of the evening things are helping you?' Tom says, with marginally more enthusiasm now than previously, 'Well... sometimes they are ... yeah'. Lynne asks if she needs to put the 'go to bed' reminder 'a bit earlier now?' Tom continues to yawn. Gently, Lynne says, 'You're still very tired, aren't you?' With a definite tone of annoyance, Tom says quite quickly, 'That's because I keep missing the reminders' ... Lynne says, 'why's that?' and Tom says, 'because I keep on forgetting to put it on and it's always out of batteries'. Lynne says, 'Oh right' and then, 'but if it has got batteries and it goes off then it does help ... you think?' Tom says, 'Yeah', without too much energy. Lynne gently cajoles Tom, asking him to try and remember to keep it charged; then they will just think about putting the reminder back a bit, 'as you are very tired, Tom'.

Although on the surface this extract may indicate that Tom does feel the going-to-bed reminders are serving some purpose, in the linked fourth interview, Lynne states clearly that in her opinion he was just saying that because it is what he thought she wanted to hear. Additionally, she makes it explicitly clear that she realizes Tom does not see any rationale for going to bed earlier.

Lynne: I mean the things that have been put on them are things that have come from parents, us ... but I think with, especially with Tom, because it's what Dad wanted on there and going to his sessions on time was what I wanted on there, he don't see why he's got to change anyway. It's like this going to bed earlier.

Joe: He can't see why he needs to.

Lynne: So he, he can't see that he's gaining anything from using it. Do you understand what I mean? If he ignores it, he can stay up later, can't he?

Joe: Yeah.

Lynne: So what motivation is there for him to actually take any notice of it? Because Dad wants him to go to bed early.

Joe: In the observation he did, he said that he thought that sometimes when it went off it was making a difference.

Lynne: Mm.

Joe: But do you think he was just...?

Lynne: I think he was just saying that. Yeah. Because Dad's told me that, he said it hasn't.

An alternative interpretation is that in these examples, Lynne's reaction is based on a countertransference response. For Tom – due perhaps, as

Shuttleworth (1997) puts it, to his 'unusual cognitive climate' – trying to think leads to very high levels of anxiety, and it is this 'stuck thinking' that Lynne picks up in the countertransference, leading to her ability to think in a flexible, adult and empathic way being hampered by her reaction to Tom's emotional state.

However, this is only one instance, and it should be noted that on a significant number of other occasions Lynne's capacity to tolerate uncertainty is much stronger in relation to both Tom, other children and the technology tool. This is a theme that is repeated within and across the cases – namely that mental states are ever shifting, even from moment to moment. As Margot Waddell puts it:

> Mental attitudes which appropriately belong to different stages of development, infancy, latency, adolescence, adulthood, will each, at any one moment, come under the sway of emotional forces which are characteristic of one position or the other (paranoid-schizoid and depressive), irrespective of the subject's actual years [...] Such states flicker and change with the nuances of internal and external forces and relationships, forever shifting between egoistic and altruistic tendencies.
>
> (Waddell, 1998, pp. 8–9)

We see what seems to be such a shift in the immediate following section of the third observation:

> Lynne, remaining calm and unperturbed, goes on and says that she'll show it to him now, then. By way of introduction she explains to Tom what she means my making an appointment – 'Say you wanted to go to the cinema on Monday ... You add cinema....'. She says this slightly theatrically – her eyes are expressive. Tom has the phone and follows her instructions, with an expression of concentration. Lynne reaches close over Tom as he works on the phone. She peers with him expectantly. I observe that Tom is using the on-screen keyboard to type quite fluently. Tom is focused and seems engaged, although his mouth is still flat and tight, which to me seems to suggest annoyance (although he has had this expression through the observation). After setting up the appointment, Lynne guides Tom to look at it – 'Day Plan ... Week ... Month'. Tom asks quizzically, 'do the blue dots mean that I've got appointments?' Lynne says that's right. Tom then says, rather suddenly and in a whining tone, 'when am I going to get the internet back? I've been waiting thirteen, fourteen months for it'. Lynne glances at me and we both smile. Lynne says, very calmly and quite softly, 'really, that long?' Tom then says, 'will it be when they get a less expensive server?' Lynne ignores this and says that she will ask Donald to come in maybe that afternoon and

have a chat about it with him. Lynne then shows Tom how to switch between the app and the main phone functions. Tom seems quite pleased with this. She reminds him that the phone has a camera and that he can take photos with it if he likes – Tom doesn't really respond to this. Lynne asks him finally if he is happy with the phone? He thinks for a moment and then says, in a more expressive tone than much of the rest of the observation, 'yes and no'.

Tom's somewhat transient grasp on a more adult, independent inquiring function about the activity perhaps becomes too difficult to sustain, and he is invaded by anxieties, perhaps expressed projectively in his focus on the internet not working. Yet here we see that Lynne, who had previously seemed less able to deal with the significant uncertainties presented by thinking about concerns about Tom and his capacities in the light of his autism diagnosis, is now more able to deal with Tom's (perhaps more direct) projections, encouraging Tom to return to a more adult position by again invoking an interaction with Donald. In contrast, perhaps, to the previously described encounter, Lynne tolerates the difficulty of being with Tom and his considerable anxieties and is able to manage his projections, to think through the anxieties to work out what it might be that he needs and to gently push him towards a more adult way of functioning. We might consider that Lynne holds on to the uncertainty of working with Tom long enough for a 'selected fact' to arise, drawing – unconsciously at first – on her experience of being with Tom, and in particular his relationship with Donald. That Tom might respond to Donald or the mention of Donald arises as the selected fact. When reviewing the audio tape and the final transcript, I had a strong feeling that there was a marked difference in my experience of the emotional tone between the two observations. I wrote in the observation notes that Tom's 'yes and no' had an adult tone to it that evoked the depressive position; that perhaps he can here tolerate some uncertainty, linked perhaps to Lynne's greater capacity to tolerate his anxiety in this instance. The psychosocial contention is that the marked difference in my feelings is based on countertransference, and that this countertransference knowledge tells us something about what was going on 'in the moment' between Lynne and Tom (although, as is consonant with realism, not everything, and not with any absolute certainty).

Methodological considerations – the role of the work study group

I have interpreted Lynne's interactions with the app and Tom as providing evidence that she takes, at least in some instances, an idealizing position towards it – a feeling that in some way this new magical tool will allow her to avoid engaging with the very difficult uncertainties involved in working with Tom.

In other instances, there was evidence that Lynne may have taken up alternative positions. In particular, during the work study review of the second observation and interview transcripts, colleagues commented specifically that they picked up on a considerable amount of resistance from Lynne. Further, the discussion during the session indicated that I was strongly defensive about this – partly because to a significant degree I wanted the app to be successful – meaning that I was, in interpreting the material, defending against negative messages. Moreover, as Bick (1964) indicated in her original formulations of the infant observation method, part of the function of the work study group is to help the observer untangle issues that they may, because of their own emotional position, have not picked up; or, more specifically in my case, to help them identify where they may have had too strong an unconscious reaction to the material to be able to consciously judge the reality of the situation.

For example, in the interview, Lynne discusses how she had set up reminders for Tom to remind him to get ready for lunch, something he found difficult to do:

Lynne: Well what I've done was I set it up so it was like on the appointment thing and then as soon as it bleeped, I mean he'd be in a lesson at twenty past twelve, so we'd still be sitting in the lesson and then his phone would bleep to say that it was now time for him to get ready ... 'Well why do I have to get ready, no one else is getting ready?'
Joe: Aha, right.

Lynne goes on to say when these reminders were implemented, Tom was worried about being identified as different from the other children. This was not so much about him having a piece of technology which they didn't, but rather about him getting ready for lunch earlier than the others:

Lynne: He doesn't want to be seen as being different to everyone else but if we wait till ... say ... normally it's two minutes before lunch and we say, 'Right we'll finish now let's all go to lunch' cos, literally, the other kids will just get up, 'We're going to lunch!' Tom will need to go to the toilet and wash his hands. He washes his face and he then goes and finds his lunchbox and then he's late but that doesn't bother him.
Joe: Right, interesting.
Lynne: But it bothers him that he has to finish the lesson before the other students to get ready. ... but I think it's Tuesdays and Thursdays where he's in a lesson and he has to be ready for lunch, so what I've suggested is one of the lessons is mine, which is fine ... the other lesson is the other teacher ... that all the students stop when Tom's

phone bleeps. So everyone stops at twenty past twelve when Tom's phone goes ... Tom can then get himself ready and basically the other students can ... we can like finish the lesson and they can go and wash their hands and whatever, so that we're all ready then but we're doing it at the same time as Tom. Because I think that was the issue; he had to stop the lesson and he thought he was missing out, that they were still doing something else. So that was what I suggested to Tom, which he agreed with but then the phones got taken away because of the internet issue and everything, so that's what we're going back to after the holiday. Whether he uses it in the holiday for this bed thing I don't know, I really don't know.

My initial interpretation of this extract, before the work study group discussion, was that this was an example of Lynne adopting an inclusive approach to the use of new technology. Just as a teacher might get all the classmates of a child with Down's syndrome to use Makaton sign language, similarly here Lynne was adapting the whole classroom to fit the needs of an individual child. However, in the work study group discussion, colleagues read the observation and interview transcripts as suggesting a considerable degree of resistance to and negative feelings towards the app. They highlighted a number of sections from the second interview in particular, including the following extract from the start of the interview:

Lynne: So yeah ... it was very ... I mean I spoke to Dad ... I spoke to Mum and Dad about what they would like on there but Tom is very anti changing his routine.

Joe: Right.

Lynne: And I don't know whether he's going to use ... I mean, as soon as they couldn't have the internet any more Tom didn't want the phone anyway!

Joe: Yeah.

Lynne: And it was like ... well there are other things we can do with it and whatever ... and I think ... I dunno, because he had that option ... if he hadn't had that option before he would probably be alright with it but because they had the internet and he used it all the time and now it's taken away, he's sort of anti the phone if you know what I mean.

Joe: He did seem a bit negative there certainly, yes.

Lynne: I mean he wouldn't have it back. Because Patrick and Alan had theirs back for two weeks after the internet was taken off but Tom wouldn't have his back.

Joe: Does he think ... that's what he's upset about?

Lynne: Yes.

Although this extract is focused on Tom's perceptions, later extracts do indicate a generally negative trend in Lynne's thinking at this stage in the implementation. For example, later in the interview Lynne discusses what she thinks could be improved about the app:

Joe: What did you like, what did you think was good or potentially has worked well if anything?

Lynne: No, I mean obviously the actual phones themselves have been a bit temperamental with ... it's more the fact that one minute they've got them and then, 'Oh no, we're taking them away' and also, I was speaking with Tracy [another member of the research team] and John yesterday and I said, 'I just ... she said ... there's a training session on the Wednesday after we get back after the holiday' and I said, 'Oh well, what's happening with me then?'

Joe: Right.

Lynne: ... and she said, 'Oh haven't you been invited?' and I said, 'Well, no one tells me.'

Joe: They only just sorted it out yesterday.

Lynne: But then she said, 'Oh well what I'll do is I'll do that with them and then I'll come over to you' and I said, 'No, I wanna be ... I feel as though I'm over here on my own and ... [said forcibly] Tracy does come over here but just her and me doing it, I'm not sharing with the other teachers if you know what I mean [this is obviously a strongly felt issue for Lynne] and I just think ... I have felt a bit on my own over here trying to get everything done and not included in what's going on at school. But that's not your fault or anyone's, it's just I think ... it needs to be a whole school thing rather than me over here doing it on my own and, also, Patrick's residential ... I mean the people that he's with every evening need to be included in things.

This extract also illustrates how the implementation of the app ties in with Lynne's ongoing feelings of being 'left out', as well as Lynne's significant frustration in relation to the app.

It may also be that Lynne is experiencing rivalrous feelings towards the technology. In particular, her existing envious feelings in respect of the greater attention that staff on the main site are, in her perception, receiving may have been stimulated by the introduction of a new object. In her internal world, the tool may be viewed as a new toy to which rivalrous 'siblings' (her colleagues) have been given greater access. Lynne does in fact make reference on eight occasions in her interview responses to feelings of being left out (one in the first interview, six in the second interview and two in the fourth interview), and it is relevant to note that these were made exclusively in respect to questions about the app, not her feelings about working on a different site.

I think this material from Lynne serves to illuminate the potential for the use of a modified infant observation approach in the exploration of emotional aspects of professional practice. It demonstrates how counter-transference, feelings in response to the observed situation, can tell us, when used judiciously, about the emotional state of the actors in the field. It also shows how such a tool needs to be used carefully, and demonstrates the potential for triangulation between sources that the use of both obser-vation and interview material allows, as well as how the use of a work study group to review material can usefully help the researcher or research team to separate out strong identifications which belong to the researcher from the reality of the emotional field being considered.

Although it seems that Lynne was at times, particularly in the ear-lier stages of the implementation, beset by significant negative feelings, her positioning in relation to the app was more complex than that. On a number of occasions Lynne indicated, either directly or indirectly, her belief that it could make a difference to the young people she was working with. Source references from Lynne were coded to the data node 'Teacher indicates belief that the technology tool can promote autonomy' on nine-teen occasions (fourteen instances across the interviews and five from the second observation).

Thus it is reasonable to conclude that at times, Lynne had a positive ori-entation towards the app. This can usefully be considered from Waddell's perspective on shifting states of minds. At times Lynne was subject to inva-sion by feelings of rivalry or intrusion due to the introduction of the app. On other occasions, as with Tom in the third observation, her anxieties related to the uncertainties involved in working with children with autism interfered with her ability to base her use of the technology on realistic thinking about the children's needs.

Yet at other times, perhaps when she was less invaded by uncertainty, Lynne did see the potential for the technology to make a difference to the lives of the children she was working with and was able, in a Bionian sense, to come to 'know' the children. In other words, Lynne was able to engage in a state of intersubjective relatedness, whereby she could tolerate uncertainty and anxiety and utilize her experience of working with the children to decide how the tool might be used. These instances were examples of productive uncertainty in action.

This pattern of shifting states of mind in relation to the app is one that repeats itself across the other cases in this study.

Kathy – live company

Current role and career background

Kathy started work as a qualified teacher in mainstream secondary schools in Birmingham. She then worked, for thirteen years altogether, in schools for children with emotional and behavioural difficulties, latterly in a borough-wide management position with responsibility for excluded and SEN children. Kathy then 'came out of management' to work at Randall School, where she has been for the past six years. Kathy is a form tutor, as well as teaching art (her specialist area) and religious education across the school.

When asked, in the initial interview, why she decided to come and work specifically with children with autism, Kathy gives a bravura response:

> Because for the last twelve, fourteen years I'd been working with the whole spectrum of special needs, both on the 'shop floor' and managing the organization of the same, and I decided I didn't want to be in management anymore cos my time was divided ... you couldn't be in the classroom and manage but you were expected to be so ... the needs were there ... and I was brilliant with the kids, so I thought, what is the condition that makes me feel really de-skilled and that was autism, so I sought a job in that cos I thought, well I don't want to be de-skilled in any area.

Here Kathy identifies disillusionment with the conflicts engendered by being in a management role as one factor in her decision to change roles. It is also evident that she saw working with children with autism as something of a challenge. In this context, how should the declamation 'I was brilliant with the kids' be considered? As a rationale, is it a somewhat unconventionally effusive, reflective analysis of her skills, or a defensive projection of invulnerability? Such uncertainty is a common thread throughout the ensuing discussion about Kathy, her thinking and her actions. There was also considerable uncertainty for me, during the analysis of the data, in making sense of what was going on for Kathy, and the review in work study group allowed a greater sense of understanding to slowly emerge.

Key information sources for Kathy

First interview 14 October 2009
First observation 25 November 2009
Second observation 19 March 2010
Second interview 24 March 2010
Third observation 18 May (1) 2010
Fourth observation 18 May (2) 2010

Supplementary:
Observation, Kathy's class and Jill (16 June 2010)
Interview with Jill (6 July 2010).

Approach to dealing with autism and conflicts with the school

Kathy was withdrawn from involvement in the app project directly after the third and fourth observations, and was not available for further interviews or observations. Material relevant to a consideration of Kathy and her work with the children in the context of using the app was derived from additional observations of Jill, a senior support worker who was regarded as holding a teacher equivalent role in the school, working with Kathy's form class, and from an interview with Jill.

It is also relevant to note that during the 2009/10 implementation year, as reported to me by Kathy herself, Kathy's mother suffered a serious illness; she died a few weeks before the last observation.

Kathy's approach to working with children with autism can be typified as being aligned most closely to a social model of special educational needs. Of the interview source references, eight were coded to the data node 'Children with ASD are just normal' (three in the first interview, four in the second interview and one in the final interview), which was used to categorize responses that indicate expressed views synonymous with a conceptualization of autism which stresses the children's inherent humanity and views them as having (at least partially) socially determined strengths and weaknesses, just like all children. This is exemplified for Kathy in the following extract from the first interview:

Joe: What would you say is your general approach to working with autism, how that fits in with the school's approach overall?

Kathy: I'm not low arousal [chuckles] for some reason that seems to work. I'll adopt the strategies that I was advised to do and I don't do that in a hypocritical way, I can see how they work or why they work … for instance the Brain Gym, it was suggested that I do that because after the children travel into school I believe they should be allowed some time running around in the playground, for some of them an hour before they [come in]. This is *not* the rule here, so the Brain Gym was introduced to me as an alternative to me allowing them to play and, fair enough, if my class is playing then other classes might want to play. So we did the Brain Gym and it was quite formal and I thought, this Brain Gym would be wonderful if we could have some nice loud music with it, and that's worked. I'm not sure the inventor of Brain Gym wanted loud music with it but it's working and is certainly motivating the ones … they are going like that [demonstrates movement] and they've got a rhythm to do it to so, yes I will follow the strategies and the laid-down rules that we have to work to but if I could find a way of making it more stimulating or interesting I'll go for it and I will be very straightforward with the students. *I think they are people with autism, not autistic people!* [said with significant emphasis]

Joe: Tell me a bit more what that means, that difference?

Kathy: When I find myself saying 'he' or 'she' is autistic, or that they're autistic, I get cross with myself because I think that it's almost putting down ... there are people with autism and they have a condition, they are NOT autistic people. Cos saying they're autistic people almost sets them as a race apart and they're NOT a race apart; they are people who have emotions and feelings, the same as the rest of us, they just have this condition ... because I've got arthritis, I'm not ... 'Oh that's an arthritic!', I'm Kathy *with* arthritis. Why can't they be students *with* autism or adults *with* autism, not autistic people?

This extract also serves to illuminate some aspects of the conflict between Kathy's approach to working with children with autism and that of the school. The school employs a modified TEACCH approach (University of North Carolina, n.d.), part of which is the promotion of a low-arousal environment. In the extract we see that although Kathy pays lip service to the school's overall approach, it is clear that on this issue she disagrees with it.

Her consideration of her charges as being 'students with autism ... not autistic people' also reflects a wider conflict between Kathy's sense that the school should be promoting the children's autonomy and independence and her perception that the school's approach is too cautious and restrictive; that is, that they see them as autistic people, not as people with a varied range of potential. It also mirrors, to some extent, wider conflicts between the social and medical models of disability in relation to special educational needs.

The conflict between wishing to promote autonomy and independence and concerns over the restrictions on capability resulting from autism is exemplified here in the conflict between Kathy and the school. It is, however, a conflict that is present as a tension in the thinking of all the teacher cases presented in the study. This conflict is also present within Kathy's own thinking, as can be seen from the following extract from the second interview, when I refer to the initial observation I did with Lynne's class at Further Education (Post-16). Kathy refers to two of the children at FE, Steve and Danny, with whom she is familiar.

Joe: Right! I did do ... I did an observation again at FE ... I went out with them to the supermarket actually ... I did notice that they all ...

when they got to the end of the road, they all kind of stopped and waited for the teacher or teaching assistant to come and cross over the road with them so I had a query in my mind at that time ... you know, with 17-year-olds, do they actually need that?

Kathy: Steve can do. You can go to the supermarket with him and he can cross the road and you can go to the supermarket and say, 'Get the week's shopping for the flat Steve' and he'd do it without you being anywhere near him and Danny is meant to be a 2-to-1 ... you have to be with him because he does panic and call the police but, equally, you can say, 'We need the week's shopping' and from memory he can do it independently, but for the public safety you have got to be near him, given his size as well.

Joe: Umm. A difficult balance to work out.

It's clear that Kathy is, inevitably, trying to work out the 'difficult balance' between promoting the children's autonomy and independence, and working within the realities presented by their restricted capabilities. Although she tends to come down more on the side of the former, rationally she recognizes the imperative for practice mandated by the latter.

It seems reasonable to propose that the attempt to resolve these two contrasting positions in terms of deciding what to do when working with children with autism is a considerable source of uncertainty for Kathy and the other teachers in the study.

Mark

Kathy has one child in her form class, Mark, who is using the app. Mark was born in 1996, making him 12/13 during the 2009/10 app implementation period. He had a full IQ measured on WISC-IV of 84, a VQ of 89, and a clinical psychiatric diagnosis of autism on entry to the school. He has a co-morbid diagnosis of obsessive-compulsive disorder (OCD).

Mark lives at home with his parents and attends the school on weekdays. Classroom observation data, teacher interviews and informal visits to the school form initial impressions of Mark presenting as a pleasant, polite but very nervous child. He is very keen to please, and both classroom observation and reports from Kathy indicate that he is unfailingly polite to adults. On several occasions when I was in the school, Mark would come up to me and say hello, and there was a strong sense of his desire to receive adult attention.

In classroom observation he frequently has a noticeable forced smile, which tends to have a manic quality to it. Kathy discusses Mark's use of this smile, and of a high vocal tone, as being responses to anxiety. Other adults in the school, including Jill and Donald, the school educational psychologist, also comment informally on Mark's sometimes extreme nervous states. However, Mark – particularly in Kathy's presence – also has a more lively aspect to his character. He has what could be described as a flair for theatricality and humour, and this is evident in a number of observations when Kathy is working with him.

Although there is significant discussion in the interview material about Mark's autism and the significance of the diagnosis, there is no mention of the co-morbid diagnosis of OCD. There is also no reference to it in the interview with Jill, nor in informal discussion with other staff members.

Kathy comments on his playground play, indicating that despite Mark's slight frame and overall nervous disposition he likes to engage in quite rough play on the climbing frame with older and bigger children, although she notes that this type of play does not require any talking. His day-to-day relationships with other children in the school are generally positive and over the course of the 2009/10 year he develops a friendship with Phillip, who has moved to his form class from another class.

Academically, Kathy places him as equivalent to 'an early level five in a junior school', which implies that he is working just below his age-expected level.

Kathy – live company?

In the four classroom observations, Kathy comes across as an ebullient, enthusiastic teacher who injects a lot of energy into her classes, to which the children on the surface appear to respond well. There is also, throughout the observations, an ongoing interpretative tension between events that could be considered as examples of lively engagement with the children or might be regarded by some as examples of narcissistic or even close to uncomfortable crossing of personal and professional boundaries. Several examples of attempts to draw me out of a non-participant observer position, and the countertransference responses this invoked in me, were useful in helping to make sense of these events.

In the first observation, Kathy unexpectedly and jarringly reveals personal information about her son:

> I go into class at 8.50 am. There are no children there, just Kathy, Diane and two other teaching assistants/practitioners – Lorraine and Kay. [Diane is Mark's key worker]. Kathy introduces me to Diane – jokingly, 'This is Joe. He's the [app] man that everyone moans about'.
>
> Everyone says hello and seems very friendly. Kathy shows me 'Amos', her stimulus object, which is a toy baby monkey that moves and gurgles to a sequence. It is very cute. Almost out of nowhere, Kathy tells me

excitedly that 'my son's got a girlfriend', and goes on to tell me how his father is very pleased with this.

In my initial annotations to the writing-up of the observation I note:

> I feel a bit taken aback by all this – I'm not clear why Kathy is sharing what could be regarded as quite an intimate matter with me – someone she hardly knows. I feel confused/uncomfortable.

This is typical of a number of instances during the observations where I also make a note of having similar feelings.

Agency and autonomy

At the time of the first interview, Kathy had been working with Mark for six weeks. She has a strong sense that in the previous years, Mark has had too much of a reliance on various supportive aids, like an angled support for use at his desk – 'a half tent affair that was meant to stop him becoming anxious' – which were designed, in the eyes of previous teachers and other colleagues at the school, to reduce Mark's anxiety. Kathy's feeling seems to be that this level of support with Mark is unnecessary and that it is reducing his independence, as in this extract from the initial interview:

Kathy: I haven't offered it him. He brought it in and he asked for it … he can just pick it up and he hasn't asked for it at all this term. His mother is very, very caring and very, very anxious and she's mentioned that he probably needs it but he hasn't asked for it. I deliberately didn't mention it to him, but I said, 'Don't you want your work station?' … [Mark replied] 'Oh no!'
Joe: So was that because you thought he didn't … he maybe didn't need to have it?
Kathy: I didn't think either way. I just thought if he wants it he'll just say.

Kathy is clearly conscious of the difference between her approach and that of the school typically, as can be seen in this extract from later in the first interview, when she is discussing her expectations for Mark:

Kathy: I think we have to be very careful of over-nurturing. Particularly when we're at a specialist school like this. It is great … I say I feel privileged that I have the support I do to teach the different areas of the curriculum, I do, but I think that is a pitfall, that where you've got people who have worked with the same students for many, many years they are doing *too* much for them.

During the 2009/10 year, Kathy implements her stated policy of reducing Mark's reliance on aids in the classroom. This is evident in the first and second classroom observations, when Kathy makes several direct references to Mark about the aids and how he is getting on fine without them. Mark is apparently getting on well under this regime, at least according to reports by Kathy, up until early May when, one week before the third and fourth observations (and a couple of weeks after Kathy's bereavement), there is an incident in which Mark 'acts out' very seriously. I am not, until the end of the academic year, given any information about specifically what happened in this incident; however, it seems clearly to have had a significant effect on the school's approach to working with Mark. During the third observation it becomes clear that a review meeting was held which involved the senior school management and Mark's parents. As a result of this meeting, specific guidance was issued to Kathy about reintroducing some of the aids that Mark had previously been using. It seems likely that the school management's concerns about Kathy's approach to working with Mark had been brewing for some time, and that the incident provoked an exertion of the school's authority.

Kathy's approach to the use of classroom aids needs to be considered in the context of her overall approach to working with Mark, which – in line with her general approach to working with the class – was characterized by lively interactions. These interactions serve to exemplify the interpretative tension created by the observational material from this case – that is to say, was Kathy engaging in lively stimulating interaction which promoted the development of autonomy by her students, or was she perhaps uncomfortably close to crossing boundaries and provoking their anxiety? At times the material afforded itself more closely to the former, as in the following extract from the third observation:

> Kathy introduced the children to an English worksheet. It has several pages. The first is on first letters and has the alphabet in sequence with a space, as in 'A_____ B_____', to write a word. This is repeated underneath with upper and lowercase together, as in 'Aa_____ Bb_____'. Kathy is using the sheet for the children to think of words beginning with each letter and write them down. She is working more directly with Julian but frequently interjects/directs to Mark and the group as a whole. Mark has his triangular block and a grip on his pencil. He is very smiley but seems engaged with the task, looking enthusiastically at the worksheet. Kathy starts them off by asking to different children which would come first in the dictionary – to Julian, 'which will come first, Inky Snake or Bee?', to which children chorus 'B'.
>
> Kathy then asks the children to suggest words which they do for the different letters and she explains how to fill it in. She asks Mark, in reference to the bottom section if they write each letter of the word twice.

Mark shakes his head vigorously and says, 'Noooo'. Kathy goes on to introduce the following pages. The next one is on nouns, with a picture and first letters of some of the objects in the picture. Kathy asks to the group generally, 'is black a naming word?', 'Noooo', 'is cat a naming word?', 'Yes'. Mark is nodding enthusiastically. Throughout this session, Kathy is interjecting, cajoling, suggesting – her energy seems to motivate and sustain the children's engagement.

The children now start working on the sheet. There is quiet and some fairly industrious working for a minute or so. Kathy is sitting now looking at Andy's work. Kathy reads from the sheet, explaining to the group, 'Cover the snakes to make them fit the adjectives? Can you read the words on there...? [there is an exaggerated pause] ... Mark!'

Mark obliges and reads, 'long, red, yellow, spotty, furry, sad'. Kathy says, 'Now do it as though you were on stage', throwing her hand out theatrically and starting him off in a flourishing tone.

Mark says, 'LONG?'

Mark gets very animated, and goes on to say, 'long, red, yellow?' in a kind of quasi-American affected tone that does sound like an actor expositing on the stage. He does a flourish with his arm to accompany this. Kathy laughs and says, 'Well done'.

Kathy, pointing to the next page, says, 'the next page is more difficult? You've got some sentences to finish? So adjectives ... snake hisses, Julian?' Julian looks a bit unsure and Kathy says, 'a word to describe the snake'. Julian gives a response. Kathy then asks some more questions on describing words to the children and then asks, specifically to Mark, 'another one Mark?' Mark says, slightly hesitantly, 'Blue' ... Kathy repeats, sounding pleased, 'Blue? Yeah? What about a dog, what could a dog be Julian?' Julian says, 'Yellow'. Kathy says, 'Yeah? A car ... words to describe a car, Mark?' Mark hesitates, saying, 'Errrr...' and then comes up with, sounding pleased, 'Striped!' Kathy says, in agreement, 'a striped car? I'd like a striped car.' Julian then says 'a polka dot car'; Kathy echoes in a surprised and enthusiastic tone, 'a polka dot car! ... who knows what polka dot means? ... it means spotty doesn't it? What a lovely [emphasis] word. Well done!' The children then briefly discuss sunsets – 'yellow sunsets?' – and Kathy says, in a pleased tone, that she didn't know her 'class were so clever' [...]

The final sheet is on the past tense. Kathy introduces this and says, 'Who can give me something in the past tense?' There is a definite pause for a moment or two – none of the children react. Phillip is thinking quite hard – I have the sense that this is a challenging question for them. Then Phillip says, 'David Tennant leapt' [this is a reference to the actor playing the character of the Doctor in the television show *Dr Who* at the time]. Kathy says, 'Dr Who ... yeah ... that has happened'. There is some more back-and-forth questioning on the past tense and then Kathy asks Mark if he can think of anything. Mark looks a bit blank, so Kathy prompts with, 'how about Mark used to have a high voice?' Mark says 'Yeah', quite agreeably, and Kathy continues, 'but that's past'. Mark nods and seems very happy to agree. Kathy says, 'What else did you used to have?' Mark thinks for a second, says, 'Ur ... ur...', and then has a light-bulb-on look and says, 'used to have an insane sense of humour'. Kathy and Mark laugh together and Kathy says, 'you've still got that'.

This lively interaction shows Kathy modulating her responses effectively in reaction to the children and using her enthusiasm and energy to bring them with her. She also fosters and encourages Mark's expressive use of language and his theatrical flair, and my fieldnotes indicate that this feels to me like a genuine interaction from Mark. His 'rictus' smile is absent and there is an easier flow to his facial and bodily movements than on other occasions, when he appears tense and nervous.

In the moment when Mark theatrically says 'long, red, yellow', he doesn't seem like a boy with autism, who is beset by chronic anxiety. He doesn't seem like a child with a co-morbid diagnosis of OCD. He is also all those things, but 'in the moment' it does seem reasonable to suggest that Kathy has used her energy, as well as her belief that Mark is not defined by his labels and his anxious state, to draw him into a more genuine and creative relational state. There are echoes of Anne Alvarez's adaptation of Trevarthen's phrase 'Live Company'. Alvarez (1992), writing about the use of psychoanalytic psychotherapy with autistic, borderline and abused children, suggests that such children often get stuck in repetitive behavioural patterns which, although originally serving a necessary defensive function, are now just relics that prevent them reaching their potential. Alvarez proposes that the therapist needs to consider whether the child needs to be this way to deal with their own anxiety or whether, if it is just pattern behaviour, they could be challenged or enticed to consider more mindful types of communication. Alvarez's position seems to be that we should not accept autism as just 'difference', but should be active agents in reaching across the divide and using our 'live' mind to foster the reclamation of the child's mind, and by implication their agency and autonomy. With Kathy, too, it seems reasonable to propose that in some instances at least she uses her live mind to cross the boundary to Mark and draw him into a more creative and alive state. Although her use of this strategy is to a significant degree based on implicit rather than explicit thinking, the end result is largely the same.

On other occasions, Kathy's interaction with the class and with Mark was, in my perception, less sure-footed. In fact, this change in tone is seen almost immediately in the next part of the third observation:

Kathy then moves on to talk about the 'future tense, which you two [Phillip and Mark] should all be very [Emphasis] good at that as it's all about space ... if I cooked yesterday what do I say?' The children respond, 'I cooked...'. Kathy says, 'if I cook tomorrow what do I say?' Kathy and children chorus together, 'I will ... I will go to a charity shop tomorrow'. There is then a back-and-forth discussion for a minute or so on the future tense, with Kathy asking individual children what they will do tomorrow.

Kathy asks Mark, who looks a bit blank, and Kathy emphasizes, 'Will will will will...'. Mark says, sounding rather pleased with himself, 'I will go to HMV tomorrow and buy a *Dr Who* DVD.' Kathy flips her head and rolls her eyes and says, 'Oh ... *Dr Who*...', in a mock-resigned voice.

There is more discussion on 'I will' between Kathy and the adults. Kathy says, 'I will go to work tomorrow', and the adults laugh.

After a few moments, Kathy says to Phillip, in a more conversational tone, 'will you go to church on Sunday?' Phillip shakes his head and Kathy says, in a slightly jokey tone, 'are you going off church then?' Phillip puts his head down on the desk and mumbles something. Kathy, exaggeratedly, does the same, and says in a loud voice, 'Phillip, Phillip ... I can't hear you.' Phillip looks a bit irritated but springs up again and says, 'I usually go on Saturday'. Kathy asks, 'What happens there on Saturday?' Phillip says, 'I get bored.' Kathy says, 'I'm [emphasis] going to church on Saturday next term. Who with ... do you know anyone else in the school who goes to church all day Saturday?' Mark says, 'Steven...', in a rather strangulated tone. The children's expressions at this indicate recognition. Kathy says that she saw Steven's father yesterday and said, 'Can I come to your church and see what happens? And that's what I'm doing ... 'cos Steven knows more about the Bible than I do'.

Phillip says, 'and he always says that Jesus's birthday wasn't on Christmas Day, it was on another day'. Kathy says, 'it wasn't' [emphasis], but then says to Phillip, 'if I wanted ... you know you're going to church a bit ... if I was your mum and really really really wanted you to go to church ... and you go, [with dramatic emphasis] I DON'T WANT TO GO ... I could say, Phillip, you're really going to like the church service ... when you get there they're going to show you lots of *Dr Who* DVDs. You'd go wouldn't you?' Phillip looks pleased. Kathy continues, 'and Steven's church is a bit like that ... you know my reggae music'. Phillip says, 'Uh ... huh'. So when you go to Steven's church instead of all sitting there quietly, you go [in a loud voice] Ah, yeah, Praise the Lord [claps her hands] ... and they'll all be dancing around and it'll be really good ... and that's why he likes going to church because it's different ... white people and English people go too but it is a lot of fun...'. Kathy jigs her body as though they were dancing at the church. Kathy asks Mark,

'Do you ever go to church?'... he looks a bit blank. Kathy prompts with 'weddings or...', and Mark says, 'yeah ... weddings'. ... Kathy says, 'yeah ... though so that's about the future'.

Kathy then says, 'OK I want to see you all working now so go! ... no rushing ... best work as it's all things we have done before'. The atmosphere breaks, and things become more relaxed after the intensity of the previous dialogue sequence. Mark jumps up and looks at his worksheet [...]

At the time of the observation, this sequence on church attendance made me feel rather uncomfortable. It was, in professional terms, unorthodox or unconventional. However, it was arguable, particularly as part of Kathy's role in the school is to teach religious education, that she was quite reasonably taking an opportunity to explore this aspect of the curriculum with the children.

When this material was reviewed in the work study group, however, there was agreement from professional colleagues that there had been a veering off into unbounded territory. My discomfort during the observation, and the discomfort of colleagues reviewing the material in work study, was suggestive of a countertransference response to an underlying narcissistic quality to Kathy's engagement, in which she seemed to have lost a clear connection to the children. From a Bionian perspective, her ability to tolerate uncertainty and allow knowledge about them to emerge from intersubjective relatedness could be regarded as being impaired by a flight to defensive mechanisms. It is interesting to note that Mark returns to an unusual voice tone, and that both he and Phillip's levels of engagement seem to be qualitatively different in this section of the observation.

Methodological considerations on the role of the work study group

The work study group highlighted the usefulness of my countertransference response in resolving the interpretative tension inherent in this part of the observation. As can be seen from the material presented, I make a number of references to how Kathy's interactions with the children at times evokes differing feelings, sometimes very uncomfortable ones, in me.

The fact I felt very uncomfortable at times did seem to be a useful signal, suggesting that the children may also have been feeling uncomfortable – a conclusion which is supported by the observational write-up. A close reading does suggest that Phillip is very uncomfortable and that Mark has no idea what Kathy is driving at, and is finding the situation anxiety-provoking. It may be that due to my prior history as a class teacher I had something of a natural tendency to side with the teacher and a concomitant reluctance to make 'negative' judgements, and that this was affecting my ability to properly make use of the available material. As in a number of other instances, taking the material to a work study group allowed me to see past these blockages.

Again, the material from Kathy's case does, I propose, serve to illuminate how the use of a modified infant observation approach to considering professional practice can be effective in uncovering the emotional interactions at play between teacher and child in the classroom.

Varying states of mind

Kathy's general orientation towards technology in general in the first interview was characterized by a mixture of frustration and what seemed to be stronger feelings of fear and even anger. Her attitude to the app was at times in marked contrast to this.

In the first interview, in response to a question about what challenges she experienced working with children with autism, Kathy gave an answer focused on her expectations for the app:

Joe: Okay. There must be … maybe 'challenge' is the wrong word but just the kind of issues that come up … that you have with ANY class, what are the things that…?

Kathy: I'm going to sound conceited but as I say, I just think that visual images, which is one of the reasons why I think the *phone will work* because it's not communicating in writing or speech. It's largely going to be … it does have those features on it but the first thing we're going to put on there is pictures to remind them, isn't it? Because that's the way I operate anyway, being an artist … I've never found it that difficult … I've had to learn a lot about autism and about sequences and about the communicating and the ways to speak but as I say the visual communication thing, I just thought, 'I can do this, this is really excellent!' and if you look at recorded incidents in any room where I've been teaching there have been very few. I don't know whether I'm lucky or it's that particular talent for producing visual stuff works and I think that's why I think the phones will probably work.

Joe: Great.

Kathy: Because it's not lists of writing which is difficult. It's not someone talking and you're not understanding their expression. The other thing that these kids relate to, along with all their peers in the outside world, is technological equipment: DSs, computers, TVs, films like Disney and look at Thomas the Tank Engine … if you are thinking … Thomas in the story goes along lines doesn't he? … sequential pictures, so yeah I think the phone's a good vehicle.

At this stage in the implementation, Kathy had attended two two-hour training sessions on the use of the app, but had not yet started using it regularly with Mark. She was correct in identifying the use of images, in the personal trainer function, as an important part of the app. There is also a recognition, somewhat contrasting with her earlier responses in the first interview on technology in general, of the importance of technology in the lives of young people. However, there is also a somewhat manic and brittle tone to what Kathy says. The question was about challenges, yet her response ignores this; she focuses on her flair for the use of visual images and, in what seems to be a partial non-sequitur, exclaims that there have been very few recorded incidents in her classroom. Her enthusiasm for the app, given her low level of exposure to it at this stage, also seems perhaps overblown.

This perhaps overblown enthusiasm is also present in the second interview, four months later in March 2010. Kathy and Mark are still not quite fully engaged in using the app, partly due to a technical issue that had led to the smartphones being withdrawn from the children for a number of weeks at the start of the spring term:

Joe: So what do you think ... what's his feeling about it; do you have a sense of what ... how he's ... does he like it, is he happy to have it?

Kathy: Oh he'll be happy to have it.

Joe: Yes.

Kathy: Not just to please us ... cos he wants to please, that is his agenda in life; he wants everyone to be happy. But, no, he will actually like it and he will find it useful unlike his laptop computer, which he doesn't like.

Joe: Why doesn't he like it?

Kathy: He can't see the point of it, he can write perfectly well. It's boring ... can't access the internet on it...

Joe: This is the one he's got in school?

Kathy: Yeah.

Joe: Ah!

Kathy: So it's just for Quirk training really [a computer training course that Mark was attending] and, as I say, his writing is probably a year below what it would be if he was in mainstream, so I don't think there are any issues there and it's become a chore! So, no, you know, you have to remind him to get that out ... he comes in with so many aids. When he first came here he had his tent, like this portable workstation; his wedgies; his laptop ... you know, comes in over-burdened.

Joe: Yeah, I was going to say.

Kathy: So something you can just put in your pocket, it's going to be brilliant!

Again, Kathy's expressed confidence in the app is somewhat surprising, particularly given the significant technical problems involved in the implementation up to this point and Kathy's self-confessed lack of engagement with the technology. Mark's engagement with the app also seemed, from my interactions with him, to be much more uncertain at that point than Kathy suggests. In the second observation, several days before this interview, I had shown Mark how to use various aspects of the app during the observation, and his orientation towards the phone had been one more of suspicion and uncertainty than of enthusiasm.

Kathy's somewhat counterintuitive expressed enthusiasm for the app seems to be linked in her mind to her conflict with the school over how to work with Mark. The app is not considered as another classroom aid, but as something that is going to be 'brilliant'. Yet there does not seem to be any clear rational evidence on which Kathy can base such a conclusion at this point. It may be that because the app has been introduced by an agency outside the school, Kathy positions it differently from interventions for Mark introduced by the school itself. In Kleinian terms we could consider that Kathy may be engaging in splitting, projecting negatively on to the school aids based on the institution's association in her mind with a harsh judgemental internal object (the school management), and simultaneously projecting positively on to the app. This projection, however, seems to be based on magical thinking (Klein, 1923), and could be regarded as having a brittle, omnipotent quality to it. This new technology will be infallible and achieve miracles for Mark. When Kathy is in such a state of mind, she is not able to enter into live contact with Mark, and not able to use uncertainty productively to help him in his development.

At other times, however – particularly in the third observation, in May – Kathy's state of mind in relation to the app seems to be more realistic. In the following extract from this observation, Kathy has managed to set up some personal trainer interventions on the app for Mark and shows them to him during the class:

> Kathy now comes back in and now asks Mark to go and get his phone. She says, as he goes to his tray, 'Mark ... don't panic ... [gently] no rush'. She discusses with him how he is getting on with it. Kathy says to him, 'you know how you keep forgetting it in your tray?' Mark turns his head and looks surprised, and says, in a questioning tone, 'Do I?' Kathy nods and smiles and says that she thinks he does but that, 'there's nothing wrong with that ... it's normal'. Mark says, sounding surprised, 'Really?' and Kathy says, 'Yeah [...]'. Kathy talks to Mark about what is set up on the phone for him and that it now has a reminder – 'it's going to make noises to make you pay attention ... you're not the only one, Jeremy's the same, keeps forgetting it and how useful it can be.' Kathy carries on,

explaining how the reminder will work and that one of the interventions on it will be 'Don't Panic'. Mark echoes 'Don't Panic' in recognition when Kathy says this. Kathy says, 'you know last week we discussed … you wanted May Day, May Day, May Day, and then Don't Panic – Just Stop and Ask – well that's going on there'. Mark nods and says, 'Yeah', with a tone of recognition.

I observe that Kathy speaks in a measured calm tone throughout this session with Mark. She gives Mark her full attention – she looks directly at him and leans slightly forward in her chair. He also, for much of the time, looks very directly back at her. Mark says, 'Yeah … yeah…' in a slightly stressed tone in response to what Kathy is saying – again it is hard to gauge his level of actual engagement.

Kathy then goes on to say that whereas Kevin has the phone out all the time as for him it's 'fashionable', for Mark it's different– 'you're more interested in this guy than a fashionable phone'.

I then observe Mark starting the app and navigating the software. He uses the stylus a little bit gingerly but his general demeanour in navigating the smartphone seems fairly fluent. Whilst he is navigating the phone I observe that he puts his hand behind his head, almost as though scratching it to think what to do next. He also, at one point when Kathy is talking to him, gently traces the air near his face with the stylus.

Kathy then refers to the incident – 'remember Friday when you weren't doing what you were supposed to be doing?' Mark says, sounding confused and unsure, 'I was confused.' Kathy says, quite confidently, 'you were confused because you'd been caught I think … you knew exactly what you'd done … it was something you'd done before … it wasn't a new thing'. Mark nods – he seems quite calm – and says, 'I saw someone else doing it as well.' Kathy says, 'but the point was that you didn't know what to do with that confusion, did you? … and that's what the phone is going to help you with … it could be really useful in helping you when you get upset'. Then, by way of analogy, Kathy tells Mark that sometimes she gets confused and gives an example from the previous week when Darnelle made some comments in her planning book. Kathy says, 'I was cross … I wanted to cry … and I wanted to go home'. Mark nods and says, 'Yeah'. Kathy says, 'and I didn't have a phone to say, Kathy, Don't Panic … you have … and we all feel like that'.

In my fieldnotes I wrote that Kathy seemed to be much more in contact with Mark during this exchange. I also noted that I felt much more relaxed during this exchange, compared to the significant anxiety and confusion I had felt at other times when observing Kathy. When reviewing the audio and the transcript, there also seemed to be a more realistic evaluation of the role of the technology, now based on actual experience of using it. In Bionian terms, we could say that she has managed to stay with the uncertainty and maintain a greater degree of intersubjective contact, allowing her to 'know' more about what is really going on for Mark; in other words, it is an instance of productive uncertainty in play. Thus, the 'Don't Panic' intervention that Kathy has implemented on the app in this instance seems at the very least potentially attuned to his needs. My countertransference response to the observation – that is, my feeling of calmness in contrast to my emotional state in other observations – also supports the contention that Kathy handles the issue of the 'incident' here with careful attunement to Mark's emotional state.

The app still plays a role in her thinking about Mark, and although it is certainly not clear at this stage whether the app really can make a difference to Mark, his functional engagement with it in this observation does at least suggest that it is a possibility.

Tolerating uncertainty – the need for containment by the school

Shortly after the third and fourth observations Kathy went on sick leave, and was simultaneously removed from the project by the school. The incident with Mark, happening in the context of Kathy's recent bereavement, seems to have precipitated a change for the school, for Kathy and for Mark himself. Although I discussed Kathy's abrupt withdrawal from the project with Donald, the school's educational psychologist and lead for the project, no explanation for the change was forthcoming; nor indeed did I ever find out what actually happened in the incident.

Thinking about how to work best with Mark engendered considerable tension for Kathy and for the school on a corporate level. This tension was positioned around two contrasting positions. On the one hand, Kathy felt that the use of support aids reflected a broader 'nannying' attitude to Mark, which hampered his independence and was limiting his development. Kathy adopted a less structured, more energetic approach to working with Mark, which at times clearly stimulated the creative and expressive aspects of his character. On the other hand, the school seemed to have felt that the freer, less structured approach taken by Kathy, exemplified through the removal of support aids, was increasing Mark's anxiety levels. Towards the end of the 2009/10 year, the children 'moved up' to their 2010/11 academic year classes and Mark moved to Penny's class. I undertook an observation with Penny in July, in which I observed her working with Mark:

> Phillip moves quickly to his place but Mark goes more measuredly to his tray, and gets his desk support and his image-based paper day planner. He seems calm (calmer actually than any of the previous observations). I note his keyring of reminder phrases sticking out of his front pocket.

The protruding keyring flags the return of the classroom aids, and on this occasion Mark is noticeably calmer in the much more structured and 'low-arousal' environment of Penny's class. One also has to question, however, whether Mark also lost something when the break with Kathy occurred.

Review of the material from the third observation in the work study group was helpful in moving towards a conclusion about Kathy's work with Mark. Colleagues confirmed my sense that Kathy could be perceived as coming uncomfortably close to personal and professional boundaries, and that she could be regarded as being on occasion narcissistic and beset by internal anxieties that reduced her ability to be in regulated emotional contact with her students. Their response to the written transcripts was in line with my sense of anxiety both during the observations and when reviewing the material later. Yet there was also recognition that she was the victim of quite powerful forces from the corporate school body, forces that could be considered as repressive. Given the structural power imbalances that individual teachers face when confronting whole-school approaches, it is perhaps not surprising that these forces stimulated defensive reactions in Kathy, particularly in the context of the illness and death of one of her parents during this period. It was also felt important to recognize that Kathy could be thought of as having crossed boundaries that needed crossing when working with Mark and his classmates. Kathy had an explicit sense of the uncovered potential of her students that was not wholly defined or restricted by their autism diagnosis, which meant they could be more independent in their current and future lives. This sense of developing independence may have been interwoven in Kathy's thinking with the fostering, particularly for Mark, of a sort of creative social communication exemplified in their joint engagement in theatrical flourishes. Kathy was also likely to have experienced considerable uncertainty about how to work with Mark, even if this was for the most part covered by an omnipotent façade in the collected material. In particular, the tension between Kathy's and the school's positions in respect of Mark must have led her, at least on an unconscious level, to entertain doubts as to whether she was doing the right thing with him. Kathy's wild, unbounded energy may have at times been narcissistic and manic, but this may have been a reaction to the considerable external forces brought to bear on her. At the same time, this exertion of energy by Kathy, when she was in a more robust state of mind and was able to maintain a regulated emotional connection with Mark, served to create some sort of live connection with Mark, one which was at least partly based on her intersubjective relationship with him and which was not constrained by the expectations associated with his diagnosis. This connection did, at times, serve his development. It was this that he lost when the connection with Kathy was severed.

This pattern of manic energy and live connection can also be identified in Kathy's positioning towards the app. In the second interview, Kathy's reaction to the app was considered to be an example of idealization or magical thinking. There is undoubtedly an element of truth to this, but it is probably not the whole story. Kathy may have thought that engaging children with autism with this new technology was a way of fostering their autonomy and independence. Thus it wasn't just that Kathy saw the app as something outside of the school's corporate structures, but rather that it actively tied in with her explicit and implicit desires to place greater stress on fostering the children's independence. This may be a more nuanced explanation for her somewhat idealized view of the app earlier in the project. Of course, much of her engagement with the app was still likely to have been driven by this manic energy. Thinking about the app meant thinking about the ongoing tension between her position and the school's in relation to working with Mark, and would have tended to stimulate the repressed but most likely ever-present uncertainties as to whether she was in fact doing the right thing with him. Her flight at times to idealization and a kind of manic, magical thinking can be understood in this context.

Putting this another way, Kathy's ability to tolerate uncertainty, and to work through her engagement with Mark to know productively what his real needs were, was in part dependent on the function of the school in containing her anxieties and uncertainties. Bion's (1985) use of the term 'containment' in early development suggests that the unmanageable projections received by the mother from the infant are reprocessed and fed back to the infant in such a way that the infant can now think the thoughts that were previously unmanageable. This requires the mother to be in a state of reverie, an emotional state that requires considerable reserves of psychic energy. In order to achieve this, Bion (and Klein) suggest that the mother needs to be contained herself, by her husband or other adults around her, to be able to, in a sense, re-project the projections of the infant, and have these reprocessed and fed back to her in a manageable form. In simple terms, this correlates with the common-sense notion that the new mothers should be told they are doing a great job. By extension to professional practice, the teacher, in order to fulfil their role of containment and thus create the possibility of tolerating uncertainty in order to engage in a true intersubjective manner with the children with whom they work (that is, productive uncertainty), also needs the containing function of the school, of their colleagues and managers.

John – the cognitive patrician?

Current role and career background

John did a degree in biology in the UK and then went to Canada to do research to on microbiology. On returning to the UK in the early 1990s he trained as a teacher and then worked as a science teacher in secondary schools, but also at times as a teacher in primary schools. John initially came to Randall School on a short-term supply contract and at that stage had no specific experience of special educational needs or autism. John has now been teaching at the school for six years. He seems to feel that there is a good fit between him and the school, as indicated in this extract from the first interview with him:

> I've been teaching here six years and when I came here it was with *no* special educational needs background at all. But I came as a supply teacher ... and I just said, throw away the learnt and be prepared to come into an SEN school and I came here a couple of weeks after I said that and I've been here six years now and fitted in reasonably well I think.

Later in this interview, John reports his motivation for wanting to come and work with children with special needs as being based on a desire to contribute to society:

> [...] I don't know why I had a thinking that I'd quite like to do it? Possibly because I've got quite a lot of belief in God and things like that and I want to be of service to the community and not just obtaining my financial remuneration, so I suppose that's what really motivates me ... the idea of helping.

John's main role in the school is to teach science and maths across the year groups. He does not have a specific form class for which he is responsible. He was not originally scheduled to be involved as a teacher in the implementation of the app during the 2009/10 exercise; another teacher, Mitzi, originally started working on the project with Jeremy (the focus child using the app) in the autumn of 2009. Mitzi was Jeremy's form teacher. Mitzi's motivation for involvement in the project was, however, very low, and little progress was made with Jeremy's use of the app. Mitzi then left the school to take up another post towards the end of the autumn term, and John was identified by the school, partly due to his technical skills, as an appropriate teacher to take over the role working with Jeremy on the use of the app from January 2010. It is relevant to note that John did not take on the role of form teacher, and at least in the initial stages of his involvement, his main contact with Jeremy was for a few science sessions each week. However, as his involvement in the project and his work with Jeremy developed, John spent an increasing amount of time working with him.

Key information sources for John

Interviews and observations were undertaken with John as follows:

First interview 15 February 2010
First observation 4 March 2010

Second observation 25 March 2010
Second interview 26 March 2010
Third observation 21 May 2010
Third interview 21 May 2010
Fourth observation 25 June 2010
Fourth interview 25 June 2010.

John's positioning in the school

In the initial interviews and observations, John comes across as a committed but often quite anxious teacher. His approach to working with the children has something of an 'academic' air to it and he often focuses on concepts, thinking quite hard about how to get these across to the children, although not always with success. His control of the classroom is variable. Sometimes he projects his presence and authority, but at other times there is much less of a sense of authority and on several occasions the children seemed restless and somewhat unbounded with him. However, at these times John acts without rancour and there is a sense of affection between him and the children, even when they are not always behaving very well. This sense of affection is mirrored in John's positioning within the staff group. One of my colleagues on the general project team, who spent a significant amount of time with all the teachers involved with the app, commented in early 2010 to the effect that John was very much 'held' by the school. My own informal and classroom observations did also indicate that John was felt by the school to be a valued member of the team. John did, in fact, very much 'fit in' with the school.

Jeremy

John worked with one child, Jeremy, who was using the app. Jeremy was born in 1995, making him 14/15 during the 2009/10 app implementation period. He had a full IQ measured on WISC-IV of 74, a VQ of 63 and a clinical psychiatric diagnosis of autism on entry to the school. He had no other co-morbid factors.

Jeremy lives at home with his parents and attends the school on weekdays. Initial impressions of Jeremy in the school environment are of a very anxious child who finds it difficult to deal with new situations and tends to be limited in his use of language, particularly with people with whom he is unfamiliar. Teacher reports indicate, based on parental reports, that his school behaviour contrasts to that in his home environment, where he is relaxed most of the time. When he is anxious he displays a significant amount of what can be regarded as typically autistic traits, particularly repetitive behaviours and routines, echolalia, etc. Echolalia and repetitive pacing up and down were seen on a number of occasions during classroom observations. Teacher reports also indicate that Jeremy finds it difficult to read other people's emotions and gets worried that people around him are unhappy.

Jeremy enjoys using technology, receiving time out on the computer as a reward for positive behaviour. He requires lots of prompting and guidance at school and in his daily life, enacting plans or actions required for the task in class only when he is verbally prompted by his teacher or when he sees others in his peer group beginning the target behaviour.

Jeremy has a keyworker teaching assistant, Jean, who works with him for most lessons. Jeremy seems to have a relatively strong and secure attachment to her. Another assistant, Dawn, who is Jean's sister, also works with Jeremy for some lessons, and again Jeremy has a positive attachment to her.

John categorizes Jeremy's ability in maths as a high level two (the typical level expected for a child aged seven) and in science as a low level two (below the typical level expected for a child aged seven). John reported that as he does not teach Jeremy for English, he is unsure about his exact ability level; however, he felt that he was able to decode well, but often did not properly comprehend what he had read. In terms of social interaction, John reports that Jeremy is able to ask people things but often does not, even when he needs help. In observations, I do see Jeremy asking for help on a number of occasions; however, this seems to be the limit of his typical interactions with adults. When asked about Jeremy's play interactions with other children, John indicates that he doesn't think that Jeremy engages in much play with other children due to anxiety, but he thinks if Jeremy has got someone that he really knows well then he can play and interact with him. John also maintains a strong sense of hopefulness about Jeremy, which is evident throughout all the interviews.

The academic patrician? The place of theoretical knowledge

John, as with the other teachers in the study, does not have any significant prior education or training in working with children with autism. This resonates with what we know from the literature about the low level of input regarding special educational needs in pre-service teacher education in the UK. However, John showed evidence, in contrast to the other teachers, of thinking explicitly and sometimes in significant detail about theoretical aspects of autism. John's orientation towards theoretical knowledge can be seen quite strikingly in this extract from the second interview:

Joe: [...] social skills, what would you say that means for children with autism?

John: Oh I see, anything that helps them communicate with others, either understanding what someone else says or being understood themselves, I would say ... it's that situation and the thing is, is that if you can take something wrongly in what's said then an autistic person is quite likely to do that and they find it hard to bring their words to their minds … very often they've got actually a period of time that they require to process the information and if there's just one piece of information then they're given the time to process that and they're fine but if there's a lot of things going on all at once then it's just too much for them and I suppose they do a 'whitening out', I suppose we all do to some extent, don't we? If you get too many stresses it's very difficult although I have a feeling that in our cases we often try and block out all the other things, no matter how terrible they are, and concentrate on that one thing.

Joe: That's really interesting. I mean you've been referring to … I suppose you could call it aspects of cognitive functions or about them not having time to process it … so is that something, that thinking, has that come from your experience or from reading or …?

John: Partly reading and partly through hearing the people give talks here. I did do a very small amount of psychology myself anyway. I did a basic … I can't remember what it was called … a basic course in psychology at The Open University and I was going to take more with a view to doing educational psychology but it was just that I never realized it was too much of a climb and the wages too poor for half of that time, so I couldn't do it because I have to support a family.

Joe: Right.

John: So I do have some ideas about cognitive thinking and therefore I sort of understand, when someone says about the processing times, I do understand that that's a problem and you can see it in them, give them enough time [and] they'll be okay. If you try to give them one thing and then, straight away, another thing it's too much for them. I mean I try to, when I do worksheets and things like that or choose a textbook I try to get things that do a little bit, ask them a question, do another little bit, ask them a question, rather than a whole big passage and then ask questions.

The need for longer processing time is indeed a common cognitive concept used theoretically in relation to autism, as part of the overall theoretical construct of impairment in executive function (Luna *et al.*, 2007), and it seems clear from this extract that this is something that John both is explicitly aware of and makes use of in the development of teaching techniques. That is not to say that the other teachers are not implicitly aware of this concept. In fact, the category coding analysis indicates that both Kathy and Mandy, on at least one occasion each, made reference to the idea of giving children more time, but there was no associated explicit consideration of this as being based on theoretical knowledge.

John's orientation towards the explicit use of theoretical knowledge can be considered to mirror, at least to some extent, his general orientation towards teaching. In several of the observations, I had a strong sense of the importance of knowledge and of knowing about things pervading John's lessons at certain times, as in the following extract from the first observation. In this lesson, John is teaching a maths lesson, focusing on sequencing, including the use of doubling:

> There is half a minute or so of milling about and quite noisy getting ready but the children sit down quite quickly. John speaks to the teaching assistants, directing them to work with particular children. There is chatting and getting ready going on during this. John then says in a clear voice, 'good morning everyone' and they respond, 'good morning John'. Gradually the children focus on the lesson – John introduces the lesson objectives, which are about sequencing. They are up in a list on the Interactive White Board (IWB) and John reads them out, 'to recognize patterns, to recognize sequences … discuss your work'.
>
> John starts off with a doubling 'warm-up' and asks selected children doubling questions. At the start John tries to get some sort of 'doubling' slide on the IWB but this does not appear to be working. He spends a few moments trying to get it working and says, 'They all worked on our computer last night but not today, honestly, that's just typical' [laughing]. John switches to working on the flip chart and draws up a doubling sequence. He says, showing a number added to itself, 'that's all doubling is!'
>
> I observe Jeremy. John asks Jeremy, with a warm, inviting tone and as though he's got [a question] just right for Jeremy, 'Jeremy, what is double five?' Jeremy replies, 'double five is … ten', in a flat tone. John says 'well done' in a generous tone. John goes on and asks other children doubling questions. He finishes off by pointing out to the children that 'doubling is? … Times two [emphasis]'.
>
> John then moves on to the main part of the lesson and says, 'So … we're going to do sequencing'. He goes back to computer and brings up another slide, which works this time. He shows the image on the IWB which is using pictograms to show a doubling sequence, as in '2, 4, 8, 16 […]', and says, 'You could have a doubling [emphasis] sequence'. John goes through the pattern and the children echo with him '2, 4, 8, 16 […]'. John points out the additive pattern, '4 then 4 more? […]'
>
> I observe Jeremy. Jeremy focuses in and out and then gets up and walks around the back of the classroom before going back to his seat. He does this several times during the lesson, sometimes accompanied by clapping.

John then gives out a worksheet based on pictograms and identifying patterns. John initially asks Charlotte, one of the teaching assistants, to work with two children – Oswald and Karl – individually at the end of the table, showing Charlotte what the children need to do. He then draws in the rest of the group with him – 'Now I'm going to do some work with you on sequences'. He demonstrates different patterns on the pictogram sheet. John works with Oswald, Karl and Charlotte for a few minutes, making sure that they are clear what to do. The room is quieter now. John then addresses the larger group and explains the pictogram sheet: 'you have some shapes here, but the idea is that you're going to think of some shapes and then we'll have a look at them at the end'. John shows the sheet to Jeremy and points at a sequence with four pictograms in a square. John says, 'what shape is this, Jeremy?' Jeremy says '4' and John says, 'no ... it's a bit like a square, isn't it?'... John says 'Yes' very quickly.

The class carries on working on the worksheet and there is an industrious, 'academic' atmosphere.

In my initial fieldnotes made after this observation, I annotated this section of the observation as follows:

I have a sense when observing John of an academic tone to the session – a sense that there is something to learn, and that there is a possibility of learning it, and that learning and knowledge is something important in its own right.

Knowing about things is important to John, and he is also committed, as a teacher, to facilitating the development of knowledge in the children he is working with.

This extract also shows Jeremy exhibiting echolalia and pacing, as well as John's constructive attempts to engage Jeremy in the lesson at a level, in this case, appropriate to his needs.

John's thinking about theoretical knowledge

I initially identified John as having a cognitive, academic aspect to him, and felt that in some observations there was a sense of the importance of knowledge. It is also clear that even though he was somewhat self-deprecating about it, he had read a fair bit about autism, and he used theoretical constructs from typical psychological theories about autism at times in his interview responses. This contrasted with the absence of such usages by the other teachers, apart from Lynne. My initial impressions from observations, and from the early interviews, tended to confirm what might be characterized as a more cerebral approach. However, as happened frequently in the study, impressions of states of mind gained in one context did not paint the whole picture. Thus I was somewhat surprised when, in the third interview, John gave this nuanced response when I asked him what sources he drew on in working with children with autism:

Joe: And what do you draw on in coming to those ways of working ... with the children ... where does that come from?

John: It comes from the experience I've had over the years here. I guess ... not I guess, I know I've had quite a bit of teaching on autism here, both informally and formally. I haven't done a huge amount of reading on it in terms of ... after a day of working here I think it's quite difficult, especially with my family, so I find it difficult just to sit down and read on autism. That may sound terrible but it's the truth. But I have an interest in it.

Joe: But do you think it would make a difference? Do you feel that if you read loads and loads of books it would make a difference?

John: I think if I read the right books here and there it could make a difference.

Joe: Right.

John: I think if I read too much what it would do is turn me into a boffin who knew this and that about autism but wouldn't necessarily have the practical knowledge on it. But the thing is ... is what I really am working from is the empathy ... yes I suppose it is empathy ... I was just looking at you to see whether it was sympathy or empathy but we all have difficulty learning certain things and we all have times that we find that we're barraged by too many things all at once and it's overload ... and to allow empathy to guide to some extent is quite a useful thing.

Joe: What do you mean ... what does that mean...?

John: It means that I'm trying to put myself into their place; I'm trying to think how they would think in order to see how they would react and that allows me to think ... 'I give such and such, will they enjoy it, will they do it...?' etc. etc. ... 'How will they be able to tackle it ... is there too much writing for them?' In many cases the students will reject the work if there's lots of writing but if I've made it a multiple-choice option they'll go for it and things like that. So all the time trying to think ... what would make it attractive to them and how would they learn from it etc. ... bearing in mind that they do have this overload of information and so on.

John is suspicious of too great an emphasis on theoretical knowledge, and gives at least equal weight to 'empathy'. When asked to explain what he means by empathy, there is still something of a cerebral quality to it – it's about working out what format of question will work best – and there is a continuing implied reference to impairment in executive function. Yet at the same time it is about putting himself in their place. There is something resonant here with how Bion approaches the relationship between intersubjective experiential relationship and theory. Even if it is still perhaps, in Bion's terms, too inflexible, at least there is recognition of the importance of the intersubjective relationship to the human other in mediating how theoretical knowledge is applied.

I return to this theme of the relationship between theoretical knowledge about autism, empathy and professional practice in the final interview:

Joe: I just wanted to come back briefly to ask, we talked previously quite a bit about your view of autism and working with children with autism and you talked about a bit about it in this interview. You said in the last unit you were working from, in your day-to-day working with them that you were working more from empathy than from, you used the phrase of 'being a boffin', a theoretically based knowledge, although you said that was also something that could be useful. I just wondered if you might say a bit more about when you said about working from empathy what that meant?

John: Yes, I mean I don't mean to say I've got no knowledge of autism, I am sure I've got quite a lot although I haven't formally gone and taken a qualification in autism, so…

Joe: I mean that was my interpretation, the understanding I had was you thought the subject, the theoretical knowledge was important and could be beneficial but it wasn't as important as the ability to be working from empathy with the children.

John: Yes, I think that's probably true and in fact I think in some cases some people have got very good theoretical knowledge but can't properly empathise with the students. I mention no names at all but that can happen and if you've got the theoretical knowledge, I know that it can be a good background for practice as well, I know that from my other disciplines and good theoretical knowledge normally gives good practice but it doesn't have to, it depends whether the person is applying it or not.

Joe: So you were saying about empathy, can you say a bit more about that?

John: Well to understand that you have problems in your own life that you try to solve and they have got problems and they are trying to solve them. I do think that I have some past history which makes me think that maybe there were traits in my life of it, I don't think I am autistic but I think I might have had the odd trait, for example when I was a young adult people said, 'why do you stare when you talk?' and

I realized I was going, staring at the person and not giving normal eye contact and at that time, and I can't remember whether they taught me or where I learned it but I learned that people normally look in the eyes and look at the mouth, look at the eyes and look at the mouth, and I actually sort of re-taught myself, I am not sure whether I untaught myself the natural, that's possible because I went through a phase where I was interested in staring for a point, for the sake of it, teenagers go through daft things and so on, and I might have taught myself to stare too much, I have a feeling I did, from reading something or other. And then so I found myself however sort of teaching myself, you know to look at the person's eyes and look at their mouth and not to go sort of staring at them all the time because of course it's actually physically a challenge, not physically, mentally a challenge if I stare in their face and so on. Also I think I tended, at that same time I tended to move up to the person too close. So I was in their personal bubble. But then of course I probably am not autistic because I can appreciate the idea of personal bubble and so on, it was just somehow I hadn't learned those things, so what I am saying though is we can make those sort of social errors and so on and of course they have got this problem which makes [it] even harder to socialize and think creatively and makes ... information come at you in a way which is bewildering sometimes to us but is constantly bewildering to them. And from knowing where we get stressed and it is overpowering gives me the empathy I think to understand them a bit. I think it's empathy as opposed to sympathy there, we do sort of, have the same sort of things, we just, not at the same level.

Joe: I am just wondering how that plays out in the classroom or when you are working with them?

John: Oh that's a big question, I don't know, I have not thought about it so I don't know where it plays in that sense. It does in terms of my communication, because you learn after a while not to speak too much or to try and limit your words and if I speak to someone here, one of the students, I'll probably give a command in almost a euro speak sort of way, in a potted thing with less of the articles in it and just more of the actual subject and noun, so it has an effect on that, it has an effect on work I produce for them to use, always trying to make something simple, trying to make it so it's visually pleasing, visually comforts rather than alarms ... I don't want to see a dog's dinner, I mean I would be fine with that but an autistic person could well freak at seeing something like that. You know it's the same sort of feeling going into an exam, a maths exam and thinking [gesture] the questions, you know, and a bit later we actually draw a breath and we look at it closer and we see it's not such a problem. I suppose they are always going [gesture] in their lives. Does it cause me to [think about] other things, I am sure it does; I am sure it causes me to do a lot of thinking about what are the pitfalls in something that I wouldn't otherwise think of.

Joe: It sounds to me that you are saying like your, you know your self-awareness, how maybe some things, at one time they are difficult for you kind of helps you in understanding how things can be difficult for them.

John: Yes, I think it does, I think also I have some theoretical advantage on that, not from autistic study, not studying autism itself so much as studying a little bit of psychology and in terms of recall and you've got recall and recognition, a difference between recognition and recall, how much harder recall is than recognition for example, so that, you know, realizing that quite a number of them have that problem of recall makes me put things in multiple-choice style rather than get them to think it out straight from jumbled thoughts. I suppose in a sense I am supplying them with something in their minds, later on they might put it in the right way but initially they have it down in front of them and the choice of the GCSE science papers that I take for them, you've got a choice at the moment between totally multiple-choice and totally written and I take the totally multiple-choice options for them because I think that much better for them. Also in terms of the psychology I did, [it] had things about attention, you know if you've got more than one source of information coming to you at once what do you tune out, do you hold the other while you partially attending to it or you know does it get ignored completely and I understand that as well from the psychology. And that of course has an influence on knowing what they are like. I think, this is how I see it, that they find it hard to attend to more than one thing at a time. We, when we attend to things we attend to this, we keep an ear out as it were to what's going on around us and we sometimes tend to one or two or three things at the same time and I don't think that they do, I think because of the confusion of things that they have to keep to the one thing otherwise they are going to lose track of what on earth they are doing at all.

Joe: Interesting.

John: I hope I've conceived them properly.

John is certainly not autistic, but it does seem plausible that his experiences of not matching to social conventions in some instances as a teenager have given him a sense of what it feels like not to fit in that he has drawn on in working with the children, and which may even be a significant aspect of his motivation to be at the school.

In my fieldnotes for this interview I noted that the interview left me with something of a disconnected feeling. When I reviewed the transcript, this lengthy extract did seem to have an oscillatory or jumpy quality to it. One the one hand, John seems to be suggesting that he is drawing on his experiences in relating to the children and getting into their shoes. On the other, there is considerable discussion of psychology. The two aspects are oscillatory in that there doesn't seem to be a smooth connection between them.

Interestingly, John talks about attention from a psychological perspective:

> [...] you know if you've got more than one source of information coming to you at once what do you tune out, do you hold the other while you partially attending to it or, you know, does it get ignored completely...

This, in a sense, is the question posed to caring professionals by Bion, and this extract seems to indicate the tension experienced by John in achieving this partial attention to intersubjective relationship at the same time as making use of theory. My countertransference response to the material – that it made me feel disconnected – perhaps points towards the difficulty that John had in keeping these two types of knowledge in mind at the same time when working with the children. This tension is quite possibly exacerbated by the difficulties in making connections between concepts experienced by the children with whom he is working. John may feel under an unconscious pressure to help them to repair these connections, or to maintain them for them; this may be easier, given his internal dispositions, for him to focus on than the more challenging task of engaging with them intersubjectively.

We can see this tension being played out in the context of the positioning of John and the app, and concurrently in the relationship between John and Jean (Jeremy's key worker assistant), Jeremy and the app in the fourth observation.

Closer to the action: achieving intersubjective relationship?

The fourth observation is of a lesson on maps and coordinates. At the start of the lesson, as I come into the class, John tells me that his wife and children were sick over the weekend so he is feeling quite tired. After that, Jeremy, who had gone to get his smartphone from the office where it was supposedly charging up, comes back into the classroom. At the start of the lesson, John is quite jumpy and anxious. It is likely that this anxiety relates to being observed by me, but also to what seems to be a significant level of uncertainty and linked anxiety about how to use the app with Jeremy.

The lesson then starts properly with John demonstrating finding a coordinate position on a map on the interactive whiteboard. The boys are fairly attentive and there is some good-natured calling out and joking between John, Jean, two other teaching assistants and the boys during the demonstration, as in this extract:

> One of the icons is a pub [public house] and there is some good-natured joking about this. John says jokingly to the children, as he places it, 'that's where you go to have a drink'. There is a general laughing, 'Oooo...' sound from the children. The teaching assistants laugh as well.
>
> John finishes the introduction, still sitting at the PC, turning round and saying in a loud, confident voice, 'I want you to do that', smiling and pointing his fingers up (a bit like a double Churchill V sign). John then moves on to showing them a follow-up activity, an internet-based, more complex coordinates-based map. He spends a minute or so locating this, and shows them how to access it on the computer.
>
> He says, 'I'd like you to click on the hyperdrink'. He laughs, comfortably, and says jokingly, 'that's because of all that about a public house before ... hyperlink ... click on the hyperlink'. One of the assistants says, jokingly, 'Drink Up ... Drink Up...'. John clicks on the link and shows the class the map, which has some relief contours and looks more complex than the previous one. John says as he is showing it, as an aside to the adults, 'It might be a bridge too far'. Jean interjects, 'Let's see how they get on with the first one'. John nods, for a moment seeming slightly unsure, and then says more confidently, 'I'll help you boys with it', generally to the class.

In my contemporaneous write-up of the observation, I note in relation to this:

> I have a sense of the class – the children and the assistants – almost holding John – being understanding of his 'eccentricities' and perhaps sometimes perceived lack of authority. I might extend this to the school as a whole. I remember, when John was initially involved in the project four or five months ago and was clearly stressed at the time by the additional responsibility (which he had not had any time allocation for at that point), that Tamar (a fellow researcher on the general project), had said, based perhaps on his perceived lack of ability in her eyes, 'I think they look after him really well though'.

It is relevant to note that Jean seems to have a more accurate estimation of the ability level of the children, and his hesitation suggests that he is happy to defer to her evaluation of the situation. This is on one level entirely reasonable, as Jean, being a teaching assistant, works with this group all the time, whereas John only has them a few times a week. At the same time, however, it also suggests that in this instance John doesn't quite find the range of the children – that, despite his detailed responses regarding thinking about their needs, he doesn't quite get on the right level. The contrast with Mandy's case later on, in particular, is quite instructive. This interpretation is, I think, bolstered by my feeling (which I would consider a counter-transference response), expressed directly in the observation narrative, that John is to some extent being contained by the class, rather than the other way round.

There does seem to be something of a pattern here for John, rather than just one isolated incident. There is corroborating evidence for this interpretation from the comparative category coding. The data node 'Could be closer to the action', used to denote instances where the teacher seems not to have gauged the needs of the children, had four source references from four separate sources for John. For Kathy, seven source references from three sources were also coded to this data node, but none were coded to this data node for other teachers.

The next extract is from around the halfway point of the lesson. The children are now working semi-independently on completing a worksheet which involves finding coordinates on their own map. John now moves to working with Jeremy on using the app:

> John now goes over to the other side of the classroom to where the phone was charging (it is around 10.15 am) and gets the phone and stands behind Jeremy, tapping it, frowning and muttering, '... enough charge...?'
>
> Jeremy turns round and shows John his sheet, standing up, and John looks at him, with their backs to me. Jeremy looks attentively at the sheet with John – 'C6 ... good ... C8 ... yes' […] and so on, and then, 'Well done, Jeremy'. John then says, 'Now Jeremy, I would like to spend five minutes talking...'. He doesn't finish but nods at the phone which he has given to Jean, who is sitting down at the table. Jeremy seems markedly stressed as he says this. He starts echolalia – 'say ... say ... say […]' and starts to wander about in a little circle by the table. John says, I think to me and Jean, 'He's stressed already, isn't he?', but Jean says, calmly and non-committedly, 'He's alright'. Jeremy sits down but continues echolalia. Jean starts the phone up and gives it to Jeremy. John stands over him and starts to explain, but the other teaching assistant sitting at the computer with Robbie behind John calls out, 'What do you do here?' John interrupts and rushes over to the assistant, saying something about 'primary maths resources'. He is over there very briefly and then darts back to Jeremy. He takes the phone and apparently sets a personal trainer intervention running on the app.

It is relevant to note the difference in reaction between John and Jean. John sees an overt display of echolalia, which is typically an anxiety-related behaviour. Yet Jean stays calm and is able to stay with the anxiety which this new technology, making new demands, is no doubt provoking in Jeremy. She can stay with it and perhaps to some extent process it for Jeremy, and possibly also for John as well, at least for a short time.

It also seems possible that for John, the uncertainty and anxiety felt in respect of the app is linked to his ongoing tension about how to work with these children – that is, what the balance is between 'empathy' and use of theoretical knowledge.

The observation record continues:

> John then says, methodically, 'what we're going to do Jeremy, is to know that this will help you ... yeah? ... you're going to talk with Jean...'. Jeremy – 'say ... say ... say'. John – 'you're going to ask her questions.' Jean confirms – 'ask questions?' – and John says, 'Yes'. Jean starts looking at the phone with Jeremy and says, quizzically, 'The battery's low'.
>
> I decide to move to the other end of the table as I am concerned that my presence close by may be making Jeremy more stressed.

We sit as shown in Figure 5.1.

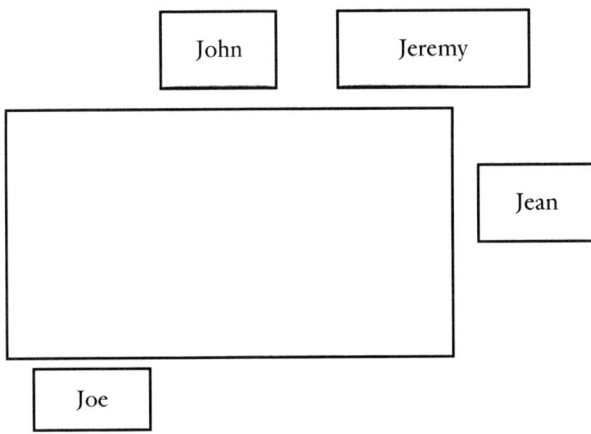

Figure 5.1 Seating arrangements during observation

John also moves off, saying in an aside to me that he'll let him get on with Jean so he doesn't get too stressed. Jeremy seems to be navigating the phone, as before, quite confidently, and gets the idea clearly. He reads the questions that the personal trainer prompts in his typical monotone – 'How many brothers and sisters have you got? What are your favourite sweets? What is your favourite TV programme?'

Jean answers the questions brightly; she smiles and seems to be enjoying it. So to the first question she says, 'Dawn ... Dawn's my sister'. I notice that with this question, as with the others, Jeremy doesn't make much of a register of the answer and moves on to the next question.

However, Jeremy also seems to have somewhat relaxed. He has stopped the echolalia, smiles occasionally and seems quite focused on the phone. At the end of the sequence, the personal trainer plays a short video of Harry Hill (a UK television comedian). Jeremy reacts to this very positively – he moves back in his chair, smiles broadly and really seems to like it. Jean asks Jeremy if he would like to 'ask questions to anyone else ... to John?' Jeremy nods. Jean signals to John, who has been hovering, and he comes and sits by him. He takes the phone and clicks through some screens. John seems a bit unsure and Jean gives John some prompts as to how to use the app. Jeremy repeats the series of questions to John, 'What's your favourite sweet?'... John replies, 'Oh ... chocolate', said in a somewhat luxuriant tone.

I note that as with Jean, Jeremy doesn't give any follow-up responses to the answers, and stays looking at the phone. Before the end of the personal trainer sequence, I notice Jeremy looking quizzically at the phone. John looks with him and says that it's running slow and that it must be the battery. The reward video doesn't seem to run this time and, a bit abruptly, Jean says, 'are you finished ... do you want it to get charged up?'

Jean goes on and says, 'Well done Jeremy ... shall we let him have free time for doing well?' John says yes and nods and Jeremy gets up, leaving the phone on the table, and goes over to one of the computers. John says to me in an aside, smiling, that he had these conversational prompts on a key ring, but they have put them on the phone as well. John goes on and says, 'He hasn't really got it in to his head that the phone is there to help him ... and that that's what I was trying to do there'. Jean then says to John, 'we could add on to those questions, couldn't we John?'

In my fieldnotes, I note that in this instance the atmosphere feels relaxed and open, in contrast to previous instances when John was working with Jeremy alone, when things felt tighter and more constrained. This is also apparent directly from the observation narrative where, in contrast to the earlier parts of the observation, John and Jeremy both seem much calmer and focused and seem to be able to work with the app constructively, to explore what it can be used for. It might be that Jean's previous interjection, 'He's alright', had potentially – by at least partially processing the significant anxiety and uncertainty present in the session – opened up a space where they could better tolerate the no doubt ongoing uncertainty linked to the app, allowing them to engage in work on the app.

In the work study review of the material, colleagues noted how Jean was much calmer than John. They also suggested that it is possible to identify a male/female principle in play here, with Jean as the female containing principle creating a nurturing holding environment that facilitates Jeremy in learning. In (necessary) contrast, John is the paternal one, more cognitively based and driving. It could be argued that both functions are required if Jeremy, or children in general, are to engage in growth and learning. In a way, Bion's clinical approach can be considered as overcoming, or merging, what Gabriella Mann (2002) characterizes as the psychoanalyst's "oedipal struggle" between Papa-Freud and Mama-Klein, between interpreting and holding, phallus and breast, patriarchy and matriarchy' (p. 74). We might also add the struggle or dialectic between knowing and not knowing. Mann writes this in relation to Bollas' (1999) work suggesting that discussions about theories advocating holding and those advocating interpretation are misguided, as it is impossible to have without the other. The derivation from Bion is clear. When Bion directs the analyst to work without memory or desire, the cognitive function doesn't disappear from the consulting room but merges, in the transformation of 'O', inescapably with the empathic, intersubjective function. This is the core of productive uncertainty, in which, based on Bion's epistemology and clinical guidance, both theory and relationship 'in the moment' are iteratively intertwined.

In our material here, it is possible to suggest that although no one person achieved this, when John and Jean worked together in their professional roles, *they* intertwined holding and interpreting, empathy and cognition, which gave Jeremy the support he needed to engage with the app.

Flight to theory

I have considered John as holding a paternal cognitive function. At the same time, I have identified the tension he seems to experience – revealed substantively in interview responses, as well as in my countertransference response to observational material – between being 'empathic' and using theory-based approaches to autism. This conflict can be further seen in the third observation. On this occasion, a maths lesson, John is working with Dawn, Jean's sister. As in the fourth observation, John makes time for Jeremy to work on the app. In this extract, the children are working on a shape and space task:

Jeremy has come back to his seat now and has started cutting out his shapes. He suddenly turns to Dawn, and in a high-pitched staccato says, 'Sorry Dawn ... sorry Dawn ... are you angry, Dawn?' He looks towards her but doesn't make eye contact. He repeats this a few times, 'Angry? ... Angry? ... Angry?' Dawn says, soothingly, that she isn't angry at all. John, who has been watching from the front of the desk, says in an aside to me that he wonders whether it might be possible to have emotional expression recognition characters on the phone. I feel confused for a moment and John says, 'It's relevant...' and I make the connection. I say that I have seen face recognition software for children with autism and John nods and says, smiling, that maybe we could load that on the phone.

Again we see, this time with Dawn, a maternal empathic position contrasted with a paternal cognitive position. My feeling of confusion perhaps serves to reflect the greater note of dissonance between them. It is no doubt possible to have emotional recognition characters on the app, but John, with his technical understanding, probably knows that this is outside of the scope of the current project. There seems to be something of a flight to theory and cognition, rather than an appropriate use of it. Perhaps it is easier for John to think about a technological solution which might bring certainty and regularity to Jeremy's often difficult to understand behaviour, as opposed to having to process the quite difficult feelings of anxiety and inadequacy that Jeremy is projecting in this instance.

This pattern or theme seems to surface again in the subsequent third interview, in which I ask John about his perceptions of Jeremy's behaviours when they are working with the app later in the observation:

Joe: Right! One of the other things that I noticed ... one thing that I noticed that during the lesson and also when you were working with him on the phone ... echolalia he was like ... repeating this phrase ... it sounded to me like he was saying, 'say ... say ... say'... I wasn't quite sure what it was.

John: Yes, I'm not sure myself but I do know that he has quite a number of those echolations ... is it echolations?

Joe: I don't know [laughs].

John: Yes I think I should try and look it up. It's not a noun, it's a verb isn't it.

Joe: What does it signify to you when he's doing that?

John: Well I would say it's displacement behaviour; he's doing something because he's not feeling quite comfortable. I think you might have noticed as soon as he had the instructions for the lesson he went into a little bit of a routine of his, his own, again because of displacement and the funny thing ... well, not funny but the interesting thing is he could do it; he was quite good at it really wasn't he, he wasn't bad.

Joe: Do you mean when he went to get a glass of water?

John: Yes.

Joe: Yes, I remember you commented on that.

John: Yes. The glass of water and also he sat there and there was that period of not doing anything and when he was asked what did he need he said 'Scissors' so he sort of knew that he should be acting but he didn't want to act until he was confident. I don't know how we can get that using the phone. If we could, if we could get him sort of prompted; that might help as well. That might require him … you can't do it by a buzzer of course but I'm just thinking if we can get him trained whereby he's looking for the prompt for him to help him … 'What do I need?' … 'Go get it!' … that sort of thing you know […]

John is clearly thinking hard about Jeremy here, and the presence of the app also seems to be a spur for his thinking more about Jeremy and his needs. Yet there is something of an arid, scientific quality at play here, which seems divorced in a sense from Jeremy.

Scientific theory and technology are linked paradigms. For many people, and quite likely for John given his background, technology represents the expression of scientific discovery and its regularized expression in the world. The app as a piece of technology seems to be acting, for John, as an object that sits somewhere between John and Jeremy, acting in a sense as a barrier to allow John to distance himself from a true intersubjective experience in relation to Jeremy. This seems to parallel instances of John's use of psychological theory, which at times also seem to get in the way of John being 'close enough to the action'. This is, of course, a danger which John himself has clearly identified in his interview responses.

We could regard John's use of the app, in this instance, as being to some extent an example of what Bollas (1992) names a 'terminal' object. Bollas describes a whole variety of object types, including transformational and terminal objects. Objects are not just people but can be physical inanimate objects, landscapes, flora and fauna or cultural genres, such as a type of pop music. Bollas identifies the transformation that takes place when the mother's processing of the infant's projections results in a developing experience of the self. On an unconscious level, the self continues to seek out objects that will also facilitate ongoing transformations, making use of its 'idiom' in the object world (ibid., pp. 59–65). Healthy individuals will express this desire by making creative use of music, painting, novels, etc. as transformational objects. A terminal object, in contrast, '[…] ends the self's disseminative movement. It ends the natural forward movement of those departing trains of thought that are the elaboration of any person's idiomatic experience of life […]'

(Bollas, 1995, p. 75). The use of terminal objects is dry and arid, and lacks a quality of live relatedness.

Bollas tends to use these object categories in quite a fixed way, so an object that is transformational will typically always be transformational for an individual. As such, I do not apply his use of these categories in an identical way in this study as, in fact, it seems quite clear that both John and other teachers have multiple and changing identifications of the app. Yet Bollas' idea of a terminal object does seem relevant to John's positioning towards the app, in that the same arid quality seems to be present in John's use of the app in this particular instance.

Back to Schön and Bion

Schön (1983) highlights the limitations of technical rationality when applied to professional practice, illuminating in particular the failure of the technical rational model to resolve the tension between theoretical knowledge and tacit knowledge and the actual practical application of knowledge in professional practice. His approach to resolving this tension is to propose a new paradigm, 'reflection-in-action', in which theoretical knowledge co-exists, in some rather ill-defined way, with tacit practice-based knowledge. Schön characterizes this idea of 'reflection-in-action' with the example of a tightrope walker:

> [...] the know-how is in the action [...] a tight-rope walker's know-how, for example, lies in, and is revealed, by the way he takes his trip across the wire, or that a big-league pitcher's know-how is in his way of pitching to a batter's weakness, changing his pace, or distributing his energies over the course of a game [...]
>
> (ibid., pp. 50–1)

Schön tries to elaborate the idea that the 'know-how is in the action' by referring to how such professionals talk about this. So he describes how pitchers talk about 'finding the groove' or how jazz musicians talk about 'having a feel for' their material when improvising. As we saw in Chapter 2, both sociocultural and cognitive interpretations of Schön have their limits. Nevertheless, when he uses phrases like 'being in the groove' or 'having a feel for', Schön's idea of reflection-in-action seems to require that there is some way in which knowledge of some kind is flexibly made use of 'in the moment', in response to ongoing events. I have gone further and argued that Bion's quasi-mystical dialectic offers one way of interpreting what Schön is trying to get at in his idea of reflection-in-action, of conceptualizing the relationship between how theoretical and tacit knowledge, or John's 'empathy', intercalate 'in the moment' of working with the child.

Let's come back to the tightrope walker. As Schön intimates, if they sit on their unicycle, balancing on the rope, and start consciously thinking 'Is the pole pushed too far out, did I check the rope properly?', then we can guess what is likely to happen. If we reinterpret this in Bionian terms, we could say that they need to suspend memory and desire – the desire for certainty based on knowledge – and rely on their unconscious intuition. True, in this the intuition is in relation to the manipulation of a physical object – although, as exemplified with John, Bollas (1979, 1992) has shown how we can extend Bion's ideas to objects. The emergence of the selected fact – 'this is the time to move the pole up a few millimetres' – arises based on the walker's use of his free-floating attention in relation to the physical task. Yet the walker still might have a body of theoretical knowledge about tightrope walking – 'check the rope is tied at both ends carefully before you start, don't tip your pole over too far to one side' (I am not a tightrope walker, but I imagine it works something like this). They make use of and can to a greater or lesser extent consciously talk about this knowledge in relation to their practice (knowledge that can't easily be put into language *yet* is one, but only one, way of conceptualizing what tacit knowledge is). In Bionian terms, this doesn't disappear when the tightrope walker is on the rope; rather, it is made use of unconsciously as a preconception which is then saturated by the actual experience of that particular tightrope experience. From this perspective, theoretical and tacit knowledge are tightly intertwined in dialectic tension, so tightly that they almost merge – not the merging of a sociocultural interpretation of Schön, and not quite the stark separation of theory and practice that cognitive interpretations imply either, but rather a different epistemology where theories remain free and flexible, both general and specific, and where they are continually adjusted (the dialectic) to the moment-to-moment experience.

In the classroom, teachers too often have the experience of 'being in the zone'. In fact, it is precisely when they have thirty children all vying for attention at once that they could be typified as demonstrating 'reflection-in-action'. Their (extensive) body of knowledge – about behaviour management, about teaching techniques, about approaches to teaching maths, about how to model column addition – is not at the forefront of their conscious minds. Teachers don't have the luxury of taking ten seconds in the midst of a classroom exchange to think about what they will say or do. Often they need to make decisions and react to events instantaneously, 'in the moment'. Similar to the rope walker, their knowledge about teaching doesn't disappear; it is made use of unconsciously as a preconception, which is then saturated by the actual experience of that particular teaching experience to create a saturated formation, a thought translated into action – that is, the decision to choose a particular teaching strategy in a particular moment. We might modify Schön's concept of reflection-in-action, when viewed through the lens of Bion's ideas, so that it becomes intersubjective reflection-in-action – where memory and desire are pushed to the background to allow the 'selected fact' to emerge from the matrix of knowledge, predicated on a dialectic view of theoretical and tacit knowledge. Importantly, the tension – or, perhaps better, dialectic – between the two types of knowledge, the productive use of uncertainty, is what leads to really knowing about the other. It is this function which seems, in some of the vignettes presented about John, to have got lost, and which my countertransference responses sometimes pick up on. The open, flexible possibility of a concept that the app might represent, or any other concept that a therapist (or teacher) might bring to bear on a situation, has been prematurely saturated, or ossified. The desire for certainty, for clear unambiguous knowledge, for scientific certainty – which is an understandable and very common desire – has pushed John (or he has allowed himself to be pushed) to a flight in to theory.

For Bion, knowledge about the analysand arises first from intersubjective communication, mediated through the transformation of 'O'. Bion uses the grid (see Table 2.1) as both a system of notation useful to the analyst when reflecting on the analytical session and an outline for how thoughts and concepts emerge. When focusing on implicit and explicit knowledge, the key move in the grid is from rows D to G. The move from D to E is from preconception to conception, where an unsaturated state of mind meets with a negative realization (this doesn't quite fit, this doesn't quite work), and if the uncertainty can be tolerated and a flight to an attack on linking avoided, it is possible for a conception to arise. This move from preconception to conception is essentially experiential; it involves the analyst being in direct unconscious communication with the analysand. It is inherently implicit, and is not based directly on reference to a set of theoretical knowledge.

Combining the horizontal and vertical aspects of the grid, then, when conceptions become saturated, the analyst (or the patient) may engage in attention, research and action (columns 4–6), which is intertwined with the abstraction of conceptions into more advanced construction of thoughts (rows F and G). This construction of thoughts is, for Bion, based on noticing similarities between phenomena and developing links between them – as Grotstein put it, engaging in 'symmetrical thinking for the purposes of comparisons' (2007, p. 313). This happens as a process in the consulting room as the analyst uses his cognitive function, in collaboration with the analysand, to explore the meaning of the shared intersubjective communications in which they are engaged (the emerging conceptions). This process of abstraction does not happen in a vacuum, however; rather, the analyst makes connections to an existing body of psychoanalytical theories – a body of professional knowledge. It is, however, a circular iterative (or dialectic) process – the use of the cognitive comparative functions, attention, research and action, is bounded by the need to realize that any arising conception must inevitably have a new unsaturated component. So the arising system of knowledge, or theoretical framework, still has to be grounded in the ongoing intersubjective relationship. The analyst needs to keep checking, on an intersubjective level, that the abstractions they have made still correspond with the experience they are having with the analysand. They need to check that they still relate to the personal 'O' of the analysand. As Grotstein stresses, for Bion, explicit thinking – an articulated theory, a comprehensive interpretation – can only be valid if it arises, is directly articulated to, implicit thinking that equates to an experiential knowing of a human other. Bion's epistemology shows us, and shows us to an extent based on acute empirical observation or experience, that any theory needs to be connected to the intersubjective experience of the professional and the client. The professional, just as the analyst, must get to know the client and use theory in a way that remains true to that intersubjective experience, to the personal 'O' of the client. Further, they must also build a new theory about that client that again remains true to that same intersubjective experience. This is where uncertainty is productive. This is where memory, desire and understanding risk a flight to premature certainty. This is, at least in some of the material presented, what John opts for – as most of us probably do every day of our lives, in order to quell the anxiety, to make things manageable, to be able to get through the lesson, the analytic session or the doctor's consultation. But Bion's epistemology, based on his clinical experience, directs the analyst to eschew memory, desire and understanding, to hold 'in the moment' – in Schön's moment, to hold in a psychoanalytically constructed quasi-mystical place long enough for the tacit intersubjective knowledge of the other, intertwined with but not subservient to theoretical knowledge, to come through the unconscious to the surface. It is the waking dream in which we come to know the other. We can speculate that if Bion directed this mode of thinking to analysts, he might direct it to the community of caring professionals as well. Certainly, in my mind, that community might at the very least take a moment to reflect on the import of what this mode of thinking might mean to them. It is true that the space the caring professional has to respond to such a directive may be limited; it may be, at times, squashed out of existence altogether by policy directives, time and resource constraints and other pressures. It is also true that, as we have seen Bion himself clearly acknowledge, laws and systems have their uses; categorical systems of knowledge paradoxically make the world manageable for 'the ordinary people', which I take to mean both the group in relation to the messianic mystic but also the individual in his ordinary moments, compared to the individual when he achieves the status of the mystic and achieves intersubjective knowing.

All this is true, but Bion's epistemology inescapably then raises the question: if they lose sight of the shared intersubjective experience between them and the client, in what kind of activity is the caring professional then engaged?

Varying states of mind

I identified my feelings of disloyalty towards John that arose in the work study review of the fourth observation. It is perhaps appropriate to revisit these feelings here, because as well as my no doubt strong personal identifications, there is also a reasoned case for redressing the balance. An important point, again identified during the work study review, is that John was one of only two male teachers in the school, although there were other male staff. My own experience of working as a male teacher or lecturer in largely female environments has made me aware of the fact that there is a tendency for the male, cognitive function to be projected on to the male teacher. An unconscious 'female' desire to get rid of the dangerous or difficult cognitive function associated with maleness can lead to it being projected, in this case on to John. So we might consider that as well as the school 'holding' John, he may well have been holding something for them, and this could have included struggling with the place of psychological theory and of technology, both potentially dangerous and difficult constructs, in their work with children with autism.

It is also important to note that the observational record showed John holding a variety of positions in relation to Jeremy and the app. It was probably the case, as I have illustrated above, that at times he did not get, in Bionian terms, the balance between intersubjective relationship and use of psychological theory right. At times he used theory and knowledge as a way of escaping from the need to tolerate uncertainty, with the app also playing a role. This meant that sometimes he wasn't 'close enough to the action'. We might consider that in contrast to the next case, Mandy, he didn't have as good a sense of the 'in-the-moment' needs as might have been possible. Yet on a number of occasions, sometimes with the support of Jean and Dawn and sometimes without, John did in fact demonstrate a nuanced and empathic interaction with Jeremy, as can be seen in the following extract from later on in the third observation:

> Jeremy gets up quite abruptly and goes to the back of the room to the sink to get a glass of water. This initiates a discussion between John and Dawn, with me sitting in the middle, as to whether Jeremy's behaviour in getting up to get water is related to stress. Dawn agrees that it probably is and John says that he thinks it's related to when he is starting a piece of work. Jeremy comes back to his seat and John says to him, 'What do you need?' His voice tone is soft and rhythmic. Jeremy says, in his staccato high tone, 'Scissors' and goes over to get a pair of scissors. He holds his hands out in front of him slightly and his mouth is thin – he has a tense expression. John says, in a bold warm voice, 'Well done Jeremy, that's right'. During this exchange I observe John. He seems calmer in this observation, although also perhaps more tired. His movements are slower; I observe him stroking his hands together behind his back.

As with so much of the material in this study, applying a psychodynamic lens to the classroom shows us how, when dealing with the myriad complexities and multiple, changing interpersonal interactions presented by every classroom, let alone one working with children with significant impairments in social communication, it is not possible to speak about teachers having a single state of mind or a single position. There may be predominant patterns and modes of operating, but these do not lead to rules or definitive conclusions. In fact, the clearest conclusion may be that just as the classroom varies in multiple ways, so do the states of mind of the teachers that inhabit it.

Mandy

We were initially introduced to Mandy in Chapter 2, where we saw her finely modulated interactions with Angus, Piers and the other boys in her class.

Current role and career background

Mandy started out as a mainstream secondary physical education (PE) teacher, took thirteen years off to raise a family and then went back to teaching this subject, as well as some French, in mainstream schools. She also spent a short period working in a primary school. Mandy has been at Randall School for thirteen years; teaches PE across the school, and a few years ago was given responsibility for teaching Maths. Mandy is also a form teacher. She indicates that she is thinking of retiring in a few years.

When asked, in the initial interview, her reasons for coming to work at Randall School, Mandy replied:

> Basically I was getting old and they don't like older PE teachers and young PE teachers are cheap and I was doing maternity cover; six months here, six months there. It was continuous because I must have been doing a decent job and my name went around. The last school I went into had a very good special needs department and I spent two or three weeks in there *after* my maternity cover had finished and somebody there said, 'There's a job going at Randall, do you know anything about autistic children?' … I said, 'Not a thing' … she said, 'Well "so-and-so" is autistic!' and I followed this child around for a couple of days and found it quite interesting so I thought, 'Well, go for it!' and then I got myself a full-time job … Hooray! … so basically it was to get a full-time job. It wasn't that I was desperate to come into special needs education, I wanted a full-time job and nobody wanted an ancient PE teacher.

Mandy's overtly stated rationale is that nobody else wanted an older PE teacher. In fact, this theme of anxiety about being too old or in danger of being on the scrapheap surfaces a few times in later interviews. However, Mandy's reply also indicates a desire, somewhat understated, to learn more – after tracking a child with autism for a few days she found it 'interesting', or perhaps more than just interesting. No doubt both motivations played a part in her decision to move to a specialist setting, and to stay there for an extended period.

Key information sources for Mandy

> First interview 7 October 2009
> First observation 26 November 2009
> Second observation 19 March 2010
> Second interview 27 March 2010
> Third observation 24 May 2010
> Third interview 28 May 2010
> Fourth observation 29 June 2010
> Fourth interview 8 July 2010.

In the initial observations and in informal exchanges Mandy displayed what was initially interpreted as a negative stance in relation to the app. For example, in the initial training session for the technology tool, run by research colleagues, Mandy adopted a flippant stance that suggested the activity was a significant inconvenience for her and she would rather be doing something else.

Kevin

Mandy has two children in her form class, Kevin and Marlin, using the app. Kevin was born in 1995, making him 14 during the 2009/10 app implementation period. He had a full IQ measured on WISC-IV of 102, a VQ of 114, and a clinical psychiatric diagnosis of autism on entry to the school. He also had a diagnosis of epilepsy, although there was no evidence of this affecting his behaviour during any observations. Kevin has been placed in the year above his actual age group, making him the youngest member of this class. This placement was made, I understood from Mandy, because the school felt that Kevin would do better socially with this group of slightly older children.

Although both Kevin and Marlin made use of the app, more of Kevin's interactions were observed, and the theoretical issues stimulated by his use were considerably more interesting. As such, the focus in the presentation of the case will be on Mandy and Kevin.

Kevin lives at home with his mother and attends the school on weekdays. I was told by Mandy that his father died a few years ago (no more specific details on his death were indicated to me). Kevin presents on initial meeting as quite a typical teenager. He walks with something of a 'teenage slouch', he dresses in quite an up-to-date teenage style and he tends quite frequently to exhibit a form of teenage bravado, often being outspoken and sometimes tending not to follow rules too closely. He is popular amongst his classroom peers, is extremely motivated by sports and is particularly keen on football. However, underneath the exterior, closer observation and reports from Mandy indicate that Kevin has in fact had very significant problems with social interaction previously and has very low self-confidence both socially and in relation to his academic work. Mandy indicates that he is working at entry level in all subjects, around two years below the average level expected for his age, except in maths, where in the summer of 2010 he started on roughly age-appropriate GCSE (school graduation certificate taken at age 16) related work.

It becomes clear over time, via informal comments from Mandy and Donald, that Kevin had several previous failed placements in mainstream schools. Although these comments were not greatly detailed, Mandy indicated that Kevin had found social interaction in mainstream schools very difficult and at least partly found the intense social interaction required in the schools he had attended very anxiety-provoking.

Certainly, close observation of Kevin during observations and interview reports from Mandy indicated that Kevin had significant issues with social interaction that were masked by his teenage bravado. He had sporadic angry episodes and had in the past refused to take part in exams and opted out of certain classes such as Personal, Social and Health Education (PSHE).

There is an ongoing uncertainty, expressed by Mandy, about whether or not Kevin does in fact have an autism diagnosis. Mandy reports that when Kevin was experiencing his very significant difficulties in mainstream settings, his mother, desperate to find a solution for him, took him to see a psychiatrist who was, in Mandy's words, 'giving out diagnoses like confetti'. Initial observations of Kevin also tended to raise questions as to how the autism diagnosis applied to him. One of the researchers on the general project, on initially meeting with and interviewing Kevin in the autumn of 2009 (in the initial phases of the project), independently raised the question of whether he did in fact have autism. Certainly, Kevin's presentation as a typical teenager, with what seem to be quite advanced social interaction skills in the Randall School setting with peers and adults, also raised this question in my mind. However, it should be noted that all children at Randall School must have had a psychiatric diagnosis of autism to be admitted to the school.

Kevin demonstrates nicely how, even for teachers working in special school settings, the existence of a diagnosis and issues about its interpretation can potentially be a source of uncertainty for them. Mandy discusses this uncertainty in relation to his diagnosis, as well as her assessment of his social functioning and possibilities for main school placement, in the following extract from the third interview. In this, I was initially asking Mandy about her aspirations and hopes for Kevin in the future:

Joe: Umm ... what about with Kevin? Well again, not just specifically with the phone; what things do you want...?

Mandy: With Kevin it's acceptance of being 'here' is the main thing and possibly making the best of what he can do here, [whispering] ... he asked ... to move to the mainstream school ... he really wouldn't...

Joe: What do you think would happen to him?

Mandy: He'd be excluded on day three ... I am seeing if I can get him up to Mookles Secondary School to do a BTEC [entry-level technical qualification] in PE because, again, he lives and breathes sport. They did have a boy once before but I think the whole education these days is so money-orientated it will be, 'Oh yes we'll have him, at so much a week!' Whether it's going to be out of our league I don't know but I've just started enquiries up there to see what we can do with him up there and then he'll have his entree into mainstream but supervised and only three times a week. So he will be with boys on a level playing field because he can do sport. Theory he's going to find hard and his mother and I have discussed this and I've discussed it with him as well. But he's prepared to give it a go if we can get him in there. So we will see.

Joe: Okay. Assuming that he stays here and that kind of acceptance ... do you have any strategies in terms of helping him with that, with that acceptance of where he is? I suppose it's also, presumably it's also ... an acceptance that he's got autism; is that part of it as well?

Mandy: Umm, it's acceptance that ... he should ... one of his targets at the moment is that he should just accept praise because he doesn't do it, he doesn't accept it happily you know and boosting his confidence. According to his mother he has very little self-confidence out of school. If you see him in the class you wouldn't think that...

Joe: Well...

Mandy: ... it's all bravado...

Joe: It seems like bravado but I mean it does go a little bit brittle to me as well sometimes, I can see that.

Mandy: ... yes. So we need the self-confidence ... out of school ... he's a sports ambassador at the moment and he's had to teach, along with a couple of the others, *every* class in the school to do something and he's been fantastic with the little kids. He can be so kind and so caring and we might well go down that route with him and make him a Sports Leader or something like that so he feels some self-worth ... that has got to be built up in him I think really. I don't think the all-exam route is for him at all. He might decide later on that 'Yes okay, I ought to do some NVQs' [another technical skills qualification] or something like that when he's 18 or 19 possibly, but I don't think GCSEs are his style at all at the moment.

In the second interview, Mandy discussed Kevin's perception of his diagnostic label, saying 'he hates it' and that he is both very much aware of having this label of autism and feels very self-conscious about it. Later, in the third interview, Mandy returns to this theme and we jointly reflect on whether or not he does have autism:

Mandy: Kevin will probably wish to leave as soon as he's 16. Whether his mum will be able to keep him in education or not I doubt ... he has an older brother who's working and I'm sure that's what he's after, getting out to work as soon as he can. So that means just two years to build self-esteem in him and get him to realize *how* society works. She says he's very unsure of himself when he's out and about. I don't know if we can improve on that because he's not with us to go out and about much. If he was at the Hostel then there would be all sorts of independent skills ... presumably she's doing that sort of thing with him at home?

Joe: So his lack of confidence and self-esteem, my understanding from what you've been saying is that it's linked to him being unsure about himself.

Mandy: I think so.

Joe: Do you think that's part ... of his autism being unsure about the world, or is it nothing to do with his autism?

Mandy: I really don't know. I think a lot is linked to the death of his father.

Joe: When was that?

Mandy: What, two years ago, three years ago ... gosh, how long has he been here? ... three years ago...

Joe: Right.

Mandy: And he was SO angry about that.

Joe: Oh!

Mandy: But I hear that his father was a bit bipolar. Perhaps Kevin has a touch of that, I don't know. But he was such an angry young man when he came to us. Having been excluded from various places and NO social skills at all. Just all *anger, anger, anger*! Even now you have to be careful how you tell him off; you can't just ...'You shouldn't be doing that!' It's either got to be done quietly or jokingly because ... he considers it rejection ... I'm not a psychologist and I really don't think that deeply about them [laughs] ... I don't know.

Joe: Umm! ... but my sense from what you're saying there is that you're not ... quite sure that it's his autism or whether it's just *him*.

Mandy: I wonder if he has autism? He has no social skills but he must have a diagnosis of it to be with us.

Joe: Yeah. I have to tell you when ... remember Anka, who was working on the project before, when she came initially and spent a bit of time with him, her question in her mind was, 'Why is he here, is he actually ... does he fit under the category?'

Mandy: I can remember Donald saying, when he came, 'Look you might not think this boy's autistic but he has no social skills', so he's just accepted as that and I think it was also the time that his dad died and his mother was at the end of her tether and it was a case of, 'We've got to get him in somewhere!' And perhaps she got the diagnosis and we were happy to accept him. It's touching wood but it's taken time ... let us hope that it continues ... we'll probably have an outburst when he comes back today. [laughs]

Joe: Oh dear. To me ... in my case ... which is very limited ... from what I've seen ... I did get a bit of a sense of him being a bit happier. When I came in last week ... before you got there actually ... they were ... I don't know what they were doing in break, they were like playing some music in the classroom ... and when I came in he'd got two bits of tissue paper that he'd stuck in his ears and he pointed that out to me and I asked him, 'What have you got the in your ears for?' and he said, 'I don't want to listen to the music' but he was laughing about it and I thought that was quite funny.

Mandy: He can be a bit of a clown but he doesn't know *when* to stop. It's like the banter that starts in the classroom; he doesn't know when to stop it, which is a social skill isn't it? You know how far to take it and it's no further. But he'll just keep going.

Mandy identifies Kevin's bereavement as a possible source of his social difficulties and flags his ongoing anger at this, perhaps often sublimated into teenage bravado. There is also a sense of his lack of control and how this has perhaps at times shown up in a lack of awareness of normative social boundaries, although whether this is qualitatively different from typical adolescent boundary testing is hard to say. However, Kevin's mother's reports to Mandy about his lack of confidence when he is 'out and about' do seem unusual, and resonate with classroom observations which do seem to uncover this very 'brittle' side to a boy who, on the surface, seems like quite a normal teenager in many ways.

The extract also shows both Mandy's uncertainty about the diagnosis, and perhaps about its relevance, as well as her commitment nevertheless to keep thinking about him and trying to help him as much as she can.

Mandy experienced significant technical problems with the use of Kevin's smartphone. At one point, Kevin's phone broke down, and a significant amount of time was spent waiting for it to be replaced. Despite this, Kevin had the opportunity to use the app to try and help him with managing his behaviour at school. For example, Mandy created a prompt on the phone which reminded him at the beginning of each day of the kind of behaviour that was expected. It sought to motivate him towards this goal with the use of images and language from the world of football. Mandy was also using the phone for a period of time as a replacement for Kevin's contact book, reminding Kevin to text his mum at the end of the day to inform her of his day at school. Kevin had some involvement in working with Mandy about what interventions should go on the app. Whilst Kevin did not make very extensive use of the app, observation and interview data indicated that in general he was very positively disposed towards it. It seemed, at least partially, to be perceived as cutting-edge modern technology, which may have been linked in his mind to adulthood and independence, as well as looking cool and up to date with the latest trends. Reports from Mandy also indicated that he made significant use of other phone functions, particularly text messaging and internet browsing, partly facilitated by linking it to his home Wi-Fi network when at home (quite an advanced technical action for a teenager at the time). Kevin also personalized the smartphone, installing, for example, a password and an Arsenal football club image in the phone's start-up procedures.

Observer stance conflict

My feelings about Mandy were ambivalent to start with. Her initial apparently negative stance towards technology, and towards the app, made me wary. There was a perception in the autumn of 2009, in my mind and in the minds of my fellow researchers and the school management, that perhaps Mandy was going to be a 'problem' in relation to the use of the app. Further, on a number of occasions during interviews and observations, I had a sense of being ignored or sidelined by her.

One example is shown in my field notes for the initial part of the second observation, although there are four other similar instances which were coded to the data node 'Observer stance conflicts'.

> I go down to class and Mandy is in her office. I say good morning and she smiles and says good morning back. She says, 'You're coming in for registration'. I say, 'Yes, that's right'. There is a pause and then Mandy says, looking at her work on the desk, 'The children will be here in about five minutes. I have a few things to complete if you don't mind'. I say, 'of course, you carry on'.

In my contemporaneous annotations I write:

> I have a slight? sense – linked to the pause, of wanting to be accepted by
> Mandy and being anxious about this. The pause holds the anxiety. There
> is a sense of dismissal for me (although in reality wholly legitimate) in
> Mandy saying, 'if you don't mind'.

I also note in all of these five instances that Mandy is unfailingly polite, and
in fact always makes a point of welcoming me when I am in the classroom.
However, it is also the case that typically in these instances Mandy did, as in
the extract above, send a signal that she was short on time and only had so
much time to spend with me. In my annotations to the final writing-up of
the extract from the second observation I note that a likely explanation for
my emotional reaction to Mandy's arguably legitimate bracketing off of the
time that she has to spend with me is that I was emotionally over-invested in
the app. For me, as someone to some extent involved in implementing as well
as evaluating the app, it was important. This may have made it difficult for
me to accept at face value the perhaps more reality-based signal from Mandy
that this was only one small aspect of her work. In the work study discussion
group, when we looked at the fourth observation, colleagues suggested that
the countertransference signal I was picking up from Mandy, about her side-
lining me, may also be rooted in her concern about what effect my presence
was having on the dynamics of the interaction between her and the children
in the classroom. They considered that, based on her long experience as a
teacher, she is implicitly aware that these children need *all* of her attention
when she is with them, and having to deal with a stranger in the classroom –
whether me or an app – poses a danger of distracting her from that primary
task. This argument seemed to me to have some force, and the most compelling evidence for it is the observation of how Mandy does work with sustained
close attention to the moment-to-moment changing needs of the children
she is working with. I believe we saw this previously, in Chapter 2, when we
saw how she sensitively handled Angus, Steven, Piers, etc. in the classroom.

This pattern is repeated across the other observations, and there is evidence
for it from the category coding. Thus, in the data node 'Focus on the kids and
relating to them', which captures similar instances of focused attention to children's needs in the moment-to-moment experience in the classroom, there
are six other instances involving Mandy from across the other observations.

Reflecting on this now, it makes sense that Mandy's focus is on giving
her attention to the children, an activity which no doubt takes considerable
energy on her part. In this context, it seems reasonable that she considers the
introduction of strangers, whether technological or human, into her classroom as a potential source of distraction for both her and her very needy
students.

Working without theoretical knowledge?

When asked about her approach to working with children with autism, Mandy refers to the school's modified TEACCH approach to working with autism but highlights structure as the most important part of this for her, as in this extract from the first interview.

Mandy: For structure ... the low arousal ... the empathy with the child and always the positive attitude, so that's the school's approach but, really for me, it's the structure. Yes PE is not a low-arousal...

Joe: No ... no.

Mandy: I've always said that but the child I've just had to calm down now while he was yelling and screaming at me, I didn't say a word. I just blocked the doorway and when he'd calmed [down] we talked ... very calmly ... but it's waiting that half an hour when he's yelling and screaming at you. It's my 'free time' [laughing sarcastically]. But you need time with these kids, you really do. Yeah I think structure is the most important thing with these children but the school's approach is the whole ethos of the whole thing.

Subsumed within the concept of structure, there also seems to be a stress for Mandy on giving them time. This may mean processing time; that is, time to think through instructions or, as in this extract, time to process feelings. In the data node 'They need time to process', a sub-node of 'Teacher conceptualization of and ways of working with children with autism', there are eight source references, six from other teachers and two from Mandy. One of these references for Mandy is from the extract shown above and the second is from the fourth interview, which seems to confirm that in Mandy's thinking, giving them time means both thinking and feeling time:

Mandy: The patience is one. Give ... it's, it's not only patience to give them time to process what they're doing or what you have asked them to do, but for them also to come to terms with what you're asking them to do.

Joe: Mhm.

Mandy: Erm if you take getting on the bus scenario, it's a case of well okay we'll stand there for two minutes and just wait, hoping that those who are already on the bus don't start getting agitated, rather than saying, 'Come on, come on' all the time. No, just wait and see what happens and sometimes that works.

However, whereas John made fairly significant references to quasi-cognitive accounts of autism in reflecting on his thinking, such use of explicit theoretical knowledge is very much absent for Mandy. In fact, it seems possible that

Mandy has little interest in such theoretical knowledge per se, as is indicated in the following extract from the second interview:

Joe: And related to that question I wanted to ask … I know that the children come with quite a lot of diagnostic information when they come to the school; is that something that you make use of?

Mandy: Oh yeah! [immediate positive response] … yes … especially in PE because you'll have ones that don't like to be touched or ones that don't like to change or don't like the physical aspect of things … which you can work around if you know it. If you don't know it, if you haven't read all this information on them … I mean it might even be loud noises and things like that … if you're aware then you can treat them more as an individual appropriate to them … yes, I always try and get all the information that comes in.

Joe: What about a sub-diagnosis like you know, so they've been diagnosed with Asperger's syndrome, is that something that you think means particular things?

Mandy: Umm, I would assume, if they're diagnosed with Asperger's, they are more high-functioning than the rest of them, yep!

Here, Mandy shows what might be termed a functional interest in knowing about the capabilities and limitations of individual children coming into her class. Yet her response to my question about Asperger's syndrome indicates what might be termed an absence of theoretical knowledge. Most children at Randall School are high-functioning, so it would not seem likely that an Asperger's diagnosis in itself would indicate that much about level of functioning. I felt uncomfortable when Mandy gave this answer and moved on quickly. This feeling may have been related to my concern on Mandy's behalf that she might feel embarrassed, and perhaps I was also picking up on her anxiety about not knowing enough. Given my perceived role as the expert from a university, who in the mind of the teachers might be thought to know lots about autism, it would be reasonable for Mandy to experience such anxiety. However, in the third interview, Mandy indicates that she is 'not a psychologist and doesn't think about them too deeply'. Later in the same interview, in a discussion about how often Mandy refers queries about the children to the educational psychology service, she reports that the last time she did so was four years ago. It does, therefore, seem reasonable to conclude that theoretical knowledge about autism is not something that Mandy places too much stress on.

However, absence of explicit thinking does not necessarily imply lack of implicit thinking, or thinking which is not yet easily put into language (especially when the interviewee may to some extent be intimidated by the academic qualifications of the interviewer). In Mandy's own terms, perhaps she does in fact think very deeply about them.

This is illustrated quite well in the following extract from the fourth interview, in which I refer to my observation of Kevin's swaggering, outspoken manner in the third and fourth observations, including his florid description of how one of his classmates threw a smartphone in their shared taxi to school a few weeks ago.

Joe: Erm in the last interview you were saying about him ... the ... we were thinking about you know what are ... what are the issues that he's got that one of the things you said that he's got, when he ... And I've seen in the classroom, he'll kind of sometimes engage in this kind of banter in the classroom and he kind of goes too far and he doesn't know ...

Mandy: Yeah.

Joe: He doesn't know when, when to stop.

Mandy: Mm.

Joe: Erm so I wanted to ask you a bit more about that er erm I and I was wondering what you thought was going on in his mind and, and that...

Mandy: I think he's not too good on social boundaries.

Joe: Mhm.

Mandy: Erm and possibly if he's bored and he starts this banter and he gets others involved, he's the centre of attention and I, I, I'm not a psychoanalyst.

Joe: Of course.

Mandy: And he enjoys [being] the centre of attention?

Joe: Yeah.

Mandy: And he gets others involved and it's fun and school should be fun, but you know sometimes you have to get down to work it's not always fun, but sometimes it definitely should be fun and this is possibly why he does it. It's nowhere near as much as [he] used to do.

Joe: Right, he's getting better with it.

Mandy: But we are ... as a class we are fairly relaxed until things go wrong erm and I don't mind in the sort of quarter of an hour at the end of the day or the quarter of an hour that they've just had for break time if this sort of banter goes on, so long as it doesn't go too far and in a way if it does go on and then you teach them where the boundaries are, that I think that's now gone far enough, you know it ... it'll slowly drip in that this is as far as you take it, you don't take it any further than that.

Joe: And do you think it's been slowly dripping in with him?

Mandy: I think so, because he is changing as a character, we don't see this banter as much, part of that might be that a pupil has left the class er who was quite a stirrer.

Joe: Mhm.

Mandy: And the class as a class are a lot calmer than they were.

Joe: Mhm.

Mandy: Erm that might be part of it, it might be that he, he is learning that you don't do this sort of thing. You learn, you forget, you learn, you forget. Erm you know there are times when he obviously does forget, but all, all skills, all learning comes really, really slowly to them. So yeah, I think he ... he's getting there, I'd like to think he was getting there.

Joe: Mm. Er I mean that kind of behaviour and obviously you, you know you have a better sense, but when I had observed him doing that ... it's to me, it's kind of ... I mean it was clearly very you know ... it's not the kind of behaviour you want from children in the ... in the classroom, but to me it's kind of seeing him in some way quite typical, you know you, you often will see teenagers behaving in that way. I mean is it ... is it ... to me it's kind of you know just seen to be typical ... you could interpret it as typical teenage behaviour of a teenager who wants to be the centre of attention.

Mandy: Mm, but it's not the sort of thing as you say they would do in the classroom, they would keep it for outside and amongst their friends wouldn't they? This is where they...

Joe: ... tell me

Mandy: ... don't understand I think.

Joe: Right, uh-huh.

Mandy: That what, what you do with your mates you don't do in a different situation.

Joe: Right.

Mandy: That there are formal settings and there are your casual mate settings as it were and I don't think they can transpose the two, that's part of it I'm sure.

In this exploration, Mandy again eschews giving a privileged place to theoretical knowledge – 'I'm not a psychoanalyst' – perhaps meaning 'I'm not interested in all that psychobabble'. Yet Mandy is clearly thinking very hard here about what is going in with Kevin, what effect her influence is having on him and whether his behaviour is or is not normal. She gives a sophisticated explanation of Kevin's inability to tell the difference between formal and informal settings, and broadens this to a general rule about children with autism, which aligns with standard psychological accounts based on impairment in the theory of mind (see for example Györi, 2006).

When reviewing this extract from the transcript, it evokes in me a feeling of uncertainty. It is striking in its tentative nature, for both me and Mandy. There are lots of pauses and 'Ers' and 'Mms'. The transcript seems to suggest a significant amount of uncertainty in Mandy's thinking. Yet it is also noticeable that she stays with it; when I challenge her about whether Kevin's behaviour is typical or not, she is willing to explore this. It mirrors, for me, her sustained, calm attention to the children in the moment-to-moment of teaching which we saw in Chapter 2. One of the striking things about Mandy in most of the observations is how calm she usually is, even when quite difficult and challenging things are going on in the classroom. We might consider that this calmness reflects her ability to stay with uncertainty long enough for the 'right' resolution, the selected fact, to become apparent. I would argue there is evidence of the same process of tolerating uncertainty in this extract. The interview responses indicate that Mandy does, of course, think cognitively about what is going on for Kevin, yet the combination of observation and interview data suggests how she balances this. 'I'm not a psychoanalyst' could also be interpreted as being very close to Bion's directive to guard against the dangers of memory and desire – desire for knowledge and certainty. As Mandy's responses indicate, there is still a place for theory and cognitive reasoning, but observation of her, partially based on my countertransference response, suggests that her praxis in the classroom is closer to being based on a Bionian epistemology wherein the use of theory and knowledge is mediated first and foremost by what is primarily known from the sustained attention of intersubjective relationship. This can be seen even more explicitly in how Mandy works with Kevin in relation to the app.

Productive uncertainty – containing Kevin

Mandy was initially highly sceptical of the app. She was quite explicit, in the autumn of 2009, in indicating that she saw it as a distraction and something that was being imposed on her, as in the first interview:

Joe: How do you think it's going to fit in with what you're doing already in the classroom?

Mandy: [immediate negative? response] Awkwardly!

Joe: Can you expand on that?

Mandy: Time for me to be able to put it on the phone. The fact that if two kids have the phone and nobody else does it's got to be approached will *all* the children in whatever classes they're in, who have phones, that ... 'These two have it and nobody else does at the moment and this is *why* they have them!'

This scepticism and sense of being put upon did surface throughout the implementation, as in the fourth interview, when I am asking Mandy about how she thinks the app might be improved:

Joe: If you hadn't had that particular problem and let's say it would let you go from screen to screen without you having to come out and then go back in again, do you think … I just wondered what your sense was, of how much work is involved … is it very onerous or is it a bit of work or…?

Mandy: It's more work than I think we were expecting especially as we weren't consulted in the first place as to whether we were happy to do this or not and it's not as though we're given any time to do it; it's slotted in when you can, which is why I took it home and did it over the weekend.

However, what is telling in this response is Mandy's declaration that she took it home over the weekend. Even in the initial interviews, despite her scepticism and worries about the app and how it would work out, she still was open to seeing how it might be used. In the first interview, after saying, somewhat sarcastically, that she wished she had a magic wand to give her twenty-six hours a day so that she could fit the app in, she goes on to talk cogently about how she is going to 'find time to play with the thing so I can use it to the children's advantage'. And she was true to her word. Even though she experienced significant technical problems, across the project Mandy was, apart perhaps from Lynne, the teacher who expended the greatest effort on developing interventions on the app and working with the children to see how they could use it effectively. This orientation persisted even when considerable operational issues continued to occur in relation to the use of the app, most significantly Kevin's smartphone breaking down in late May, which was followed by a long wait for the school to arrange to have it fixed. In this context, we can see how Mandy related to the app at the end of the implementation in this extract from later in the fourth observation:

Mandy then comes in and says that she's going to interrupt Kevin for a while to talk about his smartphone. Kevin smiles weakly and looks rather unsure. Mandy comes and sits boldly down right next to him. Mandy smiles and asks him brightly how long he has not had his phone for – 'it's been about a month?' Kevin nods. They discuss plans being made to repair or replace the phone Mandy says that she did actually talk to the two men working on it and 'they did actually say that they had got it working – briefly…'. Mandy then asks Kevin what they should put on it when they get the phone back? In this sequence, Kevin tends to give monosyllabic although not uninterested answers and shrugs a lot. He has a coy smile and seems, as generally across this observation, to be quite subdued. There is, in my perception, more explicitly a sense of vulnerability about him. He glances at me, quite nervously, perhaps being aware of being observed, a few times during this sequence. He speaks quite softly and at times his responses to Mandy are hard to hear. Mandy asks him how may reward points he had on the phone? Her tone continues to be bright but also, as before in this observation, modulated in response to Kevin's responses – softer when he is softer and anxious, but also leading – as in, said brightly, 'You had lots of reward points in there, didn't you?' Kevin says that it was about twenty. Mandy says, 'Right, so you must have been using it every morning?' and Kevin nods, looking quite pleased. Mandy then asks Kevin how much he personalized his phone, prefacing this with an aside to me, smiling – 'this is for Joe's benefit'. Kevin shrugs and doesn't say anything – he glances down at the floor. Mandy follows up rapidly with, 'You put loads [emphasis] on there'; Kevin nods and says, 'bit of music ... pictures...'. I ask, from across the table, 'what music did you put on, Kevin?' Mandy replies and says, 'lots of music'. I repeat, 'what ... Kevin?' He looks coy and looks down. He glances at Mandy, who smiles at him, and he says, 'I dunno ... just like any music that I like', in a voice that suggests, 'why expect me to say anything else?' I smile. Mandy says, encouragingly, 'come on ... what about the screen saver?' Kevin nods, looking pleased now. Mandy follows up with, 'you had a password on it?', and he nods again and then says 'Oh yeah ... I had the Chelsea badge on the back'. Mandy says to Kevin, 'I mean you personalized it quite a lot ... you really did, but it would be good if you actually had the SIM card back as then you could text ... in fact it was promised when we came back three or four weeks ago and it hasn't happened ... bit disappointing'. Kevin nods again. Mandy then asks whether he has done any other things, in a soft tone. 'What other things?' Kevin says, almost muttering, 'internet'. Mandy follows up brightly with, 'what do you find worth doing on the internet?' Kevin shrugs and says, 'look up the news!' Mandy says, slightly tentatively, 'so when it did have internet on it you used it as a tool to look up facts and figures about things', and Kevin nods. Mandy continues, smiling, 'about football ... which is your love, we all know that'. Kevin seems to be in agreement.

Mandy says that she will chase them up again (about getting the phone back) and that 'it would be great [emphasis] to have it back'.

Mandy then says in aside to me, 'Ok, do you want any more than that or have we done our stuff?' I nod assent, Mandy goes 'Wahay!' and I say, rather languidly, 'Thank you Mandy ... thank you very much'.

In another aside to me, Mandy repeats that the 'computer guys' got [the smartphone] working but only very briefly, sounding quite frustrated.

In the work study group's review of this part of the observation, colleagues suggest that Kevin is in fact more engaged with the smartphone than the other children in the study. Although Mandy really has to pull it out of him, it is clear that he likes the smartphone a lot, that he is attached to it in some emotional sense and that he is upset it is broken. We also see here more clearly what lies behind his adolescent bravado. I have a clear feeling when observing him, which I would categorize as a countertransference response, of emotional vulnerability. He is tentative and anxious and quite strikingly relies on Mandy to provide him with a source of stability in the encounter, a role which she fulfils very well. Her calm, balanced approach helps to contain his anxieties, allowing him the space to think. It is an example of productive uncertainty at play in the classroom.

Work study colleagues plausibly suggested that Kevin was very much aware of and affected by my presence. When I ask him a direct question, he is coy and looks down – not the response of a confident teenager to what is on the face of it an innocuous question. I'm an unknown object in his mind and clearly a source of anxiety. Yet with Mandy's containment, Kevin is able to moderate this anxiety and reveal what he really feels about the phone.

This exchange between Mandy and Kevin also further illuminates the potential power of a modified infant observation approach to interpretivist research. In a typical ethnographic approach I might have asked Kevin directly what he thought about the smartphone. It is quite likely that, projecting his anxiety associated with being pressed by a stranger, he would have said something like 'It's rubbish', and that would have been that. Yet the power of this technique is that it allows us to emotionally dig under the surface and get closer to the emotional reality of the actors. My countertransference response 'in the moment', a feeling of vulnerability when observing Kevin, signalled there was something else going on here. Further, the use of the work study group as an auxiliary ego, in this instance at least, allowed the uncovering of what may have been going on for the Mandy–Kevin dyad emotionally 'in the moment'.

Penny

We were first introduced to Penny in Chapter 3, where her experience in the classroom served as an exemplar of teacher uncertainty about working with children with special needs, something we have seen much of in the first four cases.

Current role and career background

Penny is originally from Brazil. After completing an undergraduate teacher education course specializing in humanities, she worked as a volunteer at a centre for adults with autism run by a charitable organization. She worked there for a few months and then heard about a job with a Portuguese family living in the UK, who were looking for someone to help care for their son, who had autism. After working there for two years she then came to work at Randall School, initially as a one-to-one support worker but then soon after in a teaching position. Penny has taught different areas of the curriculum, focusing mainly on geography and history but also teaching English, Art and work-related learning. In the past few years she has started teaching modern languages, initially French and now Portuguese. She is also a form teacher for a mixed Year 8/9 class (ages 12 to 14).

When asked, in the initial interview, her reasons for starting to work with children with autism, Penny suggests that it was something that she fell or drifted into, and that she enjoyed it and so decided to carry on with it. She does report that during her degree studies she worked at summer camps with children with Down's Syndrome, following which she was offered the job working with a family with a child with autism.

Key information sources for Penny

First interview 14 October 2009
First observation 24 November 2009
Second observation 17 March 2010
Third observation 19 March 2010
Second interview 19 April 2010
Fourth observation 24 May 2010
Third interview 18 June 2010
Fifth observation 29 June 2010
Sixth observation 6 July 2010
Fourth interview 8 July 2010.

A number of observations and interviews needed to be rescheduled as a result of absence due to sickness, etc., which partly explains the slightly unusual pattern of observations and interviews indicated.

Penny's children

Penny had three children using the app, but the presentation of the case focuses on Oscar, who we were initially introduced to in Chapter 3, as well as Luke, one of Oscar's classmates who was not using the app.

Oscar

Oscar was born in 1996, making him 13/14 during the 2009/10 app implementation period. He had a full IQ measured on WISC-IV of 116, a VQ of 126, and a clinical psychiatric diagnosis of autism on entry to the school, with no co-morbid diagnoses. He lives at home with his parents and attends school during the weekdays. Penny reports that Oscar does well in his schoolwork and is studying at a generally age-appropriate level, with an expectation that he will be starting his GCSE programme in due course. He is friendly and sociable with other children. However he has difficulties with executing sequenced tasks and organizing himself, particularly in regard to life skills such as getting up in the morning, going to bed in the evening, and being organized in school. Penny reports that he has a lively interest in technology.

Luke

Luke was also born in 1996, making him 13/14 during the 2009/10 app implementation period. He had a full IQ measured on WISC-IV of 102, a VQ of 106 and a clinical psychiatric diagnosis of autism on entry to the school, with no co-morbid diagnoses. He lives at home with his parents and attends school during the weekdays. As he was not using the app, Penny did not report specifically on Luke's academic or social skills as part of the study. However, my observations of him in class indicated that he was pleasant and generally cheerful and eager to please, although somewhat hesitant to join in with the rest of the class.

Productive uncertainty

As we saw in Chapter 3, Penny comes across as a competent and caring teacher who is well attuned to the needs of the children with whom she is working. This can also be seen in the following extract from the sixth observation, which takes place towards the end of the academic year, mainly during the morning registration period. Luke arrives about ten minutes late, just as everyone is settling down to start the day. He arrives accompanied by two teaching assistants.

> Then Luke arrives. The two assistants are holding him tightly by the arms on either side. He has his head down and has a pained expression. They stand opposite Penny near the entrance. Penny is also standing up and has that calm but expectant 'what's coming next?' expression again. One of the assistants holding Luke says, in a tone tinged with anger, 'Perhaps you should tell Penny what you've been done ... kicking ... hitting ... and trying to bite'. Luke looks down at the ground. His lips are pursed and at an angle. He looks almost quizzical, as though to say, 'what's

going on with me now?', and also somewhat ashamed. Penny has a calm expression and says very calmly, in contrast to the assistant, with a tone of teacherly disapproval, 'Oh Luke...', then picks up a laminated card off the first table and says, 'would you like a sticker today?' Luke nods and Penny says, 'you have to be ... you have to be good...'. She then tells Luke to sit down and one of the assistants sits him down at the front table and sits next to him. Penny sits down and doesn't take much more obvious attention of Luke, and switches gear to start the registration period. Her lips purse and she has a more dour expression, and she sits up straighter in her chair. Her demeanour suggests, 'Right. Now we're ready for business'. Penny starts the register, saying 'good morning' to each of the children in turn, prefaced by their name, in an authoritative tone. Penny then goes through the lunch menu, checking what options the children want.

The contrast between the teaching assistants' demeanour and actions and those of Penny is quite striking. She doesn't respond, as quite a few teachers might have done, to the assistant's invitation to hear about what Luke had been doing. She judges that Luke is overwhelmed by his feelings at that point and supports him in calming down by offering him a sticker, as well as remaining very calm in contrast to the agitated state of both Luke and the assistants – although it is relevant to note that it is the assistants who have had to drag him into the classroom and not Penny. Her exclamation 'Oh Luke', in a calm voice of 'teacherly disapproval', signals that Penny is in control of the situation, even if no one else is. She also verbalizes both what Luke needs to do at that moment – 'you have to be good' – giving a signal to both Luke and his classmates that in the classroom there are expectations and boundaries for behaviour. Penny judges that Luke needs some space to regain his emotional composure and, by purposefully ignoring him, creates that space, at the same time as signalling – just from her 'ready-for-business' tone and body language – to the class as a whole that she has dealt with Luke and that he is fine, just as they will be fine too, and that now they will turn to their primary task of learning.

Penny's close sensitivity to the 'moment-to-moment' needs of the children, and her ability to contain the very strong emotions emanating from Luke in this vignette, is very similar to Mandy's teaching style. There is evidence to support this from the category coding. The data node 'Focus on the kids and relating to them', which included the source extract above, has four source references from Mandy and three source references from Penny. In both teachers' interactions with the children there is something resonant with the Bionian idea that by tolerating uncertainty and attending to the experience of intersubjective relationship, the selected fact about what the analysand's (or the child's) experience is can arise, in this case for the teacher.

In the fieldnotes to the initial write-up, I wrote that Penny came across as 'very competent and caring, tuned in to their needs'. When I revised the write-up after listening to the audio tape, I was trying to remember how Penny had spoken to Luke. I was unsure whether there was a tinge of annoyance in her voice. On listening to the audio, I made a further annotation, noting that 'I am struck by how fluently Penny handled the situation' and that 'there is no trace of sullenness or hostility in her voice when speaking to Luke'.

It could be argued that my unsure recollection of sullenness in Penny's voice was a countertransference response – that in fact, in phantasy, she really was annoyed with Luke. This could be the case, and it would be possible to look at all the variations between the initial write-up and the recorded audio, considering if they were in fact examples of phantastical misremembering. In considering this, I am reminded of Joanne Brown's admonitions about the dangers of 'wild analysis', and also of the wealth of cognitive research – as well as perhaps common-sense knowledge – which suggests that quite often we just misremember. So, at least in this instance, I would argue that the audio represents what really went on more accurately than my misremembering. I think the case study material presented so far does demonstrate the potential to use countertransference as a tool to investigate the emotional states of the actors in a research field; however, this particular case of misremembering also shows that we need to be careful, perhaps very careful, about how we use this tool. Reference to audio recording is, I contend – as demonstrated in this example – one useful way of validating the use of countertransference as a research tool.

Balancing theoretical and tacit knowledge

In common with the other teachers, Penny's interview responses show that she is concerned about the significance of the diagnosis to her practice. Penny initially discusses this in relation to Oscar in the second interview.

Joe: You said about ... also you said in the last interview that you hadn't related those to ... you hadn't had any specialist training?

Penny: No.

Joe: I mean do you ... is that something ... would that, would that ... do you think that that's something that would help with that?

Penny: I can imagine, but I don't know, that cannot be bad, but no I don't have any training apart from my qualification of teacher. Um but as teacher in mainstream schools not special school. Obviously my twelve years' experience yes but apart from that nothing else, well training, tiny things, but not specific about autism. No.

Joe: Do you think it might help?

Penny: Could be yes, yes I can imagine.

Joe: But you don't sound quite, you don't sound quite sure.

Penny: Well you know, I see all these people all these speech therapists with lots of degrees, and stuff like that in autism and I can see Donald with his psychology, all this kind of things, and at the end of the day they cannot help me they ... it doesn't look like they can help me, I am not sure this training will help me much neither.

Joe: Okay.

Penny: But I don't know. [laughter] I don't know.

Joe: I mean I have to say that, you know, I think from all the teachers that I've ... you know I've been observing quite a lot in the classrooms and I think, you know, the team here and I think you've, you've got a very good handle actually on working with these children I mean I think ... but I think just sometimes it is difficult ... you know there is no ... sometimes there isn't any obvious ... easy answer. Yeah, kind of linked to that, I think again kind of thinking about Oscar, you said as well that 'we have to understand his interpretations'...

Penny: Well we have to understand ... I am not sure that is the right ... understand his interpretation, mainly he interprets things in very different way than the rest of us, for example yesterday for example, yesterday for some reason he hurt his back then after lunch he couldn't move, or he say he couldn't move and then he was sat down in my class in these green chairs, comfy chairs there he was sitting on there. Andy [one of the other children], poor thing, he went to ask him, 'how are you Oscar?' and Oscar snapped at him and spoke to him very nastily um and then obviously Andy was upset about it. 'Oh well never mind', [Andy] went. Today I asked him, 'say, Oscar what happened yesterday why you were not very kind to Andy? 'Oh because he poke my back' [Oscar replied] and there was three members of staff there and none of them, the three members I have asked them, they say no he didn't, he didn't touch him, he wasn't even close to him. These are his interpretation[s of] why he was upset with Andy you know ... Um I'm not sure he recognized that as a lie. I'm not sure if, if it's really he believed that this happened or just [an] excuse for him because um yesterday and Monday we had this sponsor run ... um he's quite competitive boy... um and Dwight he did more laps than him, and then Oscar he say, 'oh I couldn't win because my back was hurting', and then from there everything [Oscar's subsequent feelings] just came. Then he could be upset really because he didn't do as many laps like he wanted to do. He could be upset because maybe yes his back was really hurting or it's just his natural dislike for Andy but he ... this is... he create all this kind of thing of things he interpret things in this way or ... I'm, I'm not sure his whole interpretation or how they call it but he sees these things in very different way than the rest of people had to say.

Joe: And do you think that's ... is that part ... do you think that's part of his autism – related to his condition?

Penny: Well mum say it is.

Joe: Mum says it is?

Penny: Yes. Um I'm not sure...

Joe: What do you think?

Penny: Um I think he's just a very competitive boy and he doesn't want to recognize when he cannot do ... achieve what he want to achieve. I don't think he's able and maybe this could be part of his autism. He doesn't ... he isn't able to see what is really his excuses or [what his] abilities are. And he feels, because mum tried to err, err make him ... grow his self-esteem, [she] has been saying you're the best, you're the best, you're the best and then he believe he's the best when he maybe doesn't recognize is, I'm sorry, but you're not because you are scared, for whatever is the reason ... He is very good but not the best, he had to be the best.

Joe: Yeah and I remember you, you were saying about this before ... your view of how mum influences him. So in your mind ... in your view then certainly this kind of behaviour it's not necessarily ... my sense is that it's not necessarily to do with this autism it's mainly something to do just with his family dynamics?

Penny: Yeah I would think so, yeah I would say so ... but at the same time I ... it could be maybe that link to the autism or not I don't know, [it] is his incapacity to see really where he [is], because every time he cannot achieve what he think he should achieve there is always excuse. There is something, for example yesterday the excuse is my back was hurting ... um it's I cannot play football or the match didn't went right, it's because the rest of the team didn't play properly, but never ever his fault. He's not say, 'well I'm rubbish goalkeeper', he never ever would say something like that or 'I did something wrong in English or maths whenever, well maybe because my story was [not] interesting', no it's 'oh I was very tired, I didn't do it, I didn't bother, you know, it's this kind ... I, I know any other kids maybe would do the same, come with the same reaction you know.

Joe: You know, very difficult for them to admit that they've got any problems.

Penny: This is what I said, I'm not sure this is, this is because mum or because he's err well he's just being a boy [laughter] do you know what I ... mmm ... he doesn't want to recognize that, then maybe it is not up to them, it's just maybe here ... mmm ... hmm.

What comes across here for me is Penny's sense of being quite lost in relation to how to help the children – perhaps one of the most explicit and obvious avowals of ongoing uncertainty made by any of the teachers in the study. Much of the dialogue is hesitant and what Penny is trying to say is quite unclear in places. Although this might be partially attributed to the fact that English is not Penny's first language, she is of course a competent speaker of English, and I feel that this lack of clarity reflects her considerable uncertainty about Oscar. In particular, she is considerably uncertain about what place the autism diagnosis plays in how Oscar acts, as well in the ability of experts to tell her anything useful about the children. In the second interview, I go on to probe further as to how Penny thinks about the relationship between theoretical and tacit knowledge in her work:

Joe: Okay, okay, okay alright well linked to that you did um kind of linked to that I was … one thing I was going to ask you is in the last session we talked about diagnostic information and so I was asking you like you know when then come into the school they have all these reports and things, so you said about you know that could be useful sometimes?

Penny: Yes this is what I said that this is what I know about the kids when they come here first time. I know about assessments done in previous schools or, or assignments from um the psychologists or whenever it's from err when they came before they came to this school plus observations that Nigella um mainly Nigella [speech and language therapist] does with the students before they come to the school, to this school, then look at the information, it's like, I have to say, sometime it just rarely, usually um just 20 per cent is useful, because sometime it hasn't been updated for a long time or these kids have been off of the school for a long time and many things happen between that time and the time the report was written and now they really will … there are certain things err you can take from them and then the rest I have to say is just, you know, just looking, observing and giving some time to … for you to learn about the kids really … these kids mainly too they behave so different ways, and [in] certain different environments that maybe what the psychologist say is not really what is happening in the school and other environments.

Joe: Sure but you, but you said it can be helpful sometimes, I was gonna ask, do you … could you think of an example where, where it was helpful … where you thought oh that was really useful to know?

Penny: Yeah but I said in majority has been helpful but maybe just really, really useful maybe just 20, 30, 40 per cent of the actual report.

Joe: No, no I, sure, sure I understand but I just wonder if you could … can you tell me about something specific?

Penny: Oh no I cannot, I cannot, I cannot. I mean I cannot remember now any...

This response has some resonances with Mandy's discussion of the use she makes of specialist colleagues in the school. It's almost as if both teachers know there is an expectation that they should be doing this, but really find it hard to remember any time that they actually have. It is probably important to differentiate two positions here. One of these – which is indeed present in the literature on professional and teacher thinking, as discussed in Chapters 2 and 3 – is that theoretical knowledge is in fact not very useful to teachers. Neither Schön nor Bion, however, can be taken in any reasonable way to be suggesting that knowledge is not necessary. Neither a sociocultural nor a cognitive Schön can be considered as suggesting that professionals should not know something about their profession, that there should not, for example, for an engineer, be useful things about mathematics, physics, metallurgy, that might come in handy when building a bridge. I doubt that Schön or his interpreters, whatever their theoretical position, would suggest that doctors would not be better doctors for knowing something about anatomy, physiology, chemistry and a host of other things. Bion certainly was not suggesting that psychoanalysts would be better psychoanalysts by knowing nothing about psychoanalytical theory. What Bion was saying is that the analyst needs to use the theory and 'dream with it' in the session so that its application to the analysand, 'in the moment', can somehow approximate to the 'O', to the reality of the analysand and their needs then. For Bion, theoretical knowledge and tacit knowledge are in a very close dialectic. The theory's use is then something akin to both the generative potential of myth (and messiah) and the recognition of common features, constant conjunctions, in what becomes known about the analysand, so that the myth and the reality can be joined together, through the emergence of the selected fact, in pursuit of truth and growth. This is an uncertain process. The analyst and the analysand never quite know what is myth and what is 'scientific', but they get further by sticking with the uncertainty than by rushing to certainties. In this way, uncertainty becomes generative and productive. I think that, perhaps in bold contrast to Schön's key thesis about the problems of technical rationality, it is fair to argue that Bion's ideas perhaps do not hold so well when applied to bridges. The constant conjunction of a bridge is, Bollas notwithstanding, from most useful perspectives a pretty fixed thing. When applied to human bodies and medicine, I think we have to consider our stance in respect to the relationship between mind and body when considering where physical medicine sits in the continuum between engineer and psychoanalyst, just as we might conjecture as to where the tightrope walker sits. For the caring professions, however, where the subject matter is people and their lives, emotions and phantasies, the application seems much clearer. In fact, we might turn

Schön on his head and suggest that the caring professions are the interesting ones, the ones where the pain of uncertainty can yield to productive uncertainty; that life lived grappling with this is life lived with fear, with anxiety, but also with reality, or the chance at least of grasping something close to it. Nevertheless if, as Bion argues in *Attention and Interpretation*, theoretical knowledge has a central place in practice, the same should be true if we apply his mode of thinking to professional practice in the caring services. We might then, from this stance, consider Penny and Mandy as lacking something. The empirical evidence suggests fairly clearly that they do not have – in contrast certainly to John – many theories of which to make use. We could then argue that the dream-work with which they can engage is perhaps not as rich as that of someone whose unconscious mind has models and myths and theories contained within it. After all, the theory, the expert opinion, might fit – albeit imperfectly, albeit always with an unsaturated component, albeit only for that lesson – and perhaps not in the next, but still it might fit, and the teacher who can make use of theory and expert knowledge flexibly is more likely to come closer to what it is that the child needs. Productive uncertainty needs fuel, and fuel that is grounded in both intersubjective relationship and the development of theory. From this perspective the idea that tacit knowledge is simply knowledge not put into language yet, and that such unarticulated knowledge is good enough for our patients or our children, whilst glibly seductive, seems in the end impoverished. Putting it another way, yes, Penny and Mandy were good teachers, and their ability to contain both their own anxieties and those of their children was an invaluable strength, but they would have been even better teachers if they had greater access to theoretical knowledge about autism. In a way, this is similar to the argument that I made above about John and Dawn. We need teachers who can combine the Papa Freud of John with the Mama Klein of Penny and Mandy.

Summary

In this chapter, I have aimed to demonstrate how productive uncertainty is something that we can see in play in real classrooms with real teachers and that a modified infant observation approach can be used as a way of investigating this. I think the possibility for countertransference responses to be used as an investigative tool to tell us about the emotionality of the actors can be seen across the cases, particularly in the first four.

The empirical data has also demonstrated, I contend, the ways in which the innovations I introduced into the use of a modified infant observation technique can serve to bolster the validity of the conclusions drawn, and act as a bulwark against the possible dangers of 'wild analysis' in the use of countertransference. I will further review the 'effectiveness' of the techniques used, and implications for further research, in the final chapter.

Chapter 6

Teacher uncertainty

A pervasive phenomenon

Productive uncertainty in practice

I have argued that the area of special educational needs, and autism in particular, is a fertile crucible for illuminating and exploring the concept of productive uncertainty. However, my contention is that uncertainty pervades the work of teachers in the classroom, and concomitantly that the concept of productive uncertainty has application in many areas of school life.

I have considered uncertainty though a melding together of the theories of Schön and Bion, using Bion to 'plug the gap', as I see it, in Schön's model of the reflective practitioner. Another way of looking at this is to say that I inserted (injected?) into Schön Bion's ideas about moving from not knowing to knowing in the context of both coming to know the intersubjective other and promoting their 'becoming'. Schön's ideas, whether conceived of as sociocultural or cognitivist, have been deeply influential on how we think about the practice of teaching. A number of reflective practice models, such as Kolb's experiential learning model (Kolb, 1984) and others, for example, by Tripp (1993) and Moon (1999), have in a significant way been influenced by or derived from Schön. In different ways, all of these accept Schön's premise that reflection, which sometimes or perhaps often happens 'in the moment', can facilitate, as Kemmis puts it, a dialogue between theory and practice (2005, p. 394), which ultimately leads to improved practice. Kolb, Tripp and Moon, as well as others, might also be thought of by many as suffering from the same relapse into a cognitive or rationalistic conception of the relationship between theory and practice of which Erlandson and Beach (2008) and Kemmis (2005; see also Carr and Kemmis, 1986) accuse Schön. More importantly, in my view, they also could all be usefully enhanced by a greater emphasis on the place of intersubjective relationship in the work of professionals in the caring services.

This line of argument does, perhaps, suggest that productive uncertainty might have its greatest potential application for teachers in relation to emotional aspects of school life, such as issues of behaviour management, understanding and dealing with emotions, self-esteem and personal, social and emotional education. It could be argued that it has much less relevance to the academic, cognitive aspects of the classroom. Consider a secondary school lesson in which a class of 16-year-olds are learning advanced mathematics for their public examinations. Is it as relevant there? We can certainly conceive of uncertainty, and emotionality, at play: adolescent anxieties about identity, expressing themselves in the formation of transient gangs within the group; the encroachment of objects of generational identification into the lesson when someone notices that a practice exam question uses the name of a pop singer; pair groupings, real or imagined, between boys and girls and the activation of issues of sexual identity, which can easily cross over into phantasy identifications with the teacher. Salzberger-Wittenberg *et al.* (1999), Coren (1997) and Dykes (1987) have written eloquently about how emotions, and anxiety in particular, lie under the surface in the classroom. In Bion's epistemology, emotionality and thinking are closely intertwined; thinking and thoughts arise from anxiety, or at least the toleration of it. What is this anxiety primarily about? It is about the uncertainty of peer relationships, the uncertainty of sexual identity, and so on. However, it is also about the uncertainty represented by the blank piece of paper in the examination hall.

In the arena of special educational needs, and autism in particular, questions about the relevance of expert knowledge derived from psychology and psychiatry to how we think about particular diagnostic categories throw into relief the relationship between theory and practice. This could be seen in action in a number of places in the empirical data presented in this book. Melding Schön and Bion, I have argued that productive uncertainty, based on an intersubjective understanding of the other, suggests a way of working effectively with theoretical knowledge – including the diagnostic categories common in special educational needs – that maintains an understanding of the autonomy and potential for 'becoming' of the other. This argument can be extended. Teachers make use of assessment data, as well as existing preconceptions, in how they approach working with all children, not just those with a particular label. Banding children into higher, middle and low-ability groups for particular subject areas in primary schools, or streaming in secondary schools, also involves using a framework of assessment, partly based on policy directives which at least to some extent can be construed as relating to an expert body of knowledge. Yet this sits in tandem with the teacher's tacit or, in John's terms, 'empathic' knowledge of the child. I would argue that from Bion's perspective, the teacher's intersubjective 'knowing' of the child, and through that their involvement in or commitment to their 'becoming', is just as relevant in the mainstream classroom with the mainstream child as in the case of the teacher in a special school working with the child with autism. I will aim to demonstrate this argument by presenting some case material derived from another study which used a modified infant observation approach.

An example of working with a 'mainstream' child

The following vignette is derived from a series of self-observations of my work as a primary school teacher. These observations were done using a modified infant observation approach, quite similar to the method used in the main empirical study in this book. The key difference is, of course, that it was a self-observation of my own practice, rather than an observation undertaken by an external researcher. The material was taken to a work study group which consisted of a group of teachers and a child psychotherapist as facilitator. Each week one teacher would bring material from a self-observation of a particular incident of interest with children in their classes. The general approach was similar to the method used in the main study, in that an observation record was written up as soon as possible after the lesson. However, audio recording was not used.

The observation relates to a time when I was teaching a year four class (ages 8–9) in a faith school in north London. It was a small school, with one form per year, and the intake was largely from middle class families. The focus of the observation was Nathan, 8 years old at the time, an intelligent boy who was very quick at maths and showed a lively interest in the world, with a particular enthusiasm for football and science topics. Nathan generally got on well socially with the other children. His mother was a senior teacher at the school and Nathan had been in the school since the age of five.

> We had had a long morning session, doing the usual literacy and numeracy stuff. It was a hot summer afternoon, and everyone seemed to be a bit restless, a bit ratty even. I was a bit tired and somewhat dismayed as I sensed the restlessness of the class. Would they want to listen to me? Probably not, I thought; the boys would much rather be out playing football. But I had a lesson to teach and I needed to start the topic. So I waded in – history – the ancient Egyptians. I asked the children to brainstorm with the others on their table about what they knew already about the ancient Egyptians. I knew that they were all interested in this topic as they had, over the last few weeks, kept on asking me, 'When are we doing the Egyptians?' They started to talk to each other enthusiastically (I thought hopefully about the Egyptians).
>
> I notice that Nathan (he sits at the back of the class but right in my line of sight) has turned away from his partner and is looking at the wall. He has curled his legs up and is kneeling on his chair rather than sitting on his bottom. He is twisting the top half of his body towards the wall and looking absent-mindedly at the times tables poster on the wall directly behind him.
>
> I ask for people to share their responses. Hands go up and Nathan turns round, immediately engaged, hand shooting up and rising out of his seat. Several other children also respond in this way; they are quite an excitable

class. We listen to some responses about pyramids and mummies. During the responses, Nathan is showing attention; he appears to be listening to what the others are saying, but he is jumpy, moving about in his seat, shifting his body weight around, sometimes rising a touch out of his seat and then sitting down again, moving his leg up, curling it underneath him as he sits. He is also playing with his pencil, twisting it about on his desk. I am not too bothered about his 'jumpiness'; this is normal for Nathan and he is listening. The pencil annoys me though. I am always going on at the class to sit with 'nothing in their hands', which some of them find very difficult.

After two responses from other children, I ask Benji to speak. Benji begins to tell us about Tutankhamen. Nathan can contain himself no longer; his hand shoots up and he shouts out, interrupting Benji, 'I have a model of Tutankhamen at home. It looks like real gold...'. I close him down and say that we need to listen to what Benji has to say as it is his turn to speak. Nathan's expression changes. It goes from enthusiastic to put-out, annoyed. His leg curls up again and he turns away from me to face the back of the classroom. He is muttering under his breath. I find this very annoying. In fact, Nathan is extremely annoying a lot of the time. But I take a deep breath and aim to remain calm. I say (calmly), 'Nathan, we will hear what you want to tell us, but you need to wait until it is your turn.' Nathan turns round again; he seems to be on the verge of tears. He looks very upset. He is kind of clenching himself in a bit, his head is low down towards the desk and his arms are folded quite tightly. He replies in an offended, almost strangulated tone, 'You never pick me. You never listen to what I want to say'. On one level I am offended by this, as Nathan is one of the most vocal members of the class, but on another not too bothered as I can see where he is coming from. Somewhat unusually for me, I enter into a 'mini-counselling' session, calling across the rest of the class to Nathan, 'Nathan, I know that you want to tell us what's in your head and that you think it's really important. But I'm not going anywhere ... I'm going to be here in the class with you for the whole afternoon. There will be time to hear what you want to tell us, when it is your turn.' Nathan continues to mutter to himself and seems to be starting to explain his position in more depth, muttering to the boy opposite him. I look at him directly and he quietens down. He still seems very annoyed, and has his arms crossed and his head towards the desk. I ignore him for the moment and take some other responses from around the class.

After about five minutes, he seems to have calmed down and is listening to the other children. He is sitting up straight, although he has started to play with his pencil again. Eventually, Nathan puts his hand up and I ask him to speak. Nathan stands up in his place and in a very animated way tells us all more details about some other aspect of Egypt that another child had just been discussing. I praise him for his good general knowledge and for sharing what he knows with us. He sits down. We continue to listen to another two responses. I notice that after a few minutes, Nathan has again curled up in his seat and is now examining the computer poster behind him on the back wall of the classroom.

I now ask the children to fill in a worksheet featuring a big pyramid, inside which they have to fill in what they know about Egypt. I walk around the classroom, seeing how the children are progressing. Nathan is working enthusiastically now, although his writing is quite slow, as is typical for him. I notice that as he is writing, he is talking to the boy opposite him – I'm not quite sure about what – his ability to talk effort-lessly and continuously is not a new feature in my classroom, but I am glad to see him in a better mood. I say to him, 'That's a good start, Nathan, see if you can finish in the next ten minutes'. I smile at him and he smiles back. The previous bad temper and tension of the earlier part of the lesson seems to have lifted for both of us.

After history I ask the children to take out their reading books and read. Most, although not all, of the children do this. Nathan gets out of his seat and walks over to my desk. He looks at me entreatingly, coyly – this is the very sweet, although manipulative side of his nature – and says to me, as though taking me into his confidence, 'Shall I bring my model of Tutankhamen in tomorrow for the class to see?' I feel at once exasper-ated by the fact that he is manifestly not doing what he has been told and 'charmed' by his manner. I sigh and say, 'Yes, Nathan, that would be very nice, but now I want you to go back to your seat and open your book'. He goes back to his place and does in fact open his book and start to read.

After reviewing the transcript, part of a series of four that I did for the work study group, I made the following additional note which related to something I had observed in the summer before I started teaching Nathan's class:

Last year one of my colleagues had Nathan's class. I remember going into their classroom to ask for something. The teacher was in the proc-ess of yelling at Nathan; she was clearly very annoyed with him. This culminated in her sending him to sit facing the wall at the back of the classroom. I remember being a bit mystified by this, and also remem-ber recalling the incident at the start of the current year, when Nathan seemed so sweet and charming to have in class. I remember feeling a bit superior to my colleague at the time.

Nathan is a source of considerable uncertainty. The boy who initially presented as angelic becomes a greater mystery. In much of my interaction with him reported here he engenders anger, perhaps an emotion exacerbated by the fact that he refuses to sit easily within the initial category of angelic child that I perhaps unconsciously wanted to assign him to. His behaviour makes me have to work at understanding him, work at relating to him. There is no easy category in which I can place him, much as I might want there to be. I need to hold with the uncertainty, to move from in fact not knowing Nathan to coming to know him, here very much 'in the moment'. It seems, from the self-report of the vignette, that I did manage, at least to some extent, to stay with this uncertainty and, as with Mandy, to maintain an adult, caring function that allowed me in some way to process the communication coming from Nathan. This was something like 'I am needy, I am not just one of thirty, I am me and I need to be noticed', and might also have had elements of 'I'm the head's son, I'm more important than all these others'. In some way, I managed to recognize this in Nathan, and to let him know that I recognized it – that I understood that he was not just someone who could be easily defined, but a real, living, breathing individual who needed my understanding. At the same time, I think I managed to give him some reassurance that even though there were twenty-nine other little competitors, adjunct siblings, there still was something of a space for him, even if not necessarily more space than for anyone else. It was possible, hopefully, for him to be able to see, in this instance in just a small way, that he could 'become' as an individual.

This is also, in some small way, an example of Bion's exhortation to be without memory or desire. My memory of Nathan as the angelic child and my desire for him to be that child were both very strong. It was only, however, through moving away from them that I was able to be properly in intersubjective relationship with him 'in the moment'.

It is relevant to note that, as is perhaps suggested by the vignette, I did not always manage to maintain such a containing adult function with Nathan. In common with his teacher the previous year, I too was quite often was overwhelmed with frustration when dealing with him. Just as with the teachers in Chapter 5, my state of mind in relation to Nathan was not a fixed condition.

Of course, myriad interactions like this, with myriad children – normal children, special needs children, any type of children – take place every day in classrooms across the world. For Nathan, the primary task of the classroom – of learning, in this case about the Egyptians – was, as for his classmates, inescapably bound up with his emotional interaction with his classmates and teacher. Emotionality and, in Bion's terms, knowing the intersubjective other has a very large role to play in most classroom situations. This is further demonstrated, I hope, in the following vignette.

A second example: 'I can't do it'

In this second vignette – derived in the same way as Nathan's, as one of my series of four self-observations from the same class taken to work study group review – the focus is in a way much more clearly on difficulty with learning – not, however, difficulty associated with a particular diagnostic condition such as dyslexia or dyscalculia, but rather the everyday difficulty that many children not thought of as having special needs encounter in the classroom.

Jim is a 9-year-old boy who has always had a tendency to be quite lively. He finds it hard to sit still and his behaviour can be silly at times. Over the year, I developed a good relationship with Jim. At the end of the autumn term his parents sent me a letter saying how I was having a wonderful effect on Jim as a teacher. In the two months prior to the self-observation, however, Jim had seemed less engaged with his work. A discussion with his mother indicated that he felt less able than some of his friends, who seemed (to him) to be quicker at their work than him. The extract also makes reference to Max, a boy with what was probably an undiagnosed autism spectrum disorder, who was a source of considerable uncertainty in my work and who frequently needed a significant amount of attention in class.

> This interaction takes place on a Thursday morning, before morning break. The class are working on subtraction involving borrowing (e.g. 45–28). We have revised the written method for this as a whole class and I have asked the children to complete a worksheet to practise the method. I am working with another (much less able) boy, Max, on Jim's table, and I am sitting opposite Jim's place next to Max. Jim appears very jumpy and suddenly gets out of his seat to put something in the bin. Then he gets up again to sharpen his pencil. I am watching him at the same time as working with Max. I am feeling frustrated that he is not starting his work, and annoyed that he is causing me to pay less attention to Max. After a few minutes I say, 'Jim, why are you not getting on with your work?' He just shrugs his shoulders, but starts to write in his book. I continue to work with Max. After about five minutes, I notice that Jim has started to play with his flexible ruler; he is bending it around his face. I get out of my seat, walk over close to him and say in a sharper voice, 'You should have finished the sums by now'. Jim replies, 'But I can't do it!' I reply, 'Of course you can, look, everyone else is getting on with it'. At this point, Jim's best friend, Duke, who is very quick at maths, walks towards me from behind Jim, saying that he has finished his work. Jim then seems to crumble; he sits down quite suddenly at his desk and puts his head in his hands, tears starting to flow. I feel very moved by his distress, particularly as at that moment I have remembered that even though his maths skills are generally very good, he has found this type of sum hard in the past. I crouch down next to Jim and put my hand on

his shoulder. I say to him softly, 'All right, Jim, it's OK, it's OK to find this a bit hard, it doesn't mean you can't do it. You just need to have it explained to you. Do you want me to explain it to you?' Jim shakes his head, continuing to cry. I continue, 'You're very good at maths, I think you are, just because you find one thing hard, doesn't mean anything. You'll understand it very soon'. I could see that he needed to calm down so I said to him, 'When you feel ready, you come and ask me to explain it to you'. Jim nods slightly and I stand up to conclude the lesson.

After my plenary session, during which Jim has sat up straight again and seems to be recovered, he comes up to me and says, tentatively, 'I'm ready now'.

Jim was clearly finding the idea of 'not knowing' very hard to tolerate. In the work study group, we discussed how I had in fact become aware over the year that much of his jumpiness may derive from this fear of engaging with 'not knowing'. Jim also has an older sibling who I taught in the previous year, who is now in his first year of secondary school, with whom Jim is very competitive. Perhaps he has a fear of being forgotten, again perhaps related to his dynamic with his older brother, and his silly behaviour is an attempt to provoke recognition.

On reading the vignette, it also seems that I had a strong countertransference response when Jim started to cry, which I was able to hold on to in some way during the lesson. Putting this another way, rather than resort to a flight to certainty when he started to cry ('Come on, pull yourself together now, Jim'), I was able – perhaps even only for a second or two, which might have been all that was necessary – to tolerate the uncertainty and difficult projection from Jim when he cried, so that my 'O' could resonate with his 'O' and the selected fact – that perhaps he found this type of sum hard and needed reassurance – could emerge. When I then reflected this back to him in a calm way, showing him a way to think about his difficult feelings, this allowed him to bear his frustration long enough to engage with his 'not knowing' and actually attend to the primary task of the group and of himself as a learner – to engage with the maths problem.

This demonstrates another aspect of productive uncertainty, where the ability to tolerate the frustration of 'not knowing' and thus engage with the difficult task of learning, the primary task of the school, allows the individual child and the group to 'become' productive in their engagement with the curriculum and learning. In other words, I think this material from Nathan and Jim serves to indicate how it is possible to consider the application of Bion's epistemology to the professional practice of the teacher in relation to cognitive and academic areas of the curriculum.

There are, of course, existing theoretical frameworks for thinking about how emotionality can be used in the service of academic success – in particular, the set of theories loosely defined as emotional intelligence.

Emotional intelligence

Dianne Hoffman, writing from a humanist rather than a psychoanalytic perspective, perspicaciously notes:

> Although few would disagree with the goal of having a positive emotional climate in their classrooms, and in principle there is nothing wrong with the idea of pursuing success, the larger question concerns what the consequences are for human relationships when the focus is on behavioural and cognitive skills and when emotion is valued as a means to success rather than as a good in itself. Unless a parallel emphasis is placed on the qualities of relationship that arguably should contextualize skills and behaviours, the discourse risks promoting a shallow, decontextualized, and narrowly instrumentalist approach to emotion in classrooms that promotes measurability and efficiency at the expense of (nonquantifiable) qualities of relatedness.
>
> (Hoffman 2009, p. 534)

It seems likely that Bion (and probably Schön, at that) would be in agreement. Although there has been something of a backlash, both theoretical and empirical, against this 'instrumentalist' approach to emotionality (Lendrum *et al.*, 2009; Lendrum *et al.*, 2012; Bibby, 2010), cognitivist applications of Goleman's concept (2006) to education are very much alive and well. For example, a search on the database PsycInfo for the terms 'emotional intelligence' and 'education' returned 165 peer-reviewed articles for the period 2008 to 2013. My aim here is not to review or summarize these, but rather to point out the ongoing influence of this approach to emotionality. In contrast, the concept of productive uncertainty developed in this book, whilst certainly not denying the potential place of such cognitive accounts of emotionality in a teacher's repertoire of theoretical ideas, critically sounds a note of warning against conceiving that an instrumental approach to knowing the other can be effective. Lendrum's work has shown that the implementation of the Social Emotional Approach to Learning (SEAL), a skills development programme largely influenced by Goleman's concept of emotional intelligence that has been widely trialled in English schools, tends to lead to failure in genuine engagement and adoption if it is just used as a 'tick-box' approach. From the perspective developed in this book, it could be argued that an instrumental conceptualization of emotionality, particularly – as it very much is in Goleman's work – where this is both split off from and subservient to cognitive function, in fact both derives from and serves to perpetuate a flight from proper emotional connection. Rather than dealing with the messy uncertainty that goes along with entering into proper subjective relationship with a student, teachers can seek refuge from that uncertainty in schemes where emotions are neatly categorized, sanitized and split off as just one more element of the curriculum. Personally, I think it unlikely that teachers will consciously make use of such schemes in this way. However, by commoditizing emotions in this way, they create a climate whereby it is much easier for teachers to make the dangerous mistake of pursuing refuge in the promises of memory and desire, in the promises of a deterministic categorical approach to education, where the difficulty of getting to truly know children can be avoided. It may be something of an act of speculation, but it is nevertheless a useful thought experiment to consider how I might have acted with Jim in the vignette above if I had been following a school scheme underpinned by Goleman's emotional intelligence.

Is it really relevant?

My argument in this book could be interpreted as implying that teachers need to be not only teachers but therapists as well; that teachers should know more, not about emotional intelligence, but rather about psychoanalytic theories of emotionality. I am – as I hope I have made clear, and would like to make even clearer here – not arguing that teachers should learn about psychoanalysis. Rather, I am making a theoretical case, exemplified by empirical material, that the concept of productive uncertainty derived from Bion points towards a particular stance that teachers should adopt, and should broadly be encouraged to adopt, when thinking about the relationship between theoretical and tacit knowledge in the classroom.

Nevertheless, my extensive use of psychoanalytic perspectives does raise the question of whether psychoanalysis is a useful tool for teachers. I have addressed this issue elsewhere (Mintz, 2007; Mintz, 2008) and it has more recently been considered by Bibby (2010) who, drawing particularly on Britzman's work, gives a very nice summary of how different psychoanalytic frames, not just Bion's, can be brought to bear on education. It is also worth bearing in mind that there is a very long history of debate on this issue, going back at least to the Freud/Klein controversies (see King and Steiner 1992). I have also, for a long time, been quite taken with Susan Kegerreis' (*née* Dykes) take on this issue, where she raises explicitly the question of how relevant psychodynamic thought actually is in the classroom (Dykes, 1987). Her answer is that it is the possibility of creating a space to think about the relationship between themselves and their students that psychoanalysis offers to teachers. Of course, teachers working in busy classrooms do not have the same luxury or comfort of therapists in achieving the type of therapeutic interaction that Bion considers. This is a significant critique. That being accepted, I think it is possible to argue that psychodynamic theory provides some important insights into the relationship between teacher and student and teacher and student group which allow teachers to interpret the meaning behind the behaviours of all the players. As with the example of the work study group discussion of Jim's case, bringing these often unconscious meanings into conscious awareness can help teachers understand what is really going on and appraise situations more accurately, thus choosing appropriate strategies and reducing stress levels. Psychodynamic theories may help them better process and understand the interactions between themselves and their children, leading to a greater grasp of the emotional factors behind their own actions and those of their charges. That said, there are big questions still unanswered, related to training in particular, and the need for some sort of supervision if teachers are really to make an informed, even quasi-clinical use of psychodynamic concepts – as well as all the associated cost implications of that – which make problematic any sustained use of psychoanalytic concepts by teachers in any widespread way.

The key argument I make in this book, however, is not about teachers making use of psychoanalytic theory or becoming quasi-therapists. It is rather about what Bion's epistemology can tell us about professional practice, and I think I have successfully argued that the idea of productive uncertainty, based on Bion's ideas, has something very useful to offer teachers. It can push us as a profession towards a more nuanced, developing type of thinking where the state of not knowing can be tolerated, where we can allow the 'selected fact' to emerge in the teacher's mind. It will not be solely informed by a diagnosis, a theory, a behavioural approach, emotional literacy or a government directive, although some or none of these may play a part. Nor will it be too overly cognizant of what genetics or neuroscience, or the consequences of these when translated into a particular diagnostic label, tell us about the autonomous, choosing human other in the room with us. Rather, it will be rooted in an open receptivity to the truth of the relationship between the teacher and the child, in an acknowledgement of the potential of productive uncertainty.

Chapter 7

The wider picture

Broader application and implications
for policy

Uncertainty in the caring services: implications for health and social work

In a 2007 *New Yorker* article, Jerome Groopman, an American doctor who has written widely on the use of theoretical and tacit knowledge in the professional practice of doctors – albeit not from a psychoanalytic perspective – discusses the ways in which doctors use heuristics, general rules of thumb or patterns of recognition, based on both their medical training and their experience working with large groups of patients. In the emergency room, doctors who need to make rapid decisions rely on this heuristic approach. However, as Groopman points out, over-reliance on heuristics can lead to mistakes when the individual case does not quite fit the expected pattern (Groopman, 2007).

We can see Schön's shadow here. Shulman (2005, p. 18), discussing his research on medical education, notes the inherent uncertainty of medical practice and, by extension, medical education and writes: 'Professionals can rarely employ simple algorithms or protocols of practice in performing their services'. Doctors make use of heuristics, but as both Shulman and Groopman recognize – echoing Schön – these heuristics are not the same thing as rigid rules; they are an indeterminate space where theoretical and expert knowledge meets experience, and the particular experience of the patient or problem in front of the doctor. Both Schön and Shulman argue that this is the same category of experience whether we are talking about teachers, social workers or doctors.

We can also see the shadow of Bion in Groopman's writing. In the same *New Yorker* article, Groopman gives an example of his feelings for a patient clouding his judgement when treating a young man with bone cancer. In this case, when the patient presented, he recognized him from previously seeing him regularly running around the university campus. This small connection lead Groopman to feel 'rather affectionate' about this particular patient. Groopman recounts how this affection led him, during the treatment, to fail to ask the patient to turn over during an examination so he could check for any problems not visible from the front. This meant that Groopman missed an anal infection which had significant consequences for his progress, although the patient did survive and made a partial recovery. Groopman notes that at the time of the examination he may have made a decision based on what he hoped to be true – that is, that the patient was recovering well.

This case example is very evocative of Bion's call to the psychoanalyst to be without memory or desire – memory of what the doctor thought that patient was eliding with desire for what he wanted that patient to be in the future; not a messy, unhealthy, difficult, dying patient, but a simple, easy, living, healthy patient. I could draw a parallel to my desire in relation to Nathan, discussed in the previous chapter, to be an angelic, well-behaved child who is easy to teach, rather than a difficult, hard-to-understand child whose behaviour is a mystery.

So, then, how far can we go in applying the lens of productive uncertainty across professional groups? Productive uncertainty is predicated on the emergence of the selected fact, this quasi-mystical knowing that arises through the intersubjective relationship with the other. It is, as I argue, a knowing that we can legitimately regard as informed by theoretical knowledge, through its dialectic tension with tacit knowledge. It is a theoretical knowledge that is localized to the individual across from us, not one that is twisted too far by pre-existing categories that do not match what we have learned from experience about them. It is a contingent and evolving knowledge. This resonates with what both Shulman and Groopman are saying about medical practice.

We can, I think, make the case that relational knowledge is at the heart of what teachers do for much, although probably not all, of the time in the classroom. The child, in phantasy at least, always wants to be loved by their teacher, and their teacher cannot escape loving (and hating) them back, even if they want to. This is similarly true for the psychoanalyst and the analysand. It also, at least to some extent, applies to the doctor and patient. It is true that sometimes patients might just want the doctor to be an engineer, to locate the mechanical/biological fault, fix it and send them on their way. However, there are all sorts of identification from patient to doctor, and transference, love, desire, hate, as we saw in Groopman's example of his bone cancer patient, are clearly often there too. It might be that the balance between love/desire and engineering is somewhat more weighted towards engineering in the case of the doctor than in the case of the teacher. We can argue about this balance across teaching, social work, nursing and medicine, but in all these professions it remains a significant aspect of practice.

In all of these professions, there is a tension in how to balance the use of theoretical and tacit knowledge, which often takes place in the shadow of societal and policy debates. I will now consider what a Bionian lens focused on the practice of the caring professions more broadly, as opposed to just that of teachers, has to tell us about developments in policy.

Issues in policy and practice

Bion considers the transformation of the unknowable 'O', the intersubjective relational knowledge gained in the consulting room, into words or categories that can be communicated to the analysand as something of a necessary evil. As I have pointed out already, this tension mirrors broader ontological and epistemological concerns in social science as to how we can relate the particular or the local to the general. David Byrne, although not very interested in psychoanalysis, is concerned about how social science conceives of the local and contingent nature of the social and natural world. His answer is that we should turn to complexity theory (Byrne, 2005, 2011). In my view, there are some relevant lessons to be drawn from how Byrne, drawing on particularly on Ragin (1989), uses complexity theory to grapple with this issue of local versus general in relation to how we might get a handle on what psychoanalysis is, and what this tells us about my attempt to extend productive uncertainty to other professional contexts.

> The general significance of complexity theory and its potential as a frame for science has been asserted frequently since the early 1990s […] Despite assertions that complexity theory represents a foundation for postmodern science, the complexity project necessarily confronts the subjective relativism of postmodernism with an assertion that explanation is possible, but only explanation that is local in time and place. Complexity science addresses issues of causation with cause, necessarily, understood as complex and contingent[…]
>
> (Byrne, 2005, p. 98)

Byrne rejects postmodernist and extreme constructionist accounts. In Pawson and Tilley's (1997) terms, he rejects Hermeneutics II, whereby not only are all beliefs, attitudes and feelings just knowledge constructions but also we cannot get past these, so there is no possibility of coming to know, even in a messy, partial way, anything objectively about the world, and in some postmodernist accounts objectivity cannot ontologically be possible. Rather, Byrne opts – again in Pawson and Tilley's terms – for Hermeneutics I, which is something like Hammersley's (1992) realism, whereby if we get close enough to the subjects of study in social science, if we derive thick descriptions rather than the misleadingly reified accounts of psychology, then we can in fact get past the constructions and say something about what the world really is.

In opting for Hermeneutics I, Byrne also draws a line between some aspects of 'hard' science and social science. For Byrne (2011, ch. 1), the chemistry and engineering labs deal with something quite different to the biological and social sciences. For these, at least at a macro rather than a quantum level, cause is not understood as complex and contingent but as simple and direct, in the classical scientific sense in which cause is simply and directly reproducible given the same conditions. However, for social and many biological (and medical) phenomena, cause is complex and contingent. Byrne is less clear on whether this is 'necessarily' just epistemologically, or whether it also applies ontologically. Either way, the relationship between the local and the general in Byrne's account of complexity is not at all straightforward. This brings us to another key point raised by Byrne in his exposition of complexity science; what might be thought of as the second key issue for social science, the place of agency.

> [...] complexity theory challenges the nomothetic programme of universally applicable knowledge at its very heart – it asserts that knowledge must be contextual. Moreover, it breaks down the boundaries between natural and social as objects of knowledge and action, and necessarily places human social agency as of crucial historical and potential significance for the constitution of planetary reality as a whole, precisely because human agency can change system trajectory.
>
> (Byrne, 2005, p. 97)

In complexity science, as with critical realism, human agency is given as much weight as social and historical forces. It is still a constructionist account – the individual is constructed to a greater or lesser extent by such forces – but at the same time there is a spark of the individual, the Kantian soul, that actively chooses, potentially changing 'system trajectory'. It is in this possibility for a changing of trajectory that Byrne, similar to Margaret Archer (2000), identifies the space in which what is local may not simplistically be made general and vice versa.

It is also worth noting here that for me, Byrne, and realism in general, owe a fair bit to Kant (which Byrne acknowledges) – for without Kant's transcendental idealism, it seems to me that their scope for injecting agency in to the equation is much more limited. In a way, as I have intimated in Chapter 2, in my view Kant's ontology is still – even with its problems, and even after 300 years – the realist's best defence against the assault of determinism coming from both Hermeneutics II and cognitive and neurological science. It allows the injection of agency and it is this permission, in the end, that allows for (or, perhaps better, creates) the complexity in how local relates to general.

How then, does this apply to the argument between particular and general in psychoanalysis? Well, Byrne is interested in how social science is applied on the larger scale – to matters of social policy, to how policy on housing or public health can be evaluated and made sense of. His relevance for psychoanalysis lies, though, precisely in how he uses complexity to link local and general. The nomothetic programme of hard science cannot be easily applied to social situations precisely because their cause is complex and contingent.

Further, it is non-reductionist, involving systems that are open and that have emergent properties which are not predictable from a simple knowledge of their constituent parts. Nevertheless, complexity science also posits that it is possible, in the Hermeneutics I sense, to generalize from local situations. Byrne argues that comparison across local cases – if we have enough cases, and when done with enough sensitivity – does allow us to derive indications as to how things have developed, and how they might be different. He sees Ragin's fuzzy qualitative comparative analysis (1994) as a possible method for achieving this.

Here then is the relevance to psychoanalysis, to Bion and to my insertion of Bion into Schön's account of professional practice. A professional practice based on a nomothetic hard science, or the temptation to engage in the enticing illusion that such a nomothetic scientific view of analysands, or children, or students, or clients, or even patients tells us all we need to know, represents a false dawn. Social science is complex and contingent because people (and Byrne means both their social selves and their biological selves) are complex and contingent. In parallel, professional practice should also be based on a complex, contingent view of what people are. However, in common with complex science, attention to the experience of many local cases can (and must) give professionals useful knowledge that can be applied to other cases. This might be in the form of heuristics, flexible rules based on direct experience of cases or rules about cases derived from research and theory. Bion's lesson is that the application of such rules, and categories to individuals by caring professionals needs to be done with care. Each new case needs a somewhat new model, one that is attuned to the needs of the individual. And very often in the caring professions, although not always and with varying degrees across different professions, one key source of information about the individual is that which is derived from intersubjective relationship, which is an inherently uncertain engagement.

I am aware that to some extent I am stretching the analogy between Byrne's complexity science and professional practice too far. Byrne is interested in large-scale social policy, in 'big' cases, not really in individual interactions. Yet I think it is clear that for Byrne, what happens in big cases depends on individual interaction, individual interpretation and meaning-making. Social policy is largely implemented by people, and most often those people are professionals in public service. The domain of the caring professions is one in which social policy is most substantively brought to bear. Putting it another way, social science and social policy needs to take account of agency because individual agency does change trajectories, on both a personal and wider canvas. Moreover, contextualizing Byrne's account, we also need to take account of agency because developing humans' potential, allowing them to 'become', in Bion's account, is also part of the project of the social sciences and of social policy. As Byrne puts it, 'social science in a dialogue with collective experience has something to contribute to the resolution of the human condition' (2005, p. 99). Bion's message here is that the professional, in engaging in knowing the other, in engaging with the uncertainty that is inherent and inescapable in knowing the other, in searching for the answer to what it is that the child or the student or the patient needs 'in the moment' – for what pre-existing category will properly fit (or evolve to fit) with the person known in inter-subjective relationship – also facilitates the other in 'becoming', in achieving their potential. The process of engaging with uncertainty is a productive one for the person with whom the professional is working. A view of humanity that is too skewed towards the nomothetic precludes this. Although Byrne does not make this point directly, I think it follows from his argument that a social policy on professional practice that is based on inflexible use of categories, on applying the gold standard of randomized controlled trials as what tells us about human experience, is not one that will easily or productively 'contribute to the resolution of the human condition'. Further, a wider policy framework that is based on inspection, performativity, crude outcomes – narrow assessment models in schools linked to punitive inspection regimes come to mind – will tend to militate against the productive use of uncertainty. Of course, such policy frameworks are closely linked to the nomethetic view of science as an answer to society and its problems – do a test to find out what works, then repeat what works everywhere. The danger is that this echoes down the policy chain and we end up with professionals who – sometimes implicitly, but sadly sometimes explicitly too – buy into the promise of the false dawn of categorical certainty.

It is also worth noting that Byrne's analysis points, in common with Sacks and Furedi, towards the different dangers posed by sociocultural or overly constructionist accounts of what professional practice is, which skew our view of professional practice too far towards a historically determinist view or one where the emphasis on blurring the distinction between product and process leaves too little room for taking account of the real individual in the room. Extant debates on policy in social work serve as a good example of this.

Policy and social work practice

Andrew Cooper, who has a background in social work and psychoanalytic psychotherapy, considers the dangers of a categorical view of the work of the professional from an explicitly psychoanalytic perspective. In his book *Borderline Welfare*, jointly authored with Julian Lousada (2005), he reports on his experience of a residential conference where social workers, mental health workers, psychiatrists, nurses, managers, administrators and service users, representing five mental health trusts in England, had come together, with an overall conference theme of partnerships amongst stakeholders in the mental health system.

Cooper reports:

> By the end of the conference we found ourselves rather depressed, even though there had been much energy, enjoyment, and creativity in the work done. It felt churlish to admit to these negative feelings. When we reflected, it seemed possible that this underlying state of mind was connected to the seeming absence, in the minds of the participants and their transactions with one another, of any live and lively sense of users as real persons, and themselves as practitioners who drew on their own subjective resources in order to engage with the predicaments and sufferings of the users. In one session, individual trust groups compiled a case study or profile of a potential service user, for one of the other trust groups to work on. To us, the profile that emerged of a service user seemed one dimensional, as though he or she had been assembled from an off-the-peg repertoire of 'issues', 'problems', 'events', and 'diagnoses'. When the group was handed a case profile produced by another group it had the same quality. The discussion of how to respond to the case was conducted almost entirely in terms of service relationships, service functions, and the parcelling out of aspects of care amongst the system. Most strikingly, the vocabulary in which these profiles were assembled and analyzed seemed to derive from a procedural or policy language rather than a practical language or clinical language.
>
> (Cooper and Lousada, 2005, p. 38)

This extract reflects Cooper's substantive theme – that government policy on welfare is split. On the one hand, the progressive policy of the welfare state aims to tackle social inequality. On the other, all the messy problems tied up in this – ill health, poverty, disability, mental illness, poor housing – can be portioned off for a professional class of public servants to deal with. Welfare is, in unconscious terms at least, pushed to the margin, to the borderline. Cooper also identified oscillation between these two positions, between different states of mind in the body politic. At times, welfare is a good to be promoted, and the caring professions are idealized and praised. However, at the other end of the oscillation, welfare and its recipients are perceived as persecutory, depleting the state of resources, taking advantage of normal people; in this view, those in the caring professions are either colluders in this state of affairs or incompetents who take the responsibility for failures in service provision. Cooper builds on quite a long tradition of the application of psychoanalysis to organizational function, going back of course at least to Bion's work on groups. He also builds on the seminal work of Menzies (1960), who describes how intrapsychic processes become expressed as interpersonal processes which affect the processes adopted by organizations. In her analysis of nursing in training hospitals, she describes how nurses continually have to confront situations which stimulate anxiety, including dealing with death, bodily functions and sexual arousal arising from intimate involvement with patients. The organization develops structures which are designed to reduce this anxiety, such as depersonalizing the patient ('the broken knee in cubicle three') and spreading tasks involving the care of any individual patients amongst lots of nurses. Tasks are also very heavily defined – faces must all be washed at 8am, no visitors after 6pm. These task definitions mean that individual nurses do not have to experience the anxiety of taking responsibility for their own choices, but also stifle creativity and flexibility in response to changing needs. But these defences do not truly resolve the underlying anxieties, which cannot be consciously thought about or expressed – leading to considerable stress for the nursing staff and concomitant high levels of sickness and termination of training. In effect, the aggregation of individuals' internal anxiety states is expressed in social structures within organizations that act as defences against anxiety.

Cooper extends this argument to public policy in relation to the caring services. In other words, Cooper stresses that at least partially this process of depersonalization, of over-reliance on categories rather than interaction with real live people, is a defence against anxiety on the part of society as a whole. In fact, Cooper (op. cit., p. 40), perhaps following Bollas, conceives of policy itself as a psychoanalytic object, and one invested with a particular valency due to its origins in government. This object was potently 'in the room' at the mental health trust conference.

Both Cooper and, earlier, Menzies were consciously drawing on and were influenced by Bion in their formulations. In the extract from Cooper and Lousada above, the dead quality of 'problems', 'events', 'diagnoses' is what arises, in Bion's terms, when the professional flees from the task of containment; flees from the pain and uncertainty of intersubjective relationship with a real, living, breathing, ultimately unknowable, ultimately uncategorized other and seeks refuge in memory and desire. The memory of procedures and rules that worked before, the desire for a procedure and a rule that will bring certainty; that will work again without the painful work of knowing the messy problems of the other.

Cooper also leverages Bion's analysis at different levels – the individual professional, the organization and the policy system. Policy as a (splitting) psychoanalytic object is a useful heuristic that helps us link the levels together.

As I have argued above, to Cooper's concerns about policy as a defence against uncertainty or anxiety, I would add parallel concerns about the discourse of scientism and determinism. We can partially conceive of this as another line of defence against uncertainty. If the human sciences can tell us what we need to know, if brain research can define what we are, if special needs psychology can define what autism and ADHD and all the other terms are, then we don't need to engage in the uncertain pain of getting to know individuals. In Byrne's terms, the schoolhouse and the hospital and the mental health trust become the engineer's workbench. In some sense, and for some of the time, of course, they are in fact that. Take just one example – the doctor's workbench has conquered polio, and indeed might one day conquer autism. If that happens, how many parents will opt not to have a neurotypical child? Social constructivism, it could be argued, although much less sanguinely, has conquered the didactic of the Victorian school room. Hand-washing protocols, applied to nurses and doctors, have vastly reduced infection rates. Following Kant, no one realistically doubts or should doubt the fruits of science. The danger is when we miss Byrne's distinction, when we tip over into thinking that people are just things, or just 'problems' and 'diagnoses' – and problems, at that, which are amenable to the deterministic rules of the physical sciences writ large. Byrne reminds us that the local agentic human being who can change trajectories is not so easily translated into a general principle. In a similar vein, albeit coming from a radically different starting position, what Bion flags up for the professional practice, what makes the injection of his ideas into Schön relevant, is the recognition that people are not things, and that when the psychoanalytic object of policy or determinism or both pushes us too far towards that position, the caring professions are entering dangerous territory – dangerous because it demeans and devalues the other, dangerous because as professionals we lose vital knowledge that comes from engaging intersubjectively with the other, and dangerous because our application of knowledge derived from theory and expertise cannot be properly applied to the individual case if we don't remain open and flexible in its evolving application to that uncertain human other. The benefits that come from uncertainty, from productive uncertainty, are in danger of being lost not only by teachers, but also by their colleagues across the caring professions.

Chapter 8

Conclusions and recommendations

Reflections on a modified infant observation approach

In the empirical study, I employed a modified infant observation approach which included several innovations: the use of interview and observations; the use of audio recording; and the employment of a comparative category coding approach.

Reflecting on the use of such an approach to thinking about professional practice, I think it proved effective in allowing me to come to reasoned judgements about teachers' emotional experiences of dealing with uncertainty in the particularly uncertain context of working with children with autism and new technology. Applying psychoanalytic techniques, particularly the use of countertransference to identify teachers' emotional states, did in itself provoke uncertainty within me in my role as a researcher. As I noted, in a number of instances, particularly in Kathy's case (see Chapter 5), I was aware that the conclusions that I was drawing about the subject's emotional experience were potentially open to criticism as part of the ongoing debate about how psychoanalytic techniques can and should be applied as part of social research methods. However, my use of these techniques within a realist perspective, where particular regard is given to issues of validity, does, I think, avoid the dangers of 'wild analysis' (Brown, 2006), even where I make what could be regarded as critical judgements about the emotional states of the subjects. The use of audio recording to allow cross-checking of what was remembered to what was said, as well as cross-checking between interview responses and observation data, does lend greater weight to the interpretations made. In addition, the combination of whole 'gestalt' analysis of cases and cross-case comparison facilitated by category coding of source text provides a reasonable basis to defend the credibility and trustworthiness of the material and the conclusions. The use of work study review, an integral part of the Tavistock infant observation method, proved crucial in allowing me to differentiate between my own transferences and the emotional states of the participants. That is not to say that there are not uncertainties involved.

Indeed, in the coding analysis, one of the data nodes used most frequently was 'Uncertain state of mind', used to denote my uncertainty about the particular emotional state that a subject was experiencing. The process of infant observation implicitly involves grappling with the uncertainty of what the situation means and developing the capacity to move through the frustration of such experience towards the knowledge that can be derived from open intersubjective connection with the subjects (in Bion's terms, knowing based on contact with 'O'). This also very much applied in my own use of a modified infant observation approach in this study.

Further, I certainly recognize that there are significant dangers for researchers – as Brown (ibid.) discusses – of over-identification with their research programmes and their status within academe, which can interfere with the application of psychoanalytic technique in social research. Yet, also in this case, work study review served to help identify my significant commitment to the success of the app project and the ways in which this might interfere with the judgements I was making about the emotional states of the subjects in the study.

Nevertheless, as I considered in Chapter 2, adopting a realist interpretivist position does not imply that social research actually allows us to come to an objective, reified conclusion about the truth of a particular subject's experience. The subject's experience is complex, as well as being variable. As Byrne points out (2011, p. 83), the dangers of the Platonic backhand in social research are all too real. Nevertheless, the application of psychoanalytic techniques, such as countertransference, in a properly regulated format can, I contend – once we have ourselves, as researchers, gone through the productive experience of engaging with the uncertainty of what particular emotional reactions might mean – tell us something of the truth of the emotional experience of subjects in social research.

How do teachers deal with uncertainty?

I now come to the essential project of this book. Eschewing on ontological grounds a sociocultural interpretation of Schön, I used Bion's quasi-Kantian approach to plug my perceived gap in reflection-in-action. Starting with Grotstein's perspective, I considered that Bion proposes that the analyst come to know and understand the analysand via a dialectic between 'knowledge' derived from intuitive, empathic intersubjective relatedness to the human other and the use of conscious cognition and theoretical knowledge. Bion's emphasis is, though, somewhat weighted in favour of the former, and his directive to abandon memory and desire indicates clearly that it is the productive space provided by uncertainty, by 'not knowing', that can truly lead to a genuine understanding of the human other. Moreover, Bion's use of 'O' places a particular value on human agency, human potential and the possibility of 'becoming'. It is only in the toleration of uncertainty in the encounter between analyst and analysand, that the analyst can transform the 'O' of the patient into his (i.e. the analyst's) own personal 'O', and into cognitive knowledge that will help the analysand in achieving that potential. It is only in the space that this knowing of the other opens up that externally derived theories can be properly applied. I contend that, for professionals in the caring services, this metaphysical intertwining of intersubjective relatedness and theoretical cognition is what happens when, 'in the moment', they reflect in action.

Transposing this conception of intersubjective relatedness from the couch to the classroom, and other spaces, is a jump, but it is one I make which I believe is supported by the use of a psychosocial approach in illuminating how teachers deal with uncertainty. This is particularly illuminated in the case of teachers working with children with autism, where the ongoing preoccupation with the development of social and life skills make issues of agency and potential so very potent and relevant. However, as I hope I showed in Chapter 6, much wider application of this approach can be made across the curriculum.

The empirical case studies of John and Mandy in particular serve to show how this productive uncertainty can be seen 'in action'. John, a teacher with truly good intentions, thinks hard about theoretical and expert knowledge. He is also, after Bion, well aware of the dangers of an over-reliance on this type of knowledge. As we saw in his third interview, John says, 'I think if I read too much what it would do is turn me into a boffin who knew this and that about autism but wouldn't necessarily have the practical knowledge on it'. However, as I believe the case material amply demonstrates, on some occasions when working with the children John is 'the academic patrician', and at times he takes refuge in the supposed certainty of expert and theoretical knowledge. A particular example is shown in the observation extract where John, in thinking about Jeremy's echolalia, responds in a way which I describe as having something of an arid, scientific quality to it, which seems divorced from the reality of the human other with whom he is working. I conjecture this is the same arid quality that Cooper reports on in his account of the mental health trust conference. On this and other occasions, John loses touch with the children, coming out of intersubjective relatedness with them – and because of that, he ultimately 'knows' less about them, about what they need and about how he could support them in achieving their potential.

In contrast, Mandy places relatively little stress on theoretical knowledge, and has little demonstrable verbal access to theoretical knowledge about autism. Similar to John, she is suspicious of the potential efficacy of specific expert and theoretical knowledge. For example, as we saw in Chapter 5, in her third interview Mandy says that 'she is not a psychologist and doesn't think about them too deeply', and then indicates that she has not actually made any active use of the expert knowledge residing in the educational psychology service for a number of years. However, in contrast to John, observation indicates Mandy is much more able to tolerate uncertainty when interacting with the children. For example, we saw how Mandy interacted with Kevin as we talked about Kevin's experience of using the app. In this vignette, the very anxious and troubled teenager below Kevin's usual brash facade was much in evidence, and it was striking to see how effectively Mandy, through her nuanced, 'in-the-moment' reactions, provided him with a source of stability in the encounter. There and in many other instances she managed to maintain intersubjective relatedness to her children with autism, which ultimately results in her being better attuned to their needs and, I would argue, better able to promote their individual development and autonomy or, in Bion's terms, their 'becoming'.

However, as I argued in Chapter 5, Bion's epistemological framework suggests that a teacher who has access to both characteristics, so to speak – who can flexibly integrate the theoretical with the tacit – is likely to be most effective in meeting the needs of children. In other words, what productive uncertainty points towards is the bringing together of the Papa Freud of a John with the Mama Klein of a Mandy.

It is relevant to note that my countertransference responses, and their validation and exploration in the work study group, are very significant in coming to these conclusions about Mandy and John. Indeed, judgements about whether Mandy or John are in intersubjective contact at any particular time are based largely on the use of this psychodynamically derived antenna.

I contend that the data reported here, derived from a psychosocial approach based on infant observation, does provide evidence to support my assertion that for teachers working with children with autism, reflection-in-action is usefully considered in Bionian terms. I also go further, and extend this argument to the teaching profession and the curriculum as a whole. It could be argued that teachers working in mainstream settings might have a greater focus on academic rather than emotional or social development issues. However, in the UK at least, policy developments such as Every Child Matters (DfES 2004) have led to an ongoing broadening of the role of teachers to encompass children's mental and emotional wellbeing. More importantly perhaps, a psychodynamic approach to thinking about education, as set out so eloquently by Coren (1997) or Salzberger-Wittenberg (1999), would point us towards an understanding, as indicated by Bion, of the centrality for teachers of intersubjective relatedness in the development of 'knowledge'. That is not to say that there will be many occasions on which this intersubjective knowing takes what we might call a back seat. The primary task of the school is still learning, and children come to school in order to learn. Even if we accept Bion's intertwining of emotions and cognition – his view that all learning is at root an emotional experience – learning is still sometimes just about facts, information, 'hard' knowledge, skills, capacities. At times – many times – the group and the individual in the classroom are on task and engaged in the work; there is an air of certainty; my description of John's expectation of learning as 'the academic patrician' accurately captures the scene. At these times the need to engage with uncertainty, even if not wholly absent, is much reduced. Perhaps I have not given enough attention to a schema of knowledge types in this book, but it is not really the main thrust of the work. Yet it is also the job of the teacher to switch between different states of mind when needed, and it will often be needed; to also engage in the productive uncertainty of coming to know the other. Putting this another way, teachers who can reflect on and develop their practice so that they can intertwine the Papa Freud of a John with the Mama Klein of a Mandy, who can maintain a productive dialectic between the intersubjective encounter with the other and their use of theoretical and expert knowledge, will have greater capacity to allow the children they work with to 'become' and develop as emotionally and cognitively healthy autonomous individuals.

How should teachers deal with uncertainty?

As I have argued, Schön's conception of reflection-in-action leaves a gap regarding what actually does go 'in the moment' when caring professionals work productively with clients. We can plug this gap, I contend, with a conception of intersubjective relatedness based on Bion. Specifically, this implies that for teachers, engaging in a professional encounter involves them in making use of a body of professional knowledge, as well as simultaneously engaging in the struggle to come to know the human other. Bion's injunction to abandon memory and desire is important because it suggests to teachers that they should have the courage to grapple with uncertainty, something which too skewed a focus on theoretical knowledge may serve to draw them too far away from. In parallel, Bion's linking of uncertainty with development, with 'becoming', also warns that a cognitive discourse based on determinism can potentially lead teachers towards the dangers of the false dawn offered by categorical certainties.

Linked to this, I have also argued ontologically, based on Grotstein's interpretation of Bion's idea of 'O', that for us to conceive of the human subject as having a meaningful notion of agency implies that a kind of productive uncertainty is inherent in how that agency arises. Bion's later project implies that human 'becoming' – that is, the creative development and flowering of the person – involves the individual grappling with coming to know their own personal 'O'. It is the analyst's task, through the exercise of their free-floating attention unhampered by memory and desire, to help the client in their journey to reaching this state. It is a difficult, challenging, uncertain process that is all too easy to turn away from, particularly through flight to the comfort of certainty.

Teachers – particularly those working with children with special needs, but also more generally – are often concerned with developing the autonomy and agency of their children. Using Bion's ideas to plug Schön's gap also implies, therefore, that teachers should give cognizance when thinking about how they work with their children to the productive role of uncertainty in facilitating both the professional coming to know the child and the child coming to know themselves.

So my theoretical merging of Schön and Bion, as supported by the teacher cases presented in this book, suggests that uncertainty should be thought of as a good thing. Teachers should be encouraged to engage with and tolerate uncertainty, and concomitantly or equivalently to place a premium on maintaining intersubjective relatedness with the children with whom they work. My analysis does not suggest that theoretical knowledge is not relevant for teachers. Bion's psychoanalytic approach is firmly based on the use of theory and models, but they need to be used flexibly. He calls for analysts to engage with and recreate these theories and models in their own terms, in particular so that they fit the needs of the analysand across from them. What I argue here is, first, that the first port of call for teachers should be their interaction with the child as a human other; second, that teachers should be open in recognizing that uncertainty can be productive; and third, that teachers should recognize that encountering uncertainty in their work with children can be very difficult, but there is more to be gained by staying with the struggle than by fleeing from it too early, into the promise of expert solutions. Putting it another way, it may not be practical or even desirable for teachers to abandon memory and desire, but it is still crucial for them to recognize the dangers inherent in clinging to them too strongly.

Productive uncertainty: policy implications

In Chapter 3, I noted the lack of curriculum input on special educational needs in initial teacher training in the UK. Given this, it was perhaps not surprising that none of the teachers at Randall School had any in-depth specialist training in autism. Would Mandy in fact have been a better teacher of children with autism if she had undertaken a postgraduate qualification in SEN, if she had access to the academic/cognitive material of a Papa Freud? I have argued strongly on (albeit only) theoretical grounds that, if we stay true to Bion's epistemology, then she would. I would also argue that those developing training programmes for special educational needs should make teachers aware of the importance of a model of professional practice that has the struggle with uncertainty at its centre.

This call for teachers to recognize the place of uncertainty in their work sits within the context of wider policy debates about expert and theoretical knowledge in teaching. As can be seen from the UK Education White Paper (DfE 2010), and subsequent 2011 Education Act, the policy pendulum tends to veer between on the one hand stressing the need for teaching practice to be based on expert knowledge and, on the other, declaiming that teachers can only truly learn from watching good teachers in schools. This reflects a wider international debate about approaches to initial teacher education, where although there is a general trend in the developed world towards greater location of teacher training in universities, there has also been a swing back in the past fifteen years towards minimum competency models, where competencies are conceptualized as arising from experience in school rather than from a teacher education programme (Musset, 2010). This trend has been particularly significant recently in the UK, with the very much increased focus on 'school-based teacher training', and in the US, where 'alternative routes into teaching' were taken by 31 per cent of all entrants into the profession in 2011 (US Department of Education, 2013). However, I would hope that, independent of the current political trend, my call for teachers to recognize uncertainty can be of use to teachers whatever the prevailing policy context – although it is certainly the case that policy trends which tend towards the instrumentalization of teaching can have the effect of pushing them towards grabbing the latest knowledge package dropped from on high, and thus potentially away from working intersubjectively with their students. Andrew Cooper's conceptualization of policy as a psychoanalytic object is also relevant here. Where teaching is conceived of as a set of instrumental rules, particularly where these are specified by government and thus potentially invested (unconsciously) with the imprimatur of certainty, we as teachers, and as teacher educators, can split off the need to be uncertain about the curriculum, or uncertain about our students, and seek refuge in the certainty of an all-knowing, all-seeing government.

I would argue, however, that in all policy frameworks, ultimately it is teachers and not education ministers, nor even headteachers, who work with children in classrooms. It is in those classrooms, albeit always within a wider macro- and micro-policy framework, that teachers make 'in-the-moment' decisions. This 'in-the-moment' interaction is the inescapable stuff of teaching and I contend, based on the empirical observations I have presented, that teachers will make the best use of theoretical knowledge if they do so in a context in which they recognize the paramount importance for them as caring professionals to genuinely engage in the difficult, uncertain but ultimately greatly productive encounters with the real human others that inhabit their classrooms.

This argument may, to some, seem glib or obvious. Surely, you will say, teachers know this already. Surely, doctors and nurses and social workers also know it, even if they do not always succeed in putting it into practice. Well, Sacks (2007) points out the dangers of determinist thinking when we consider how we will approach the rearing and development of the next generation and, in a similar vein, Furedi writes about the wider medicalization of social experience:

> My objection to the contemporary representation of the vulnerable self is based on the conviction that it disempowers people and distracts them from gaining a measure of control over their lives. Through cultivating a powerful sense of vulnerability, it undermines subjectivity and the sense of human agency. The continuous transmission of cultural signals that suggest that in an ever expanding range of circumstances people should not be expected to cope encourages the professionalization of everyday life.
>
> (Furedi 2004, p. 414)

This mirrors Cooper's policy analysis in which, when people are not expected to cope, it is state professionals who hold the solutions – solutions which are based on categorization, procedures and instruments. It is here that the instrumentalization of teaching, and of the caring professions, poses a risk – a risk to the professionals themselves, in terms of a deadening of their professional identity, but more crucially a risk to the children and adults that they work with. Their subjectivity and human agency, their individualism, are placed at risk in a general culture where, as Furedi has identified, determinism based on genes, or determinism based on how your parents live, or determinism based on what category you are in, undermines the possibility – in Bion's words – of truly 'becoming'. None of this, of course, is meant to belittle the need for caring professionals or their role in society. As Furedi notes, 'there was a time when enlightened mental health professionals were critical of the tendency to medicalize human experience' (op. cit., p. 415). Well, there still are some voices, such as Groopman's, who heed this call, but perhaps they are too few and far between to make enough of an impact. To me, Bion's call is the same: be critical of the tendency to make your analysand a category, to ignore the true human other across from you, to use theory and category too early and avoid the difficulty of contending with the uncertain, agentic other. Teachers who heed this call will, I contend, by following the path laid by Bion's emotional epistemology, hold on to the possibility of uncovering the possibilities that their children possess. This is particularly relevant to children with special educational needs. Ann Alvarez's work (1992), which was heavily influenced by Bion, suggests that when working with children with autism, we need to remain open to drawing them into the world of relationship and experience, to maintain the hope that they can overcome ingrained patterns, that they can 'become'. All the teachers in the study reported on here, at certain times across their varying states of mind, achieve a similar openness to the possibilities for their children and the flexibility to remain open, 'in the moment', to their needs. As I hope I have shown, such an openness to possibility, denoted by the idea of productive uncertainty, also has application both across the curriculum for teachers and, by extension, to other caring professions. The dangers of a determinist worldview when applied to professional practice, highlighted by Sacks, Cooper and Furedi, and indirectly by Fodor, are particularly acute when public policy serves to instrumentalize these professions. As Byrne warns, a flawed view of the role and potential of science in the social sciences, such that, for example, the classroom writ large is thought equivalent to the physicist's lab bench, gives false hope that procedural and categorical approaches to public policy, inflexibly applied across cases, can achieve improvements in outcomes. This same concern is at the root of Schön's project when he highlights the flaws in a technical rational model of the professions. For the caring professions, particularly when in the public (unconscious) imagination they hold both responsibility for the ills of the world and the certain solution to them, as laid down by government in its role as custodian of scientific rationality, there is also significant danger of deprofessionalization. In the UK, for example, under the Labour government of the late 1990s and the first decade of the twenty-first century, a myriad of policy directives and classroom prescription aimed to reduce the space for teacher thinking, to make teaching not a craft, not a profession, but a technician's role.

Yet the policy pendulum swings and swings. What I hope I have done here is provide some counterweight to societal policy trends which lose sight of the crucial role of the teacher's relationship with the child in coming to know their needs and promoting their agentic development. My central objective has been to introduce the idea of productive uncertainty, where tolerating the difficulty of not knowing can ultimately lead to a better, more nuanced, more flexible understanding of the human other across from you. This is particularly relevant for teachers working with children with special educational needs, but also to all those others, doctors, nurses, social workers, who also need to hold off from the flight to memory and desire which Bion so importantly warns us against when working with their patients and clients.

This may at this point, and after all this effort, seem something of a glib conclusion to some. Where is the definite policy prescription, the concrete proposals for techniques for schools and the classroom? I could propose some, but in starting to formulate what they might be I am reminded of O'Shaughnessy's critiques of Bion: that he was inexact, unclear, open to misinterpretation. As I have noted, I think these critiques are reasonable and sometimes necessary. Yet when you read his work, with its many at first opaque and difficult passages, his lack of immediately obvious precision has a logic of its own. For Bion, similar to Lacan, words represented a dangerous compromise. The false image that the child creates when they enter the world of language represents a huge loss, the loss of the imaginary, replaced with the suspect benefits of the real. When the constant conjunction leads to the selected fact or word arising, the danger is that its potential to remain unsaturated is lost. Bion, in *Notes on Memory and Desire*, proclaimed that analysts needed to make his work their own, to reinterpret it for their own practice, for their own analysands, to make of it what they will. Bion wanted his words on the page to remain unsaturated, to be uncertain to the reader, so that in the process of tolerating that frustration the reader would, if you like, come into contact with the 'O' that arises between the dyad of author and reader. This, to me, is a vision of professional practice which is very far from a view of the caring professions as purveyors of scientific instruments, procedures and categories. It is one I think Schön would be happy with. So, in a book that has at its heart been about the work of Wilfred Bion and what he might have to say about the practice of the caring professional, it would seem somewhat jarring to conclude with prescriptions, techniques and approaches. Rather, what I have to offer is a state of mind, a way of looking at professional practice. Certainly it is one that has important implications for policy in relation to teaching and the professions; however, even more importantly, it recommends to teachers and other caring professionals a way of conceptualizing their practice through the heuristic of productive uncertainty. It offers a way of thinking about the place of theoretical and tacit knowledge in that practice, and encourages their commitment, if you like, to the centrality of intersubjective relationship as a tool through which they can really come to know, in Bion's sense, the other across the room from them.

References

Aitken, K.J. and Trevarthen, C. (1997) 'Self/other organization in human-psychological development', *Development and Psychopathology*, 9(4), 653–677.

Allison, H.E. (2004) *Kant's Transcendental Idealism*. New Haven, CT: Yale University Press.

Alvarez, A. (1992) *Live Company: Psychotherapy with Autistic, Borderline, Deprived and Abused children*. London: Routledge.

APA Presidential Task Force on Evidence Based Practice. (2006) 'Evidence based practice in psychology (statement by the American Psychological Association)', *American Psychologist*, 61(4), 271–285.

Archer, M. (2000) *Being Human: The Problem of Agency*. Cambridge: Cambridge University Press.

Avramidis, E. and Kalyva, E. (2007) 'The influence of teaching experience and professional development on Greek teachers' attitudes towards inclusion', *European Journal of Special Needs Education*, 22(4), 367–389.

Barton, L. (1988) *The Politics of Special Educational Needs*. London: Routledge.

Bateson, G. (1979) *Mind and Nature: A Necessary Unity*. London: Bantam Press.

Barnhill, G.P., Polloway, E.A. and Sumutka, B.M. (2010) 'A survey of personnel preparation practices in autism spectrum disorders', *Focus on Autism and Other Developmental Disabilities*, 26(2), 75–86.

Berger, C.R. and Calabrese, R.J. (1975) 'Some explorations in initial interaction and beyond: toward a developmental theory of interpersonal communication', *Human Communication Research*, 1(2), 99–112.

Bibby, T. (2010) *Education – An 'Impossible Profession'?: Psychoanalytic Explorations of Learning and Classrooms*. Abingdon: Routledge.

Bick, E. (1964) 'Notes on infant observation in psycho-analytic training', *International Journal of Psycho-Analysis*, 45, 558–566.

Bion, W.R. (1962) *Learning from Experience*. London: William Heinemann.

Bion, W.R. (1963) *Elements of Psycho-analysis*. London: William Heinemann.

Bion, W.R. (1965) *Transformations*. London: William Heinemann.

Bion, W.R. (1967) 'Notes on memory and desire', *The Psychoanalytic Forum*, 2(3), 272–280.

Bion, W.R. (1970) *Attention and Interpretation*. London: William Heinemann.

Bion, W.R. (1977) *Two Papers The Grid and Caesura*. London: Karnac Books.

Bion, W.R. (1985) 'Container and contained', in A.D. Colman and W.H. Bexton (eds.) *Group Relations Reader 2*. Jupiter, FL: A. K. Rice Institute, pp. 127–133.

Bleandonu, G. (1999) *Wilfred Bion: His Life and Works*. New York: Other Press.

Bogdashina, O. (2006) *Theory of Mind and the Triad of Perspectives on Autism and Asperger Syndrome: A View from the Bridge*. London: Jessica Kingsley Publishers.

Bollas, C. (1979) 'The transformational object', *International Journal of Psycho-Analysis*, 60, 97–107.

Bollas, C. (1992) *Being a Character*. New York: Hill and Wang.

Bollas, C. (1995) *Cracking-up: The Work of Unconscious Experience*. New York: Hill and Wang.

Bollas, C. (1999) *The Mystery of Things*. London: Routledge.

Britzman, D.P. (1998) *Lost Subjects, Contested objects: Toward a Psychoanalytic Inquiry of Learning*. Albany, NY: SUNY Press.

Britzman, D.P. (2013) 'Between psychoanalysis and pedagogy: scenes of rapprochement and alienation', *Curriculum Inquiry*, 43(1), 95–117.

Brookfield, S. (1995) *Becoming a Critically Reflective Teacher*. San Francisco, CA: Jossey-Bass.

Brown, J. (2006) 'Reflexivity in the research process: psychoanalytic observations', *International Journal of Social Research Methodology*, 9(3), 181–197.

Brown, S. and McIntyre, D. (1993) *Making Sense of Teaching*. London: Open University Press.

Brownell, M.T., Ross, D.D., Colón, E.P. and McCallum, C.L. (2005) 'Critical features of special education teacher preparation: a comparison with general teacher education', *The Journal of Special Education*, 38(4), 242–252.

Buber, M. (1956) 'I and thou', in W. Herberg (ed.) *The Writings of Martin Buber*. New York: Meridian Books, pp. 43–62.

Burman, E. (2008) *Deconstructing Developmental Psychology*. London: Psychology Press.

Byrne, D. (2005) 'Complexity, configurations and cases', *Theory, Culture & Society*, 22(5), 95–111.

Byrne, D. (2011) *Applying Social Science: The Role of Social Research in Politics, Policy and Practice*. Bristol: Policy Press.

Carey, B. (2012) 'Psychiatry manual drafters back down on diagnoses', *New York Times*, 12 May 2012.

Carlberg, G. (2010) 'Focused systematic case studies', in J. Tsiantis and J. Trowell (eds.) *Assessing Change in Psychoanalytic Psychotherapy of Children and Adolescents*. London: Karnac, pp. 93–114.

Carr, W. and Kemmis, S. (1986) *Becoming Critical: Education, Knowledge and Action Research*. Lewes: Farmer.

Chua, S.L., Chen, D.T. and Wong, A.F.L. (1999) 'Computer anxiety and its correlates: a meta-analysis', *Computers in Human Behavior*, 15(5), 609–623.

Cilliers, P. and DeVilliers, T. (2000) 'The complex I', in W. Wheeler (ed.) *The Political Subject*. London: Laurence and Wishart, pp. 226–245.

Civitarese, G. (2012) *The Violence of Emotions: Bion and Post-Bionian Psychoanalysis*. Abingdon: Routledge.

Clark, C. and Lampert, M. (1986) 'The study of teacher thinking: implications for teacher education', *Journal of Teacher Education*, 37(5), 27–31.

Clark, M. (2005) 'Asking the right questions about teacher preparation', in P.M. Denicolo and M. Kompf (eds.) *Teacher Thinking and Professional Action*. New York: Routledge.

Clark, M. and Petersen, P.L. (1986) 'Teacher thought processes', in M.C. Wittrock (ed.) *Handbook of Research in Teaching*. New York: Macmillan, pp. 255–296.

Cobb, P. and Yackel, E. (1996) 'Constructivist, emergent, and sociocultural perspectives in the context of developmental research', *Educational Psychologist*, 31(3–4), 175–190.

Cooper, A. and Lousada, J. (2005) *Borderline Welfare*. London: Karnac.

Coren, A. (1997) *A Psychodynamic Approach to Education*. London: Sheldon Press.

Csibra, G. (2010) 'Recognizing communicative intentions in infancy', *Mind & Language*, 25(2), 141–168.

Davies, J. (2013) *Cracked: The Unhappy Truth about Psychiatry*. London: Pegasus.

Deakin, E.K. and Tiellet Nunes, M.L. (2009) 'Effectiveness of child psycho-analytic psychotherapy in a clinical outpatient setting', *Journal of Child Psychotherapy*, 35(3), 290–301.

Denicolo, P.M. and Kompf, M. (2005) *Teacher Thinking and Professional Action*. New York: Routledge.

Department for Children, Families and Skills (2008) *Inclusion Development Programme*. Online. Available from: http://webarchive.nationalarchives. gov.uk/20100202100434/http://nationalstrategies.standards.dcsf.gov.uk/node/173574?uc=force_uj (accessed 15 October 2013).

Department for Education (DfE) (2010) *The Importance of Teaching: Schools White Paper*. Online. Available from: http://www.education.gov.uk/schools/toolsand-initiatives/schoolswhitepaper/b0068570/the-importance-of-teaching/ (accessed 15 March 2012).

Department for Education (DfE) (2013) *Children and Families Bill 2013*. Online. Available from: http://www.education.gov.uk/a00221161 (accessed 23 December 2013).

Department for Education and Skills (DfES) (2004) *Every Child Matters: Change for Children Green Paper*. Online. Available from: http://webarchive.nationalarchives. gov.uk/20130401151715/https://www.education.gov.uk/publications/stand-ard/publicationdetail/page1/cm5860 (accessed 23 December 2013).

Dykes, S. (1987) 'Psychoanalytic insight in the classroom: asset or liability', *Journal of Educational Therapy*, 1(4), 43–61.

Eigen, M. (1998) *The Psychoanalytic Mystic*. London: Karnac.

Erlandson, P. (2007) *Docile Bodies and Imaginary Minds*. Göteborg: Acta Universitatis Gothoburgenis.

Erlandson, P. and Beach, D. (2008) 'The ambivalence of reflection – rereading Schön', *Reflective Practice*, 9(4), 409–421.

Fereday, J. and Muir-Cochrane, E. (2006) 'Demonstrating rigor using thematic analysis: a hybrid approach of inductive and deductive coding and theme development', *International Journal of Qualitative Methods*, 5(1), 1–11.

Florian, L. and Black-Hawkins, K. (2011) 'Exploring inclusive pedagogy', *British Educational Research Journal*, 37(5), 813–828.

Fodor, J. (1968) 'The appeal to tacit knowledge in psychological explanation', *The Journal of Philosophy*, 65(20), 627–640; also in Fodor, J. (1981) *Representations: Philosophical Essays on the Foundations of Cognitive Science*. Cambridge, MA: MIT Press, pp. 250–264.

Fodor, J. (2007) 'Headaches have themselves' (review of *Consciousness and Its Place in Nature: Does Physicalism Entail Panpsychism?* by Galen Strawson *et al.*), *London Review of Books*, 29(10), 9–10.

Fodor, J. and Piattelli-Palmarini, M. (2011) *What Darwin Got Wrong*. New York: Profile Books.

Fonagy, P. (2003) 'The research agenda: the vital need for empirical research in child psychotherapy', *Journal of Child Psychotherapy*, 29(2), 129–136.

Fonagy, P. and Target, M. (2007) 'The rooting of the mind in the body: new links between attachment theory and psychoanalytic thought', *Journal of the American Psychoanalytic Association*, 55(2), 411–456.

Freud, S. (1911) 'Formulations regarding the two principles in mental functioning', in J. Strachey (ed.) *The Standard Edition of the Complete Psychoanalytical Works of Sigmund Freud (Volume 12)*. London: Hogarth Press, pp. 218–223.

Freud, S. (1919) 'Lines of advance in psycho-analytic therapy', in Strachey, J. (ed.) *The Standard Edition of the Complete Psychoanalytical Works of Sigmund Freud (Volume 17)*. London: Hogarth Press, pp. 157–168.

Frosh, S. (1997) *For and Against Psychoanalysis*. London: Routledge.

Frosh, S. and Baraitser, L. (2008) 'Psychoanalysis and psychosocial studies', *Psychoanalysis, Culture & Society*, 13(4), 346–365.

Furedi, F. (2004) 'Reflections on the medicalisation of social experience', *British Journal of Guidance and Counselling*, 32(3), 413–415.

Gage, N. (2007) 'The paradigm wars and their aftermath: a historical sketch of research on teaching since 1989', in Martin Hammersley (ed.) *Educational Research and Evidence-based Practice*. London: Sage Publications, pp. 151–166.

Garner, P. (1996a) 'A special education? The experiences of newly qualifying teachers during initial training', *British Educational Research Journal*, 22(2), 155–164.

Garner, P. (1996b) 'Students' views on special educational needs courses in initial teacher education', *British Journal of Special Education*, 23(4), 176–179.

Goleman, D. (2006) *Emotional Intelligence: Why it Can Matter More than IQ*. London: Random House.

Gould, S.J. and Lewontin, R.C. (1979) 'The Spandrels of San Marco and the Panglossian paradigm: a critique of the adaptationist programme', *Proceedings of the Royal Society*, 205(1161), 581–598.

Gray, C. (2007) *Writing Social Stories with Carol Gray*. London: Future Horizons.

Groopman, J. (2007) 'What's the trouble? How doctors think', *The New Yorker*, 29 Jan 2007.

Grotstein, J. (2007) *A Beam of Intense Darkness*. London: Karnac.

Grunbaum, A. (1985) *The Foundations of Psychoanalysis: A Philosophical Critique*. Los Angeles: University of California Press.

Györi, M. (2006) *Autism and Cognitive Architecture*. Budapest: Akadémiai.

Hammersley, M. (1992) *What's Wrong with Ethnography?* London: Routledge.

Hammersley, M. and Atkinson, P. (2007) *Ethnography: Principles in Practice*. 3rd revision. London: Routledge.

Hargreaves, A. (1994) *Changing Teachers, Changing Times*. New York: Teachers College Press.

Hegarty, S. (1998) 'Challenges to inclusive education: a European perspective', in S.J. Vitello and D.E. Mithaug (eds.) *Inclusive Schooling: National and International Perspectives*. London: Routledge, pp. 151–165.

Helsing, D. (2007) 'Style of knowing regarding uncertainties', *Curriculum Inquiry*, 37(1), 33–70.

Henriques, J., Hollway, W., Urwin, C., Venn, C. and Walkerdine, V. (1988) *Changing the Subject: Psychology, Social Regulation, and Subjectivity*. London: Routledge.

Higgs, J. (2008) *Clinical Reasoning in the Health Professions*. London: Elsevier Health Sciences.

Hinshelwood, R.D. and Skogstad, W. (2000) 'The method of observing organisations', in R.D. Hinshelwood and Wilhelm Skogstad (eds.) *Observing Organisations: Anxiety, Defence and Culture in Health Care*. London: Routledge, pp. 175–183.

Hinshelwood, R.D. and Skogstad, W. (2002) 'Irradiated by distress: observing psychic pain in health care organizations', *Psychoanalytic Psychotherapy*, 16(2), 110–124.

Hodkinson, A. (2009) 'Pre-service teacher training and special educational needs in England 1970–2008: is government learning the lessons of the past or is it experiencing a groundhog day?', *European Journal of Special Needs Education*, 24(3), 277–289.

Hoffman, D.M. (2009) 'Reflecting on social emotional learning: a critical perspective on trends in the United States', *Review of Educational Research*, 79(2), 533–556.

Hoggett, P. (2008) 'What's in a hyphen? Reconstructing psychosocial studies', *Psychoanalysis, Culture & Society*, 13(4), 379–384.

House of Commons Education and Skills Select Committee (2006) *Special Educational Needs: Third Report of Session 2005–2006*. London: UK Parliament.

Howlin, P. (2004) 'Outcome in Autism Spectrum Disorders', in F.R. Volkmar, D.J. Cohen and R.P. Ami Klin (eds). *Handbook of Autism and Pervasive Developmental Disorders*. 3rd edition. Hoboken, NJ: Wiley, pp. 201–220.

James, A. and Prout, A. (2004) *Constructing and Reconstructing Childhood: Contemporary Issues in the Sociological Study of Childhood*. Abingdon: Routledge.

Jones, P. and West, E. (2009) 'Teacher education: reflections upon teacher education in severe difficulties in the USA: shared concerns about quantity and quality', *British Journal of Special Education*, 36(2), 69–75.

Jordan, R. (2005) 'Managing autism and Asperger's syndrome in current educational provision', *Pediatric Rehabilitation*, 8(2), 104–112.

Kavale, K.A. (2002) 'Mainstreaming to full inclusion: from orthogenesis to pathogenesis of an idea', *International Journal of Disability, Development and Education*, 49(2), 201–214.

Kelly, P. (2006) 'What is teacher learning? A socio-cultural perspective', *Oxford Review of Education*, 32(4), 505–519.

Kemmis, S. (2005) 'Knowing practice: searching for saliences', *Pedagogy, Culture & Society*, 13(3), 391–426.

King, P. and Steiner, R. (1992) *The Freud–Klein Controversies 1941–1945.* London: Psychology Press.

Klein, M. (1923) 'The development of a child', *International Journal of Psycho-Analysis*, 4, 419–474.

Kolb, D. (1984) *Experiential Learning: Experience as the Source of Learning and Development.* Englewood Cliffs, NJ: Prentice-Hall.

Labaree, D.F. (2008) 'An uneasy relationship: the history of teacher education in the university', in M. Cochran-Smith, S. Feiman-Nemser, J.D. McIntyre and K.E. Demers (eds.) *Handbook of Research on Teacher Education: Enduring Questions in Changing Contexts*, 3rd ed. Stanford, CA: Stanford University Press, pp. 290–306.

Lamb, B. (2009) *Lamb Inquiry: Special Educational Needs and Parental Confidence.* London: Department for Children, Families and Skills. Online. Available from: http://webarchive.nationalarchives.gov.uk/20130401151715/https://www.education.gov.uk/publications/standard/publicationdetail/page1/DCSF-01143-2009 (accessed 23 December 2013).

Lapping, C. (2007) 'Interpreting resistance sociologically: a reflection on the recontextualization of psychoanalytic concepts into sociological analysis', Sociology, 41(4), 627–644.

Lave, J. and Wenger, E. (1991) *Situated learning: Legitimate peripheral participation.* Cambridge: Cambridge University Press.

Leatherman, J.M. and Niemeyer, J. (2005) 'Teachers' attitudes toward inclusion: factors influencing classroom practice', *Journal of Early Childhood Teacher Educators*, 26(1), 23–36.

Lee, K.H. and Siegle, G.J. (2012) 'Common and distinct brain networks underlying explicit emotional evaluation: a meta-analytic study', *Social Cognitive and Affective Neuroscience*, 7(5), 521–534.

Lendrum, A., Humphrey, N., Kalambouka, A. and Wigelsworth, M. (2009) 'Implementing primary social and emotional aspects of learning (SEAL) small group interventions: recommendations for practitioners', *Emotional and Behavioural Difficulties*, 14(3), 229–238.

Lendrum, A., Humphrey, N. and Wigelsworth, M. (2012) 'Social and emotional aspects of learning (SEAL) for secondary schools: implementation difficulties and their implications for school-based mental health promotion', *Child and Adolescent Mental Health*, 18(3), 158–164.

Lewis, A. and Norwich, B. (2005) *Special Teaching for Special Children?* Milton Keynes: Open University Press.

Luna, B., Doll, S.K., Hegedus, S.J., Minshew, N.J. and Sweeney, J.A. (2007) 'Maturation of executive function in autism', *Biological Psychiatry*, 61(4), 474–481.

Magee, B. (2000) *The Great Philosophers: An Introduction to Western Philosophy.* Oxford: Oxford University Press.

Mann, G. (2002) 'Transformational, conservative and terminal objects: the application of Bollas's concepts to practice', in J. Scalia (ed.) *The Vitality of Objects: Exploring the Work of Christopher Bollas.* London: Continuum, pp. 58–77.

Mawson, C. (2010) 'Introduction: Bion today: thinking in the field', in C. Mawson (ed.) *Bion Today.* Abingdon: Routledge, pp. 1–14.

Melnyk, A. (2012) 'Materialism', *Wiley Interdisciplinary Reviews: Cognitive Science*, 3(3), 281–292.

Menzies, I.E.P. (1960) 'A case-study in the functioning of social systems as a defence against anxiety: a report on a study of the nursing service of a general hospital', *Human Relations*, 13(2), 95–121.

Mesibov, G.B. (1997) 'Formal and informal measures on the effectiveness of the TEACCH programme', *Autism*, 1(1), 25–35.

Mesibov, G.B. and Shea, V. (1996) 'Full inclusion and students with autism', *Journal of Autism and Developmental Disorders*, 26(3), 337–346.

Mesibov, G.B. and Shea, V. (2010) 'The TEACCH program in the era of evidence-based practice', *Journal of Autism and Developmental Disorders*, 40(5), 570–579.

Miller, L., Rustin, M. and Shuttleworth, J. (1997) *Closely Observed Infants*. London: Gerald Duckworth.

Mintz, J. (2007) 'Psychodynamic perspectives on teacher stress', *Psychodynamic Practice*, 13(2), 153–166.

Mintz, J. (2008) 'Working with children with Asperger's syndrome in the mainstream classroom: a psychodynamic take from the chalk face', *Psychodynamic Practice*, 14(2), 169–180.

Molloy, H. and Vasil, L. (2002) 'The social construction of Asperger syndrome: the pathologising of difference?', *Disability & Society*, 17(6), 659–669.

Moon, J.A. (1999) *Reflection in Learning and Professional Development: Theory and Practice*. New York: Psychology Press.

Musset, P. (2010) *Initial Teacher Education and Continuing Training Policies in a Comparative Perspective: Current Practices in OECD Countries and a Literature Review on Potential Effects, OECD Education Working Papers, No. 48*. Paris: OECD.

Nagel, T. (1974) 'What it is like to be a bat?', *The Philosophical Review*, 83(4), 435–450.

Neisser, U. (1993) 'The self perceived', in U. Neisser (ed.) *The Perceived Self: Ecological and Interpersonal Sources of Self Knowledge*. Cambridge: Cambridge University Press, pp. 3–12.

O'Shaughnessy, E. (1994) 'What is a clinical fact?', *International Journal of Psycho-Analysis*, 75, 939–947.

O'Shaughnessy, E. (2005) 'Whose Bion?', *International Journal of Psycho-Analysis*, 86, 1523–1528.

Osler, A. and Osler, C. (2002) 'Inclusion, exclusion and children's rights: a case study of a student with Asperger syndrome', *Emotional and Behavioural Difficulties*, 7(1), 35–54.

Pawson, R. and Tilley, N. (1997) *Realistic Evaluation*. London: Sage.

Polanyi, M. (1958) *The Study of Man*. Chicago: University of Chicago Press.

Polanyi, M. (1962) *Personal Knowledge: Towards a Post-Critical Philosophy*. London: Psychology Press.

Price, H. (2004) 'The emotional context of young children's literacy learning', unpublished thesis, University of East London.

Ragin, C.C. (1989) *The Comparative Method: Moving Beyond Qualitative and Quantitative Strategies*. Los Angeles: University of California Press.

Ragin, C.C. (1994) 'Qualitative Comparative Analysis', in T. Janoski and A.M. Hicks (eds.) *The Comparative Political Economy of the Welfare State*. Cambridge: Cambridge University Press, pp. 299–317.

Reay, D. and Lucey, H. (2010) 'Identities in transition: anxiety and excitement in the move to secondary school', *Oxford Review of Education*, 26(2), 191–205.

Reiner, A. (2012) *Bion and Being: Passion and the Creative Mind*. London: Karnac Books.

Rogers, S.J. and Vismara, L.A. (2008) 'Evidence-based comprehensive treatments for early autism', *Journal of Clinical Child & Adolescent Psychology*, 37(1), 8–38.

Rohlfe, M. (2010) 'Immanuel Kant', *The Stanford Encyclopedia of Philosophy (Fall 2010 Edition)*. Online. Available from: http://plato.stanford.edu/archives/fall2010/entries/kant/ (accessed 2 January 2013).

Russell, B. (1946) *History of Western Philosophy*. Abingdon: Routledge.

Russell, G. and Bradley, G. (1997) *Teachers' Computer Anxiety: Implications for Professional Development*. Dordrecht, Holland: Springer Netherlands.

Rustin, M. (2006) 'Infant observation research: what have we learned so far?', *Infant Observation*, 9(1), 35–52.

Ryle, G. (1945) 'Knowing how and knowing that: the presidential address', *Proceedings of the Aristotelian Society*, 46, 1–16.

Sacks, J. (2007) *The Home We Build Together: Recreating Society*. London: Continuum.

Salzberger-Wittenberg, I., Williams, G. and Osborne, E. (1999) *The Emotional Experience of Learning and Teaching*. 2nd edition. London: Karnac.

Scheckel, M. (2009) 'Nursing education: past, present, future', in G. Roux and J. Halstead (eds.) *Issues and Trends in Nursing: Essential Knowledge for Today and Tomorrow*. Burlington, MA: Jones & Bartlett Publishers, pp. 607–621.

Schön, D. (1983) *The Reflective Practitioner: How Professionals Think in Action*. New York: Basic Books.

Schön, D. (1993) 'Generative metaphor: a perspective on problem-setting in social policy', in A. Ortony (ed.) *Metaphor and Thought*. Cambridge: Cambridge University Press, pp. 137–163.

Sclater, S.D., Yates, C., Price, H. and Jones, D.W. (2009) 'Introducing psychosocial studies of emotion', in S.D. Sclater, D.W. Jones, C. Yates and H. Price (eds.) *Emotion: New Psychosocial Perspectives*. New York: Palgrave Macmillan, pp. 1–18.

Segal, H. (1957) 'Notes on symbol formation', *The International Journal of Psychoanalysis*, 38, 391–397.

Shulman, L.S. (1987) 'Knowledge and teaching: foundations of a new reform', *Harvard Educational Review*, 57(1), 1–22.

Shulman, L.S. (2005) 'Pedagogies', *Liberal Education*, Spring 2005, 18–25.

Shuttleworth, A. (1997) 'Turning towards the cognitive', *Journal of Melanie Klein and Object Relations*, 15(4), 647–663.

Shuttleworth, J. (2010) 'Faith and culture: community life and the creation of a shared psychic reality', *Infant Observation*, 13(1), 45–58.

Simpson, R.L., Lacava, P.G. and Graner, P.S. (2004) 'The No Child Left Behind Act, challenges and implications for educators', *Intervention in School and Clinic*, 40(2), 67–75.

Sternberg, R.J. and Horvath, J.A. (1999) *Tacit Knowledge in Professional Practice: Researcher and Practitioner Perspectives*. London: Psychology Press.

Strawson, G. and Freeman, A. (2006) *Consciousness and its Place in Nature*. Exeter: Imprint Academic.

Symington, J. and Symington, N. (1996) *The Clinical Thinking of Wilfred Bion*. London: Routledge.

Training and Development Agency for Schools [England and Wales] (2010a) *The National SENCO Award*. Online. Available from: http://www.education.gov.uk/schools/careers/traininganddevelopment/b00201451/sen-skills/advanced-skills (accessed 15 October 2013).

Training and Development Agency for Schools [England and Wales] (2010b) *Advanced Needs Training Materials for SEND*. Online. Available from: http://www.advanced-training.org.uk/ (accessed 15 October 2013).

Trevarthen, C. and Aitken, K.J. (2001) 'Infant intersubjectivity: research, theory, and clinical applications', *Journal of Child Psychology and Psychiatry, and Allied Disciplines*, 42(1), 3–48.

Tripp, D. (1993) *Critical Incidents in Teaching: Development Professional Judgment*. New York: Psychology Press.

University of North Carolina (Division TEACCH) (n.d.) *Treatment and Education of Autistic and Related Communication Handicapped Children*. Online. Available from: http://www.teacch.com/ (accessed 10 March 2012).

US Department of Education (2013) *Preparing and Credentialing the Nation's Teachers: The Secretary's Ninth Report on Teacher Quality*. Washington, DC: US Department of Post-Secondary Education.

Waddell, M. (1998) *Inside Lives: Psychoanalysis and the Growth of the Personality*. London: Karnac.

Walker, G. (2005) "Who will be the naughty one now?": using observational skills in work with primary aged children in a small school-based group', *Infant Observation*, 8(1), 19–31.

Walkerdine, V. Lucey, H. and Melody, J. (2001) *Growing Up Girl: Psychosocial Explorations of Gender and Class*. New York: Palgrave Macmillan.

Ward, A. (2006) *Kant, The Three Critiques*. Cambridge: Polity Press.

Wasserman, S. (1993) *Getting Down to Cases: Learning to Teach with Case Studies*. New York: Teachers College Press.

Wedell, K. (2008) 'Inclusion: confusion about inclusion, patching up or system change?', *British Journal of Special Education*, 35(3), 127–135.

Wing, L. and Gould, J. (1979) 'Severe impairments of social interaction and associated abnormalities in children: epidemiology and classification', *Journal of Autism and Developmental Disorders*, 9(1), 11–29.

Wing, L., Gould, J. and Gillberg, C. (2011) 'Autism spectrum disorders in the DSM-V: better or worse than the DSM-IV?', *Research in Developmental Disabilities*, 32(2), 768–773.

Woods, P. (1996) *Researching the Art of Teaching: Ethnography for Educational Use*. London: Routledge.

Yin, K. (1981) 'The case study crisis: some answers', *Administrative Science Quarterly*, 26, 58–65.

Zammito, J.H. (2008) 'Kant and naturalism reconsidered', *Inquiry*, 51(5), 532–558.

Index